A Classroom With Purpose: A Guide to Teaching Social Studies Today

⛛NCSS

National Council for the Social Studies
8403 Colesville Road • Suite 1100 • Silver Spring, Maryland 20910 • socialstudies.org

NCSS EXECUTIVE DIRECTOR Kelly McFarland Stratman
EDITORIAL STAFF ON THIS PUBLICATION Laura Godfrey, Jennifer Bauduy, Nancy Driver, Joy D. Lindsey
DESIGN AND PRODUCTION Rich Palmer
COVER DESIGN Cindy Henry

Cover Image Credits: Ga-hah-no Caroline Parker Mt. Pleasant, Courtesy of the RMSC, Rochester, NY;
Statue of Liberty, The New York Public Library; Martin Luther King Jr., Library of Congress, Unseen Histories;
Steel worker, The New York Public Library; U.S. Capitol building, The New York Public Library

To my parents, my father, an immigrant who never graduated high school, and my mother, who never had the opportunity to attend college. Though they had little, they gave everything to support their children. They cherished education and encouraged me to embrace every learning opportunity. It is through their unwavering love and guidance that I have carried this work forward—one bean at a time.

—Kristi

This book is lovingly dedicated to my parents, Madelyn and David Potts, who I dearly wish could have seen it published. Though neither graduated from college, from a young age they instilled in me a profound love of learning, reading, writing, and the pursuit of higher education. Their many hours of hard work in difficult vocations paved the way for the book you hold in your hands.

—Tim

Table of Contents

Acknowledgments

We are fortunate to have worked alongside colleagues in the field of social studies whose exceptional knowledge and experience have greatly enriched this book. Each chapter author generously shared their expertise, helping to create a resource that is both practical and scholarly. We are sincerely grateful for the care and dedication shown to this project, as well as for meeting deadlines, responding to requests, and thoughtfully incorporating our edits.

We are deeply grateful to Nancy Driver, former NCSS Director of Publications and Resources, for recognizing the potential of our proposal and giving us the opportunity to address a gap in social studies publications. Her strong early support set this project in motion. We also extend our sincere thanks to Laura Godfrey, Interim Director of Publications and Resources, whose thoughtful guidance, editorial expertise, and timely communication helped shape our work into an educational resource that teachers and students can confidently rely upon.

Many thanks to Wesley Hedgepeth (NCSS President, 2023–2024) for capturing the essence and spirit of this volume in his concise and insightful introduction.

Cindy Henry thoroughly understood our vision through her various cover design renderings, creating a final product that beautifully captured all that we wanted. We cannot thank her enough for her patience, artwork, and attention to detail. Kudos to Rich Palmer, NCSS Art Manager, for expertly and adeptly coordinating the assembly of the book in its physical form.

Thank you to Dr. Maeve Kane and her book *Shirts Powdered Red*, the catalyst and inspiration for the daguerreotype of Ga-hah-no Caroline Parker that is on the front cover.

Kristi: To my husband, Todd Girvin, and my children, Kyle and Casie, thank you for your patience, encouragement, and unwavering belief in the value of this work. Your support carried me through the long hours of writing, editing, and refining every chapter.

Tim: To my wife, Kelly, who has shared in every one of my educational endeavors since we first met in 1989 while student teaching at Johnson City High School and she was working part-time in the main office. You are truly the wind beneath my wings. To our children Chelsea, Evan, Emily, and Caleb, thank you for your steadfast love, support, and personal sacrifices. Deep appreciation and admiration of my cooperating teacher Tim Cooper for instilling all the right attributes for a successful teaching career. To my best friend since high school, Troy P. Williams, your unwavering support of this project and many others has meant the world to me. I am also deeply grateful to Rich Strum, Director of Academic Programs at Fort Ticonderoga, for our long-standing educational partnership, which strongly influenced this book. Finally, to my colleagues at Monticello Central School District, the New York State Council for the Social Studies, the National Council for the Social Studies, and the National Social Studies Leaders' Association: Thank you for your friendship, leadership, support, and camaraderie.

To all the social studies educators who strive daily to inspire critical thinking and meaningful learning in students, this book is for you. With heartfelt appreciation of our students, whose vibrant discussions and insightful questions truly inspired us over the years. Your perspectives have enriched our lives, inspired the chapters of this book, and have taught us more than you will ever know.

Please note the ideas expressed in this book and any errors of interpretation or presentation are solely the responsibility of the editors and chapter authors.

About the Editors

Kristi Fragnoli, EdD, is an Associate Professor at Siena University and the Co-Director of the Early Childhood and Childhood Education program. Prior to this post, she was a Professor of Education at The College of Saint Rose, where she served for 21 years. She is deeply engaged in research and educational community dialogue. She has a rich history of presenting at international, national, state, and regional conferences, including those organized by the National Council of Social Studies, the National Council of History Education, and the American Association of Colleges for Teacher Education. Her contributions to the field have been recognized with several awards, including the Bruce W. Dearstyne Annual Archives Award for Excellence in the Educational Use of Historical Records and the Dr. Benita Jorasky Outstanding College Educator Award for Demonstrated Excellence in Teaching from the New York State Council for Social Studies. Dr. Fragnoli is a governor-appointed board member of the New York State Archives Partnership Trust. She is also the chair of the New York Council for History Education and a member of the editorial board for the New York State Archives magazine. Her interests and research include primary document analysis, civic literacy, social justice, and student mentoring.

Timothy D. Potts, MSED, is a social studies and special education inclusion teacher for 35 years in the Monticello Central School District in the Catskills region of New York State. He is an adjunct pre-service teacher supervisor at the State University of New York at New Paltz. Timothy is a past president of the New York State Council for the Social Studies (NYSCSS) and has served as the chief financial officer since 2015. In 2017, he cocreated the NYSCSS's annual pre-service teacher conference program. Timothy is a second-term board member of the National Social Studies Leaders' Association. He is an educational consultant and cofacilitator for Fort Ticonderoga's teacher-related programs. He is a noted and longtime presenter of many innovative ways to teach social studies at the local, state, and national level. He is noted for historical thinking pedagogy centering around the design and implementation of organically researched primary sources. In 2005, Timothy was recognized as the NYSCSS Middle Level Educator of the Year and in 2018 received the NYSCSS Distinguished Service Award.

Contributors

Jason M. Chevrier is an experienced educational leader and superintendent of schools at Schodack Central School District, located in Schodack, New York. With expertise in curriculum development, strategic planning, and program innovation, he has successfully led capital projects and instructional initiatives to enhance learning experiences. He is dedicated to fostering student success, professional growth, and collaborative school environments. His research interests focus on climate, culture, and leadership, aiming to create positive, inclusive, and high-performing school communities.

Ed Finney is a technology integration specialist at Schodack Central School District, specializing in educational technology and instructional design. His research focuses on the effective integration of digital tools in K–12 education, exploring innovative approaches to enhance student engagement and learning outcomes. He is passionate about empowering educators with practical strategies to leverage technology for meaningful instruction.

Paul Gold, EdD, is a clinical professor of education and director of graduate education programs at Wagner College on Staten Island, New York. Dr. Gold was a teacher and administrator for 31 years in the New York State public school system, and two-times president of the New York State Council for the Social Studies. Dr. Gold's current focus is the continuous improvement and depth of knowledge for new teacher preparation programs for candidates completing their student teaching experience.

Wesley Hedgepeth is a social studies educator at Collegiate School in Henrico County, Virginia, where he teaches World History, AP U.S. Government, and AP Comparative Politics. He also represents the City of Richmond's Fourth District on the school board and previously served as president of both the National Council for the Social Studies (2023–24) and the Virginia Council for the Social Studies (2014–17). Wesley's primary areas of interest are in civil discourse, civic engagement, and effective professional development.

Erica Kane is a certified English teacher with nearly two decades of experience teaching in both New York City and Upstate New York public schools. In addition to her teaching role, she has also served as a union advocate, leveraging her expertise in educator representation throughout her career.

Aja E. LaDuke, PhD, is an associate professor in the Department of Literacy Studies and Elementary Education and the program coordinator for the Multiple Subject Teaching Credential Program at Sonoma State University in Rohnert Park, California. She holds a teaching certificate for Teaching English to Speakers of Other Languages (TESOL) in addition to both elementary (K–6) and secondary English (7–12) certificates. In addition to teaching language development and literacy methods courses, her scholarly interests include critical literacy, ethnic studies education, and language diversity in K–12 schools.

Bruce A. Lesh holds degrees from Salisbury University (BA) and Villanova University (MA). He is the author of *Why Won't You Just Tell Us The Answer: Teaching Historical Thinking in Grades 7–12* (2011) and *Developing Historical Thinkers: Supporting Historical Inquiry for all Students* (2023). He is currently supervisor of elementary social studies for Carroll County Public Schools, Maryland.

Darren W. Minarik is a professor of social studies and special education at Radford University. Darren's research addresses educational intersections between social studies and special education, with an emphasis on inclusive educational practices, self-determination, disability history, and civic engagement. His NCSS publication, *Social Studies & Exceptional Learners*, was the first comprehensive guide to teaching students with disabilities in inclusive K–12 social studies classrooms.

James O'Brien is in his sixth year of teaching, all six of those years spent in urban education. He received a Masters in the Arts of Teaching English from Clarkson University where his research was focused on building Standard American English proficiency in speakers of African American Vernacular English (AAVE), restorative practice, and therapeutic crisis intervention.

John M. Palella II, PhD, is the director of social studies education at Brown University, where he focuses on creating culturally relevant social studies classrooms. His research examines histories of race, gender, and sexuality; communication and media studies in social studies curricula; and the roles of media literacy and storytelling in shaping civic identity and engagement. Committed to diversity, equity, and inclusion in teacher education, Palella supports educators in developing curricula and pedagogical practices rooted in intersectional social justice.

Karen Poland, EdD, is an assistant professor in the College of Education at Niagara University, where she brings a broad PreK–20 perspective to her work. Her scholarly interests include curriculum development and teacher preparation, the history of education, and social studies and civic education. Dr. Poland is actively engaged in the educational community, serving various local and state educational associations to further advance the field.

Alyssa Sabbatino, a National Board Certified Teacher and national presenter, is the director of teaching and learning in Schodack, New York, where she oversees academic and social-emotional curricula for grades PreK–12. She specializes in restorative practices, trauma-informed care, social emotional learning, and diversity, equity, and inclusion. Her research interests include instructional design, differentiation, and curriculum alignment.

Emily Wells is a social studies educator in her fifth year of teaching and recently received a Master's Degree in Literacy 5–12 at the University at Albany, State University of New York. Emily has taught in a range of districts, from rural to suburban and inner-city, having taught grades ranging from 6–11. Emily is currently honing her practice around effectively incorporating literacy into the social studies classroom to foster a love of reading and writing in all students.

About the Cover

The cover of this book is designed to reflect the breadth, diversity, and ongoing relevance of social studies education. Each image was carefully chosen to represent a dimension of history, civics, economics, and culture—the core areas that inspire young learners to make connections between the past and the present. Together, these images tell a story of perseverance, struggle, innovation, and aspiration. They reflect the mission of social studies education: to prepare students to understand the complexity of the past, engage with the present, and imagine possibilities for the future.

As a beacon of our nation's history and a symbol of freedom, democracy, and immigration, **Lady Liberty**[1] continues to inspire reflection on the promises and challenges of American ideals. The **primer**[2] is an educational tool represents literacy, knowledge, and the foundations of learning—reminding educators that teaching is at the heart of empowering future citizens. The **$10 bill**[3] calls attention to the role of economics in shaping society. **Capitol Building Dome**[4] is not just a symbol of our nation's government but a stereogram. Just as a stereogram requires careful focus to reveal its hidden depth, so too does civic engagement demand patience, perspective, and a willingness to look beyond the surface.

Many people who were integral to our nation's development are also represented on the cover. **The railroad worker**[5], representing labor, industry, and migration, underscores the role of everyday workers in building the nation's infrastructure and driving economic change. **Dr. Martin Luther King Jr.**[6]—A central figure in the Civil Rights Movement, King's legacy reminds us of the power of civic action, leadership, and moral courage in shaping a more just society.

The image of **Ga-hah-no Caroline Parker Mt. Pleasant**[7] (Tonawanda Seneca Nation, Wolf Clan) was chosen for her importance in preserving Indigenous culture. The following was written by Laticia McNaughton, Six Nations of the Grand River Mohawk Nation, Wolf Clan:

> Born into the influential Parker family at the Tonawanda Seneca Nation community, Ga-hah-no Caroline Parker Mt. Pleasant learned leadership alongside her mother, Elizabeth, a clan mother. At a time when literacy was not common even for white settlers, Caroline learned to read and write in English, a rare accomplishment for a Native American woman during the mid-19th century. Caroline spent many years advancing her education, attending Brockport and Cayuga academies and the New York State Normal School in Albany. Her education and training enabled her to effectively manage the family's affairs, as she acted as a translator for the Tonawanda chiefs and collaborated with anthropologists to document and preserve Haudenosaunee cultural traditions.
>
> In 1853, the Tonawanda Seneca Nation Council of Chiefs raised her up as Jikonsaseh, the "Mother of Nations," a title held by the Wolf Clan. Her role in diplomacy matured alongside her Tuscarora Nation husband, Chief John Mt. Pleasant, though her work on the 1890 Indian Census later impacted her reputation in the Tuscarora community due to distrust in the U.S. government.
>
> Caroline and her family played an enormous role in the preservation of Haudenosaunee cultural knowledge through a working relationship with Lewis Henry Morgan, a founder of American anthropology. They contributed hundreds of items

A Classroom With Purpose: A Guide to Teaching Social Studies Today

to the Morgan Collection, including beadwork pieces sewn by Caroline herself, which are preserved by the Rochester Museum & Science Center (RMSC). Between 1848 and 1851, Caroline served as Morgan's primary collaborator on material culture. Her beadwork, sewing, and textile designs continue to pave the way for contemporary Haudenosaunee beadworkers.

Today, Caroline Parker Mt. Pleasant is remembered for her dedication to preserving Haudenosaunee cultural traditions in a changing world. Through her education and diplomacy, she advocated for her family and community, supporting tribal sovereignty and demonstrating remarkable accomplishments as a Native American woman in the 19th century.[8]

Visit the RMSC website for educational resources (**www.rmsc.org**).

1. *Statue of Liberty From the Ferry Dock*, 1890, Irma and Paul Milstein Division of United States History, Local History and Genealogy, The New York Public Library (**https://digitalcollections.nypl.org/items/d6b2db50-83ae-0132-8079-58d385a7b928**).
2. From **FreePik.com**.
3. From **FreePik.com**.
4. *Main Building and Dome*, 1865, The Miriam and Ira D. Wallach Division of Art, Prints and Photographs: Photography Collection, The New York Public Library (**https://digitalcollections.nypl.org/items/a06ef7c0-c571-012f-97f0-58d385a7bc34**).
5. *Worker Bolting a Steel Support*, 1931, The Miriam and Ira D. Wallach Division of Art, Prints and Photographs: Photography Collection, The New York Public Library (**https://digitalcollections.nypl.org/items/6a92c5a0-c6db-012f-8a2d-58d385a7bc34**).
6. *Martin Luther King Press Conference*, by M. S. Trikosko, August 26, 1964, Library of Congress (**www.loc.gov/item/2003688129**), colorized by J. J. Lloyd, Unseen Histories (**https://unsplash.com/photos/dr-martin-luther-king-jr-gives-a-speech-G2vxuMlATxA**).
7. Ga-hah-no Caroline Parker Mt. Pleasant, Courtesy of the RMSC, Rochester, NY.
8. Laticia McNaughton, Six Nations of the Grand River Mohawk Nation, Wolf Clan, written for the exhibit The Changemakers: Rochester Women Who Changed the World, Rochester Museum & Science Center (**https://rmsc.org/changemakers/**).

Intentionally Blank

Introduction
Building an Informed Society:
The Critical Role of Social Studies Educators

Wesley Hedgepeth

The purpose of this book is to provide practical guidance to help you build confidence and resilience as you begin your career as a social studies educator. Just remember to take care of yourself. As flight attendants say, "Be sure to secure your own mask before assisting others."

Social studies education is critical to PreK–12 student development. The National Council for the Social Studies (NCSS) emphasizes that social studies helps early learners identify real-world problems and participate in creating an inclusive, caring democratic society. NCSS (2024) explains this in its statement "Powerful, Purposeful Teaching and Learning in Elementary Social Studies":

> In the elementary years, social studies is an essential subject, critical to young learners' academic success and well-being. The success of our democracy depends on equitable access to this vital learning for all students. Social studies must be taught in every classroom starting in PreK so learners can develop into civically knowledgeable, engaged, and active adults. (para. 1)

Research supports the positive impact of social studies at the PreK–elementary level, showing that lessons in this subject not only improve literacy and critical thinking skills but also lead to higher overall achievement. According to a study published in 2020 by the Fordham Institute, researchers found that despite elementary school students in the US spending much more time on English Language Arts (ELA) than on any other subject, it is an increased instructional time in social studies—not in ELA—that is associated with improved reading ability (Tyner & Kabourek, 2020).

Moreover, social studies is fundamental to the health of our democracy. A 2018 study by the Council of Chief State School Officers (CCSSO) revealed that 44% of its surveyed districts had reduced the time allocated to social studies since the enactment of No Child Left Behind (NCLB) in 2001. This reduction is particularly concerning given that "preparing people for democratic citizenship was a major reason for the creation of public schools" (Center for Education Policy, 2020, p. 2). CCSSO (2018) also notes that effective social studies instruction has also been linked to outcomes such as

- a higher likelihood of voting and engaging in political discussions at home,
- being four times more likely to volunteer and work on community issues, and
- greater confidence in speaking publicly and communicating with elected representatives.

Despite these concrete benefits, the discipline of social studies remains marginalized, especially since NCLB.

According to a 2016 survey by the Annenberg Public Policy Center, only 26% of people surveyed could name the three branches of government—executive, legislative, and judicial—down from 38% in 2011. Furthermore, 31% of respondents could not name any of the three branches (Winthrop, 2020). Does this lack of knowledge of government possibly connect to the fact that about 90 million of the almost 245 million Americans who were eligible to vote in the 2024 presidential election did not vote (Kronenberg, 2024)? Does the dearth of social studies education nationwide link to the fact that almost half of Americans have stopped discussing politics with others (Jurkowitz & Mitchell, 2020)? Perhaps the answer to both questions is yes. Even if this is a loose association, this evidence paints an image of the marginal existence that social studies education experiences in many of our nation's schools today and underscores its critical importance for both individual development and the vitality of our democracy.

What is the purpose of social studies?

> Using an inquiry-based approach, social studies helps students examine vast human experiences through the generation of questions, collection and analysis of evidence from credible sources, consideration of multiple perspectives, and the application of social studies knowledge and disciplinary skills. As a result of examining the past, participating in the present, and learning how to shape the future, social studies prepares learners for a lifelong practice of civil discourse and civic engagement in their communities. Social studies centers knowledge of human rights and local, national, and global responsibilities so that learners can work together to create a just world in which they want to live. (NCSS, n.d., para. 2)

Ultimately, K–12 social studies education lays the foundation for students to become thoughtful, informed, and proactive citizens. By equipping them with essential knowledge, skills, and perspectives, schools ensure that future generations are prepared to navigate an increasingly complex and interconnected world while making meaningful contributions to society.

Social studies classrooms serve as powerful spaces where young minds come to understand their roles within the fabric of society. All of this is true, and yet, for new teachers entering this field, the transition from theory to practice can be complex and daunting. I recall my first year in the classroom, regularly wondering if I had the ability and necessary preparation to succeed in this field. Oftentimes, I found myself relying on my mentors for guidance and my fellow first-year educators to reflect on successes and failures. By the way, there were many failures. That is part of the job, and one of the best parts of teaching is the ability to try something else, to do better the next time. You try what you believe will best serve the population you are serving, and sometimes it just does not land quite as you expected. Other times it does, and those are amazing moments and successes you want to continue to build upon.

A Classroom With Purpose: A Guide to Teaching Social Studies Today aims to guide early-career educators through this journey, offering not only essential teaching strategies but also a deep well of resources and insights that will empower them to inspire, engage, and educate effectively. This book is more than a manual—it is a roadmap through the early stages of a teaching career, crafted by experienced educators and field experts who understand the real-world demands and unique joys of social studies education. Each chapter takes on a distinct facet of the teaching experience, designed to provide pre-service and early-career educators with the foundational knowledge and practical skills they need to thrive in their classrooms. From navigating the intricacies of curriculum standards and lesson planning to building an inclusive, culturally responsive classroom, this book reflects the comprehensive approach needed for educators to foster a meaningful and effective learning environment.

In these pages, you will find real-life examples, anecdotes, and expert advice, all geared toward helping you navigate the path to becoming a confident and competent educator. The book begins with guidance on the job search process—a phase where many new educators may feel overwhelmed or uncertain. In Chapter 1, "The Art of the Career Search: Finding and Landing the Perfect Job," Jason Chevrier, Ed Finney, and Alyssa Sabbatino present strategies for crafting a standout resume, making meaningful connections (I cannot underscore the importance of this one enough), and discovering school environments where you can flourish as a social studies teacher. It is important to understand that each schoolhouse—and oftentimes each department within a schoolhouse—has its own distinct culture, even within the same school division. Be sure that each interview in which you take part is a two-way interview. Meaning, not only are you being interviewed, but you are also interviewing the school and your would-be colleagues. How else will you know that it is the right fit? This chapter emphasizes the importance of finding a position that aligns with your values, teaching philosophy, and professional aspirations, setting the foundation for a fulfilling career. By the way, you have drafted at least a preliminary teaching philosophy within your teacher preparation program.

It is important to think about your own beliefs as an educator before entering the classroom, and know that this is likely to evolve as your career evolves. What are your career goals and aspirations? Do you think a career in the classroom is your goal? Do you aspire to move into administration? Would you like to teach at the university level or work at an education think tank or in education policy? You do not need to know the answers to these questions just yet, but keep them in the back of your mind. Later in this chapter, additional experienced educators share their own stories, revealing their unique pathways and the often-challenging realities of the classroom, alongside the rewarding connections that make teaching so impactful.

Following the job search, Chapter 2, "Navigating the Early Years" by Emily Wells and James O'Brien, includes essential tips for building rapport with students, communicating with families, and collaborating with colleagues. Wells and O'Brien emphasize the importance of community and support networks, which are vital as you embark on your teaching journey. The phrase "It takes a village" is more than just a saying—it is a fact. You are not alone. Rely on your mentors and know that both administration and parents, guardians, or caregivers can be key partners in the success of your students.

Each year of teaching brings its uncertainties; however, the first years are often more full of uncertainties. I have found that humility goes a long way with students. If you do not know something, do not lie! It might shock students the first time you admit to not knowing something; however, it humanizes you, and they will get used to it. The same goes for your colleagues—*ask for help when you need it.*

You will make mistakes. If you make a mistake, own it. We all have done it! It is not the mistake that defines us, rather, it is how we choose to learn and move forward. My students become used to me making mistakes over time, and I make sure to model humility by admitting my errors and providing transparency on how I plan to move forward. Witnessing the modeling of failure and growth is a necessary experience for our students.

In Chapter 3, "Teaching for Tomorrow: Social Studies as a Path to an Engaged Citizenry" by Kristi Fragnoli, Timothy D. Potts, and Paul Gold, you will gain a deeper understanding of how social studies is structured, the importance of addressing standards, and the complexities of fostering open and constructive dialogue on sensitive or controversial topics. This chapter also emphasizes the critical role of social studies in preparing students to engage thoughtfully with the world around them, providing strategies for nurturing civic-minded, curious, and critical-thinking students.

Perhaps one of the most challenging yet rewarding aspects of teaching social studies is managing diverse content that encompasses civics, economics, geography, and history. In an age where social studies education—in both the PreK–12 classroom and the higher education space—is under a political microscope, my primary advice for any beginning teacher is to follow state and local standards. Following these standards is your legal obligation and is the smoothest pathway to ensure continued employment. State standards provide structure and reasoning in the case someone shares a concern about what is happening in your classroom.

Nevertheless, students need to see themselves and others in their learning. Representation is critical. When students see themselves and others in the social studies curriculum, it validates their personal identities, fosters a sense of belonging, and boosts self-esteem, while simultaneously promoting critical thinking and empathy through exposure to diverse perspectives. This inclusive approach not only challenges stereotypes and biases by presenting accurate histories and contributions of all groups but also prepares students to navigate and contribute positively to a diverse society by cultivating cultural competence and informed citizenship. If your state standards do not do this, seek to change those standards. Advocate by contacting your elected officials, and volunteer to write or review standards when they are up for revision by your state education department.

Our students come with diverse learning needs, and in social studies, we face the added challenge of presenting text-rich, complex subjects. This makes it essential to consider differing student abilities when selecting classroom materials. In Chapter 4 "Building Bridges: Crafting Engaging Social Studies Units of Study" and Chapter 5 "Tapping Your Creativity: How to Create Engaging Social Studies Lessons," authors Karen Poland and Kristi Fragnoli offer invaluable guidance for designing unit and lesson plans that emphasize inquiry, inclusivity, and adaptability. These chapters focus on differentiation strategies specific to social studies and offer guidance for designing culturally responsive units and lessons. These chapters also provide a framework for creating meaningful and accessible learning experiences that resonate with every student in your classroom.

Chapter 6, "Investigating History" by Bruce Lesh, is all about empowering students to approach history as active investigators rather than passive recipients of facts. For beginning PreK–12 social studies teachers, this approach can be translated into classroom practices that stimulate inquiry, encourage critical analysis, and build a set of core historical skills. Social studies teachers can help students develop a deeper, more nuanced understanding of history. This approach not only builds critical thinking skills but also makes history relevant by showing students that the past is full of complex, interconnected stories waiting to be explored.

Creating a culturally responsive environment is another core component of teaching, especially in the social studies classroom. In a time when inclusivity and cultural awareness are paramount, John Palella's chapter, "Dreaming of Resilience, Resistance, and Joy in a Culturally Relevant Social Studies Classroom," provides strategies for understanding and addressing diverse perspectives, fostering an inclusive environment, and building strong, supportive relationships with students and their families. Culturally responsive teaching ensures that students see themselves reflected in the curriculum. Representation matters. This means incorporating diverse voices, primary sources, and historical narratives that go beyond the traditional textbook approach.

By embracing the diversity within each classroom, teachers can create a learning environment that respects and celebrates the backgrounds, perspectives, and experiences of every student. When students feel valued and represented, they are more likely to engage with the material, contribute meaningfully to discussions, and develop a deeper understanding of history and society. Palella provides actionable strategies to help teachers integrate culturally responsive practices into their daily instruction, ensuring that every student feels seen, heard, and empowered to succeed.

It is important that all educators understand differentiated instruction, especially in a diverse social studies classroom where students bring a wide range of abilities, backgrounds, and learning needs. The next two chapters—Chapter 8, "Being the Best Social Studies Teacher for Students With IEPs" by Darren W. Minarek, and Chapter 9, "Just Remember the Peanut Butter and Jelly Sandwich: Supporting Multilingual Learners" by Aja E. LaDuke—address essential aspects of working with diverse student populations: students with learning differences and English language learners.

In these two chapters, you will find strategies to adapt instruction for students who may face additional hurdles in a text-heavy subject like social studies. Minarek and LaDuke offer techniques for simplifying complex content, making lessons visually engaging, and employing multisensory approaches to reinforce key concepts. By incorporating strategies such as scaffolded reading guides, interactive digital tools like StoryMaps, and alternative assessments (e.g., oral presentations, creative projects, or choice boards), teachers can ensure that all students have the tools they need to succeed in a rigorous and inclusive learning environment.

In a world increasingly shaped by digital technologies, effective teaching now demands that we harness tools that engage students in innovative ways. In Chapter 10, "Transforming Social Studies Through Technology," Ed Finney outlines methods to enhance historical inquiry, foster collaboration, and promote critical thinking. More than merely introducing new tools and gadgets, Finney addresses crucial topics such as equitable access, digital citizenship, and ethical technology use—key considerations for the modern classroom. With the support of innovative digital resources, social studies educators can bring history, geography, civics, and economics to life in ways that truly resonate with today's digitally savvy students.

At the same time, equitable access to technology remains a critical consideration. Although many school systems now provide laptops or tablets, not all students have reliable internet access at home. In the position statement "Transforming Social Studies Through Technology," NCSS (2022b) notes that "the year 2020 was a watershed year for our nation…. The COVID-19 pandemic accelerated changes … and raised serious equity, privacy, and social-emotional learning questions" (para. 1). In response, some districts implemented creative solutions—such as offering hotspots, extending public library hours, or even deploying Wi-Fi-equipped buses in low-income areas—to ensure that all students could complete their assignments. Regardless of where you teach, it is essential to assess the unique needs of your student population before establishing technology expectations.

Building on this, digital citizenship has emerged as an increasingly essential skill in today's digital age. With the rapid rise of social media, students must learn to navigate the internet responsibly, ethically, and safely. In the position statement "Media Literacy," NCSS (2022a) highlights that "young people are immersed in a complex media landscape filled with disinformation and profit-driven narratives, yet also enriched with opportunities for participatory engagement" (para. 2). Consequently, the social studies classroom is uniquely positioned to equip the next generation with the tools they need to thrive in an environment saturated with mediated messages.

Furthermore, as technology becomes even more integral to every aspect of our lives—such as the growth of artificial intelligence—the call for ethical technology grows ever more urgent. The design and application of digital tools carry significant moral implications, influencing everything from personal privacy to social equity. Embracing ethical technology means prioritizing transparency, accountability, and fairness in digital innovation—ensuring that advancements benefit society as a whole. By fostering a culture that critically examines the impact of technology, educators and students alike can engage in meaningful discussions about responsible practices. This proactive approach not only helps mitigate potential risks but also empowers the next generation to advocate for a future where human values guide technological progress.

Teaching is a profession guided by ethics and legal responsibilities, and understanding these guidelines is essential. In Chapter 11, "Teaching in the Digital Age: Understanding Ethical and Legal Guidelines," Erica Kane discusses the foundational principles that govern professional conduct. Many national associations set these ethical standards for their respective fields. In 2022, the NCSS Board of Directors updated its Statement of Professional Ethics. There, NCSS outlines six guiding principles—Integrity, Justice, Authenticity, Civic Engagement, Responsibility, and Democratic Values—to support social studies professionals in fostering an inquiry-based, culturally competent, and socially just democratic education. These principles serve as a framework for ethical decision-making at all levels of social studies education, helping educators maintain academic integrity, promote justice, and engage students in active civic participation. While not prescriptive, the statement provides guidance for curriculum development, pedagogy, and professional conduct, ensuring social studies professionals uphold democratic ideals and equity in their teaching (NCSS, 2022c). Kane's chapter builds on the NCSS statement, helping educators navigate the nuances of professional obligations, ethical dilemmas, and legal standards, fostering a culture of respect, integrity, and accountability.

Balancing the demands of teaching with personal well-being is critical for sustaining a long and fulfilling career. Teaching can be emotionally taxing, and burnout is a real concern in the profession. Teachers are givers by nature and can often be selfless to a fault. We often feel that saying no is to the detriment of our students. The truth is that most teachers will not be able to teach for a full career without saying no on occasion, when things are just too much. Learn your limits and learn how to say no.

Finally, in their conclusion, "Hope for Teachers: A Conclusion," editors Kristi Fragnoli and Timothy D. Potts underscore the importance of professional growth and networking—not only as a tool for personal development but also as a model for our students and colleagues. My own professional journey began as an undergraduate at James Madison University when my social studies methods professor emphasized the critical role of professional association membership in a successful teaching career. She frequently referenced NCSS's (2010) *National Curriculum Standards for Social Studies: A Framework for Teaching, Learning, and Assessment* and encouraged us to join the Virginia Council for the Social Studies (VCSS) and attend our state conference. I attended my very first VCSS conference in 2009 and was immediately hooked. In addition to gaining a network of colleagues I could depend upon, I quickly learned that I could integrate new content and strategies into my classroom right away. Later, in 2014, I attended my first NCSS conference and have not missed one since.

I served on the NCSS Board from 2018 through 2025, for three years as the secondary teacher representative then eventually as an officer for four years: vice-president (2021–2022), president-elect (2022–2023), president (2023–2024), and past president (2024–2025). After seven years on the board—and much more previously and still to come—I am immensely grateful to the association for enriching my career, to my colleagues for their openness and willingness to learn from each other, and to the friends and mentors who have continuously supported and encouraged me. Although I am not yet near retirement—I likely have a couple more decades of work ahead—I will always cherish my experiences with NCSS, VCSS, and the other professional associations that have shaped my career. In the concluding chapter, Fragnoli and Potts offer more information about how joining organizations like the NCSS can enhance your career by providing invaluable resources, support, and networking opportunities, as well as by fostering your ongoing development as an educator.

Despite the challenges I have faced as an educator, I would not trade the experience for anything! Whether witnessing the spark in a student's eye who "gets it" for the first time or receiving gratitude from students, I am reminded of why I do what I do each day. A note about gratitude: From time to time, students, parents, and colleagues will write you thank you notes. Keep them! Identify a box or a file folder to store these. It is these moments that remind us of how we shape the lives of young people and are necessary fuel to get us through even the most difficult days.

Good luck on your journey! Teaching is the most noble of all professions, and social studies is by far the most relevant discipline students will engage in the PreK–12 classroom.

References

Annenberg Public Policy Center. (2016, September 13). *Americans' knowledge of the branches of government is declining.* **www.annenbergpublicpolicycenter.org/americans-knowledge-of-the-branches-of-government-is-declining/**

Center for Education Policy. (2020). *History and evolution of public education in the US.* **https://files.eric.ed.gov/fulltext/ED606970.pdf**

Council of Chief State School Officers. (2018). *The marginalization of social studies* [Infographic]. **https://udspace.udel.edu/handle/19716/36370**

Jurkowitz, M., & Mitchell, A. (2020, February 5). *A sore subject: Almost half of Americans have stopped talking politics with someone.* Pew Research Center. **www.pewresearch.org/journalism/2020/02/05/a-sore-subject-almost-half-of-americans-have-stopped-talking-politics-with-someone/**

Kronenberg, A. (2024, November 15). *How many people didn't vote in the 2024 election?* U.S. News & World Report. **www.usnews.com/news/national-news/articles/2024-11-15/how-many-people-didnt-vote-in-the-2024-election**

National Council for the Social Studies. (n.d.). *Definition of social studies.* **www.socialstudies.org/about/definition-social-studies**

National Council for the Social Studies. (2010). *National curriculum standards for social studies: A framework for teaching, learning, and assessment.*

National Council for the Social Studies. (2022a, June). *Media literacy* [Position statement]. **www.socialstudies.org/position-statements/media-literacy**

National Council for the Social Studies. (2022b, June). *Technology, digital learning, and social studies* [Position statement]. **www.socialstudies.org/position-statements/technology-digital-learning-and-social-studies**

National Council for the Social Studies. (2022c, November). *NCSS Statement of Professional Ethics* [Position statement]. **www.socialstudies.org/position-statements/ncss-statement-professional-ethics**

National Council for the Social Studies. (2024). *Position statement of powerful, purposeful teaching and learning in elementary social studies* [Position statement]. **www.socialstudies.org/position-statements/position-statement-powerful-purposeful-teaching-and-learning-elementary-social**

Tyner, A., & Kabourek, S. (2020, September 24). *Social studies instruction and reading comprehension: Evidence from the early childhood longitudinal study.* Fordham Institute. **https://fordhaminstitute.org/national/resources/social-studies-instruction-and-reading-comprehension**

Chapter 1
The Art of Career Search:
Finding and Landing the Perfect Job

Jason Chevrier, Ed Finney, and Alyssa Sabbatino

Starting your career journey is an exciting milestone, filled with possibilities and the promise of applying all you have learned. As you transition from preparation to practice, it is important to approach the job search as a strategic process. The steps you take now—from clarifying your career goals to researching opportunities and preparing for interviews—will set the foundation for a rewarding and fulfilling career. Each phase of this journey is an opportunity to reflect on your strengths, showcase your dedication, and ultimately find a role where you can make an impact. So, take a deep breath, embrace the excitement of the unknown, and get ready to begin a search that will bring you one step closer to your goals!

This chapter will support you in preparing for interviews, familiarizing yourself with common educational language and initiatives, navigating teacher evaluation systems, and understanding controversial topics in education. Finally, the chapter includes a checklist for you to use when gearing up for your job search and acquisition in social studies. Here we go!

Finding and Landing a Job in Education: Interview Preparation With Sample Questions and Advice on How to Answer and What to Ask

Congratulations! All of your coursework, studying, observations, lesson planning, and student teaching has finally paid off, and you are officially ready for your own classroom! Throughout your journey, I am sure you have tucked away many ideas for what you will do (and what you will not do) when you are offered the opportunity to become a member of the faculty and are assigned your own classroom. Remember what it took to get to this moment but do not underestimate the work and strategic preparation that should go into finding and landing the perfect job for you.

As an energetic, new teacher, you are eager and ready for your first official job. You may have a dream district in mind or be ready to take the first job that comes your way, but gearing up and preparing for this process should not be taken lightly. Do you think you may want to teach in an urban environment, or do you feel you are more suited for a suburban or rural district? Now, kids are kids, but schools in each of these areas come with their own set of opportunities and challenges, and knowing your preferences, strengths, and weaknesses will help you find success wherever you end up. Research indicates that in New York State approximately 60% of new teachers work within 15 miles from their hometown (Goldhaber et al., 2020). A similar trend is observed in California, where studies have shown that over 60% of teachers teach within 15 miles of the high school from which they graduated (Thornton & Lambert, 2024).

Resume and Cover Letter

Now that you have an idea of where you would like to be, you can work to set yourself apart from the pack. By now, you have learned a great deal about yourself and who you are as an educator. This will become important as you begin to introduce yourself to future employers. As part of your program, you have likely worked on a cover letter and resume which, in most cases, will be the first opportunity you have to make an impression. It goes without saying that, as an educator looking for a job, you should make sure there are no mistakes with spelling and grammar. Take the time to proofread and have someone else do the same for you. Be careful not to get caught up in common mistakes that deter employers like not repeating resume content in the cover letter or overusing cliches. If you choose to use cliches, be sure that you have specific examples to back them up—don't be generic! Remember, this is an opportunity to set yourself apart.

Teacher Tip: *Hiring committees can spot a generic cover letter from a mile away. Reference specific programs, values, or goals from the district's website to demonstrate your genuine interest and alignment.*

Many districts use online application portals, making it easy for employers to post jobs and for candidates to apply to these postings. For instance, in New York State, one such popular system is the Online Application System (OLAS). Most districts require that you apply through these systems. When doing so, always be sure to double-check your uploaded documents to see how they have been uploaded into the system. At times, formatting may change, making some of your information hard to follow or read. Although these systems are convenient, another flaw is that you can apply to many jobs at once. Be cautious about doing this, as we have always found it more impressive when an applicant's cover letter is personalized to the specific district. Generic cover letters might get a look, but by personalizing, your potential future employers will know that you took the time to do this and want to make a good first impression. In addition to demonstrating effort, a personalized letter also signals genuine interest in the position, schools, and community, showing that you have considered how your skills and values align with their mission. While this is not expected in all districts, in smaller or more community-based schools, it can leave a strong impression if you hand-deliver a signed copy of your resume and cover letter. It shows initiative, professionalism, and genuine interest in the position.

Preparing for the Screening Interview

Making it through the paper screening process is the first step. Though procedures vary from district to district, for teaching and administrative jobs in our district, we schedule 20-minute virtual screening interviews as part of this process. We have found these to be invaluable to the hiring process because they offer a glimpse into a candidate's personality. We all know that interviewing is stressful and that candidates can be full of nerves, but interviewing is a two-way street. These virtual interviews allow the interviewer(s) to see how comfortable a candidate can be engaging in conversation, and, if you are going to be teaching in front of students all day, you need to be able to engage in conversation. We have never used the screening interviews to dive into deep philosophical questions about education, only questions geared to allowing candidates to show us who they are as people.

Later in this chapter, we provide a list of common topics and questions used at all stages of the interview process. Questions for this process might include the following:

- Where did you go to high school? Were you involved in extracurriculars or athletics?
- What is a lesson you learned in your undergraduate experience that has shaped who you are?
- Did you always want to be a teacher? How and when did you know?
- Who are your biggest influences in your life, and why?
- What is one of the most valuable things you have learned during your student teaching experience, and why?
- What do you like to do for fun?
- What book are you currently reading, or what is the last book you have read?

Social studies–specific questions for this process might include the following:

- How do you incorporate current events into your social studies curriculum?
- How do you differentiate instruction to meet the diverse needs of students in a social studies classroom?
- How do you teach social studies vocabulary?
- What are your favorite strategies for supporting students in reading informational texts in social studies?
- Can you describe your approach to teaching critical thinking and analysis skills in social studies?
- How do you promote civic engagement and help students understand their roles as active citizens?
- How do you address issues of diversity and inclusion within the social studies content, ensuring it reflects multiple perspectives?

As you can see, these questions are not meant to make sure you were paying attention during your college courses, but rather, they are an opportunity for the district to learn more about you. Make sure you take advantage of the time to set yourself apart from other candidates. Nerves are expected, but are you able to settle in and share details about yourself that would make us want to hire you? Were you easy to engage in conversation? Did you provide genuine and reflective answers? Did your passion for the work and your sense of humor shine through? These are all qualities that will be important if you are passed onto the next round of the hiring process: the committee round.

Technology Preparation and Readiness for the Screening Interview

It is also important to keep in mind that most school districts invest significantly in educational technology, with the expectation that these resources are integrated efficiently and purposefully. Schools now provide extensive libraries of technology tools, resources, support, and professional development. When preparing for an interview, it is important to know what technology a district integrates. Does the district utilize iPads, Chromebooks, or laptops? Is it a Google, Microsoft, or Apple environment? Do they use Google Classroom, Canvas, or another learning management system (LMS)? Understanding the tools valued by the prospective district demonstrates your readiness to contribute to their instructional goals.

This information can often be obtained from the district's website. Check for Board of Education minutes (often found in a program called BoardDocs), review the district technology plan, and review teachers' websites. The research not only prepares you for the interview questions but also demonstrates your commitment to the district's goals and your professionalism.

The rapid increase in educational technology has led schools to place greater emphasis on hiring teachers who are not only comfortable with technology but who can also harness it to enhance student learning outcomes. Emphasize your comfort and skill set with instructional technology in your cover letter and resume. While you will not be expected to be an expert, having a basic understanding is important, especially regarding the district's LMS.

Teacher Tip: *Check the district's website or BoardDocs to find out what technology platforms and tools are in use. Being able to reference and speak confidently about those systems shows initiative and readiness.*

The Committee Round and Teaching Demonstration

Congratulations! You must have impressed the district with your cover letter and resume, and you must have nailed the screening interview. You just received a call that you have been selected to participate in the next stage of the process—the committee round. You are probably asking yourself, "What should I expect, and how do I prepare for this next important part of the process?"

This round usually consists of building administration and a cadre of teachers, mostly made up of members of the department. It could also include special education teachers, related service providers, counselors, staff members, and other administrators. This will likely depend on the time of year you are interviewing. Remember that first impressions will go a long way, so make sure you dress in professional attire, make eye contact with those asking questions, and keep your responses on point and concise. This will be a time when deeper questions are asked in an effort to set candidates apart. You have worked hard and know your stuff. This is your time to shine!

Many interviews require a teaching demonstration, that is, a live teaching lesson segment to see how you work with students and to view your teaching style and lesson plan in action. Do not panic if you are given the option to use the district's technology during the live lesson. Do not hesitate to ask for assistance from the classroom teacher to access the technology or post materials to the district's LMS. The classroom teacher has offered up their classroom for your demonstration lesson and should be more than willing to help facilitate your technology needs or answer your questions. Building a rapport with the classroom teacher could enhance your chances of landing the position by demonstrating your initiative and professionalism.

During the committee round, it will be important to let your personality show in addition to the content. The committee members are proud of the work they do in their school and want to make sure that you will be a good fit for their culture. Do your homework! Research the district's social studies programs and any unique initiatives, curricula, field experiences, or recognitions related to the subject. Doing this prior to the interview will allow you to share something about what is happening in the school or district with the committee. If you know someone who has students in the school, talk to them or the student. Go the extra mile to learn something about the place you would like to work. Have students done something noteworthy? Has a teacher been recognized? Does the assessment data show any trends? Are there any goals or district initiatives that resonate with you? Find a way to work some of this into your responses in the interview. The group will likely be impressed that you have taken the time to learn something about them, which shows initiative, effort, and drive. Be genuinely sincere. Who knows? You could spend the next 25–30 years of your life teaching here!

It is not uncommon for selected candidates to move on to a teaching demonstration. Seriously—no pressure! The teaching demonstration is exactly what it sounds like. You are given a topic and a class and are asked to prepare a 20–30-minute lesson. Expect all the members from the committee round to be in the room to observe. Remember, first things first. Make sure you develop a lesson plan focused on the given topic. Know your history or the particular content (e.g., global history, government, war and society, ancient civilizations, etc.). Be sure the lesson plan contains all the essential components and bring copies for the committee members to have in front of them as you teach the lesson. Be sure to know what strategies you will utilize and how you will engage the students to complete your objective. Will this be primarily lecture driven, or will students have the opportunity to be involved in small group or partner work? How do you plan to transition from one part of the lesson to the next? How will students demonstrate their learning, and how will you assess it? Think it through and show the committee that you know how to plan a thoughtful, engaging lesson.

Although the content of your lesson is important, this is an opportunity for the committee to see you interact with students. Building connections and relationships with students can be a challenge when you are just introduced, but the committee will be watching to see how you connect and talk with students, what words you choose to use, and how you respond to those who might need help. As stated before, nerves are expected, but overcoming them is important. Let your personality shine and be yourself! This can be hard to do in a contrived situation, but you will be your best when you are being yourself!

The District-Level Interview

Phew! That lesson is over and you nailed it! Now, you get the call that you are a finalist for the position. The last step in the process is a final interview, usually with the superintendent or another district-level administrator. In our district, this is an opportunity for us to meet with the top one or two candidates. It allows us to engage in conversation and get to know the candidate who we would recommend to the board of education for appointment. In most cases, we ask the building principal to share with us some of the things they might be wondering or any lingering questions that need to be answered.

This final interview is typically less about instructional strategies and more about who you are as a professional, how you see yourself contributing to the district's mission, and how you build relationships with students, families, and colleagues. You will pick up on the vibe of the interview pretty quickly—it tends to feel more conversational, but it is still important to maintain a formal and professional tone. Be sure to let your passion, excitement, and knowledge shine during this time.

To prepare, we recommend reviewing the question in the "Common Interview Topics and Questions" section of this chapter, paying particular attention to those about your core values, leadership qualities, and approaches to building school culture. Be ready to share what drew you to this district specifically, how you align with its priorities, and what makes you a right fit for this community. This is your moment to articulate not just what you can do but why you want to do it in their district.

SUCCESS!

That moment will come when your phone rings and the person on the other end congratulates you on being the successful candidate! Your hard work has paid off, and your time has come!

And until that moment comes, there may be circumstances when you do not get the job you were hoping for. It is important to remember that not receiving an offer is not a reflection of your worth as an educator, nor does it necessarily mean you did anything wrong at any stage in the process. Sometimes the decision comes down to factors beyond your control—an internal candidate, specific experience the district was seeking, certification areas, or a need for a particular skill set at that moment in time. Other times, districts might be balancing team dynamics or long-term staffing plans that are not visible to applicants.

If you find yourself in this situation, take time to reflect on the experience, request feedback when appropriate, and remind yourself that every interview is valuable practice that prepares you for the right opportunity when it comes along. Keep growing, stay connected to your professional community, and trust that your time will come.

Feedback and a Pivot

If the outcome is not what you had hoped, remember that every interview is a step forward. Take time to reflect on the experience, considering what went well and where you might improve. Reach out for feedback, if possible, and continue refining your skills and knowledge. Each application, every interview, and all the preparation bring you closer to the right opportunity. Keep your goals in focus, remain persistent, and trust that the right position is still out there, waiting for you to find it!

Teacher Tip: *Even the best answers fall flat if they sound rehearsed or rambling. Practice answering common interview questions with a friend or in front of a mirror so you can speak with clarity and confidence.*

Common Interview Topics and Questions

In addition to the specific aforementioned questions, the following topics and corresponding questions are often asked in interviews. These might come up during any of the different interviews you will experience.

1. Teaching Philosophy and Approach
- How would you describe your teaching philosophy?
- What role do you believe a teacher plays in the classroom and in the school community?
- How do you make learning engaging and accessible for all students?
- Describe a time when you adjusted your teaching style to meet students' needs.

2. Classroom Management and Discipline
- How do you establish a positive classroom environment?
- What strategies do you use to handle classroom disruptions or challenging behaviors?
- How do you ensure a balance between structure and flexibility in classroom management?
- How do you approach conflict resolution among students?

3. Lesson Planning and Instruction
- How do you plan lessons to meet diverse learning styles and needs?
- Describe a lesson plan you're particularly proud of and why it was effective.
- How do you incorporate state standards and district curricula into your lessons?
- What role does technology play in your lesson planning?

4. Student Assessment and Data-Driven Instruction
- How do you assess student progress, both formally and informally?
- Describe how you use data to inform your teaching practices.
- How do you communicate student progress to parents and guardians?
- How do you support a student who is struggling with the material?

5. Collaboration and Professional Development
- How do you collaborate with other teachers and staff?
- Describe a time when you worked with a colleague to improve student learning.
- How do you stay current with educational trends and best practices?
- In what ways do you contribute to the school community outside of the classroom?

6. Social-Emotional Learning and Student Relationships
- How do you build relationships with your students and foster a sense of trust?
- How do you incorporate social-emotional learning into your teaching?
- How do you support students' mental health and emotional well-being?
- Describe a time when you helped a student overcome a challenge.

7. Diversity, Equity, Inclusion, and Culturally Responsive Education
- How do you ensure that your classroom is an inclusive environment for all students?
- How do you integrate culturally relevant materials and practices into your curriculum?
- Can you describe a time when you adapted your instruction to meet the needs of students from diverse backgrounds?
- How do you address and support conversations around social justice, race, or cultural identity in the classroom?

8. English as a New Language (ENL) Instruction and Support
- How do you adapt your instruction for students who are English language learners (ELL)?
- What strategies do you use to help ELL students feel comfortable and confident in your classroom?
- How do you support language development while also teaching grade-level content?
- How do you collaborate with ENL teachers and incorporate language support into your lessons?

9. Instructional Technology
- How do you integrate instructional technology into your social studies lessons to enhance student engagement and learning outcomes?

- Can you provide an example of how you've used technology to support differentiated instruction in a social studies classroom?
- How do you ensure that technology use in social studies aligns with curriculum standards and promotes critical thinking skills?
- How do you balance traditional teaching methods with the use of technology to ensure a comprehensive social studies education?
- What tools or platforms do you find most effective for fostering collaboration and communication among students in your social studies classes?

Glossary of Key Terms, Concepts, and Initiatives in Education to Support Interview Preparation

The following glossary with corresponding figures is intended to support your preparation for interviews. These are basic definitions that will help you to personalize responses to the questions above, based on your own experiences, beliefs, and goals.

Academic Intervention Services (AIS): a system of academic support provided to students who are struggling to meet grade-level standards in specific subjects. AIS are typically targeted, supplemental instruction designed to address gaps in student learning and help students achieve proficiency. These services can take various forms, such as small-group instruction, tutoring, or additional time in the classroom.

Classroom Management: strategies and techniques used to maintain a productive, respectful, and safe learning environment.

Culturally Responsive Education (CRE): an approach to teaching that recognizes and values students' cultural backgrounds and incorporates them into the curriculum.

Data-Driven Instruction: the use of student performance data to guide teaching practices and personalize learning.

Diversity, Equity, and Inclusion (DEI): the intentional efforts to create a learning environment that acknowledges, respects, and celebrates the differences among students, while ensuring that all students, regardless of background or identity, have access to equal opportunities and support. It involves cultivating a culture where all students feel valued, included, and able to thrive, with tailored approaches to meet individual needs and eliminate barriers to learning.

Differentiated Instruction: tailoring instruction to meet individual learning needs through various methods, content, and assessments.

Diversity: the inclusion of individuals from various backgrounds, perspectives, and abilities, contributing to a rich and varied learning environment.

English Language Learner (ELL): a student who is in the process of acquiring proficiency in English while continuing to learn academic content in other subjects. ELL students may come from diverse linguistic and cultural backgrounds and may need specialized support to bridge the gap between their first language and English.

English as a New Language (ENL): an educational program specifically designed to support ELLs in developing English proficiency while simultaneously ensuring they have access to grade-level content in core subjects. ENL typically involves a combination of language instruction and academic support, often with an emphasis on integrating language learning into all subject areas.

Note on ELL and ENL: While "ELL" refers to a student who is still in the process of learning English, ENL is a structured program that provides specialized instruction to help these students acquire language skills. The term "ENL" refers more to the *program or instructional approach*, whereas "ELL" refers to the *student or student group* who needs additional language support.

Equity: ensuring fair treatment, opportunities, and outcomes for all students by addressing individual needs and removing barriers.

Formative Assessment: ongoing assessments, such as quizzes or observations, used to monitor student learning and adjust instruction as needed.

Inclusion: the practice of ensuring that students of all backgrounds, abilities, and needs are supported within a general education setting.

Least Restrictive Environment (LRE): the practice of educating students with disabilities alongside their peers to the greatest extent appropriate.

Multitiered System of Supports (MTSS): a comprehensive, school-wide framework that provides

Figure 1.1 *Multitiered System of Supports*

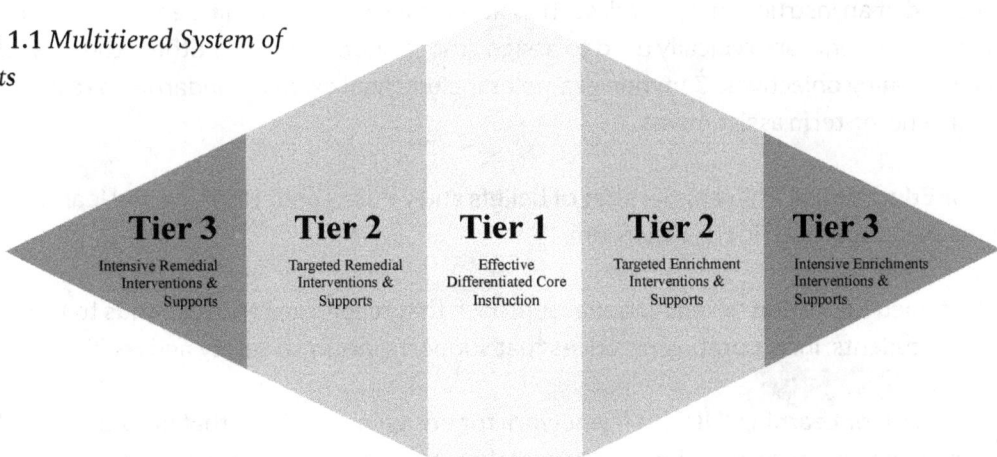

Tier 3	Tier 2	Tier 1	Tier 2	Tier 3
Intensive Remedial Interventions & Supports	Targeted Remedial Interventions & Supports	Effective Differentiated Core Instruction	Targeted Enrichment Interventions & Supports	Intensive Enrichments Interventions & Supports

A Classroom With Purpose: A Guide to Teaching Social Studies Today

varying levels of support to students based on their academic, behavioral, and social-emotional needs. MTSS typically includes multiple tiers of intervention, from universal supports for all students (Tier 1) to targeted interventions for students who need additional help or enrichment (Tier 2) and intensive, individualized supports for those with the most significant challenges or needs for acceleration (Tier 3). (See Figure 1.1)

Restorative Practices: a set of practices focused on building positive relationships and resolving conflicts by repairing harm rather than focusing solely on punishment. These are both proactive and preventative and reactive and responsive.

- **Proactive Restorative Practices:** strategies that focus on building relationships, creating a positive community, and preventing conflicts before they occur. Examples include circles, group discussions, and community-building activities.

- **Reactive Restorative Practices:** approaches that address conflicts or harm after they occur, focusing on repairing relationships through methods like mediation, restorative conversations, and conflict resolution circles.

Response to Intervention (RTI): a proactive, multitiered approach to identifying and supporting students with learning and behavior needs. RTI involves closely monitoring student progress, providing increasingly intensive levels of instruction and support, and using data to determine whether additional interventions or specialized services are necessary. RTI helps ensure that students who are struggling receive the right level of support early on to prevent more significant challenges later.

Social-Emotional Learning (SEL): programs and practices that help students develop self-awareness, social skills, and emotional regulation.

Summative Assessment: a type of assessment that evaluates student learning, knowledge, and skills at the end of an instructional period, such as at the conclusion of a unit, semester, or course. Summative assessments are typically used to assign grades or determine whether students have met specific learning objectives. Common examples include final exams, standardized tests, projects, and end-of-term assignments.

Teaching (or Educational) Philosophy: a set of beliefs and values about teaching and learning that guides a teacher's approach in the classroom.

Trauma-Informed Education: an educational approach that recognizes and responds to the effects of trauma on students, incorporating practices that support emotional safety and resilience.

Universal Design for Learning (UDL): a framework for designing curricula that provide multiple means of engagement, representation, and expression to meet diverse learners' needs.

Teacher Evaluation Systems and *You*

Based on multiple criteria, including instructional performance, student achievement, and professional responsibilities, teacher evaluation systems are designed to assess and improve the effectiveness of educators. This process can be a bit of a challenge and take some effort, but if you dive in, it is incredibly rewarding and can spark your own growth and excitement.

While the process varies from district to district, it generally includes a combination of
- classroom observations,
- review of student performance data,
- self-reflection and goal setting, and
- input from students, peers, and supervisors.

Each school district has its own way of implementing the teacher evaluation system process, including how observations are conducted, what weight is given to student data, and how performance is rated. Teachers may be evaluated on various domains such as instructional planning, teaching strategies, classroom management, and professional development.

Danielson Framework for Teaching

The most commonly used rubric for teacher evaluation, the Danielson Framework for Teaching, is used in many states and districts to provide a detailed, structured evaluation of teacher performance. Teachers are rated on a scale: unsatisfactory, developing, effective, and highly effective. The Danielson Framework is a comprehensive tool that defines good teaching in four domains:

1. **Planning and Preparation**: knowledge of content, instructional planning, and designing assessments
2. **Classroom Environment**: the physical and emotional environment of the classroom, including managing student behavior and creating a positive learning space
3. **Instruction**: the actual delivery of lessons, student engagement, and the use of various instructional strategies
4. **Professional Responsibilities**: collaboration, professional development, and reflection on teaching practices

Other State-Specific or District-Specific Rubrics

In addition to the Danielson Framework, there are other rubrics used across different states and districts. These rubrics might include elements specific to the state's educational goals or focus areas, such as student growth measures or specific instructional strategies. The following are examples of other rubrics that may be used for teacher evaluation:
- **Marzano Teacher Evaluation Model:** This model focuses on instructional strategies, including classroom strategies, the impact of teacher-student relationships, and the teacher's ability to promote student growth.
- **The Strong Evaluation System:** This evaluation system includes a detailed breakdown of teacher performance in categories such as content knowledge, instruction, and student outcomes.

Essential Factors for Teachers to Consider in the Evaluation Process

- **Preparation:** Teachers should familiarize themselves with the rubric used by their district, self-assess their teaching practices, and set professional goals.
- **Reflection:** After each observation or evaluation cycle, teachers should reflect on feedback and make plans for improvement.
- **Growth Mindset:** The process is designed not just to evaluate, but to promote professional growth. Emphasize openness to feedback and a commitment to ongoing development (Dweck, 2007).

Navigating a Polarized Political Climate in Education in the Social Studies Classroom

The political climate across the country has become increasingly polarized, and teachers are often at the center of discussions around what is taught in schools, how it is taught, and what values are promoted. While this can be challenging, it also provides an opportunity for educators to showcase their professionalism, resilience, and commitment to the students they serve. Here is some advice for you, based on the nature of these opportunities.

Stay Focused on What You Can Control! In the face of political pressures, it is essential to focus on what you can control—your classroom environment, your instructional practices, and your relationships with students. Teachers have the power to create an atmosphere of respect, curiosity, and critical thinking where students feel safe and supported, regardless of outside factors.

Building Bridges Through Open Dialogue. As a teacher, you may find yourself navigating difficult conversations. It is important to approach these moments with empathy, respect, and a commitment to fostering open dialogue. Listening to your students, understanding their perspectives, and gently guiding them toward healthy conversations can transform challenging moments into powerful learning experiences.

Stay Rooted in Standards. Let the Standards Be Your Guide. In times of uncertainty or polarization, it is more important than ever to stay anchored in the standards that guide your teaching. Whether it is state-specific SEL benchmarks, DEI standards, or Speaking and Listening frameworks, these standards serve as your compass. They ensure that your curriculum remains focused on the skills and knowledge that students need to succeed, while providing a clear and objective foundation for your instruction.

By aligning your lessons with these standards, you can create a consistent and equitable learning experience for all students, regardless of external challenges. Standards help keep the classroom focused on what is best for students, encouraging skills like critical thinking, communication, collaboration, and empathy—skills that will serve them well both in and out of the classroom.

Maintain a Growth Mindset and Professionalism. The work you do as an educator is invaluable, and staying grounded in your professional ethics is key. Remember that your responsibility is to educate and empower students—not to push any personal agenda but to help students understand the world around them. Staying informed, keeping a growth mindset, and seeking support when needed are crucial in navigating these turbulent times. Tap into your mentor, your department, your grade-level colleagues, your leadership; whoever you have as a sounding board, use them. That is what a school community is all about.

Be a Champion of Inclusivity and Respect. No matter where you teach or what the political climate looks like, your role as a champion of inclusivity, diversity, and respect never changes. By fostering an environment where every student feels valued and heard, you are helping them develop into thoughtful, compassionate citizens who can approach the world with an open mind.

Checklist for Finding and Landing the Perfect Job

Self-Assessment and Preparation
- ☐ Reflect on your strengths, teaching philosophy, and what makes you unique as a candidate.
- ☐ Identify any certifications or skills you need to strengthen (e.g., classroom management strategies).

Build Your Resume and Cover Letter
- ☐ Update your resume to include relevant experiences (e.g., student teaching, internships, volunteer work).
- ☐ Tailor your cover letter to the specific job, highlighting why you are a good fit for the school and district.
- ☐ Include any specific certifications or qualifications (e.g., ELL, SEL, special education).

Research the School and District
- ☐ Review the district's website and understand their mission, values, and student population.
- ☐ Familiarize yourself with the district's goals and priorities (e.g., academic improvement, DEI initiatives, school culture).

Prepare for the Interview
- ☐ Practice answers to common questions (e.g., classroom management, handling difficult students, promoting DEI).
- ☐ Have a concrete example ready of how you have used formative or summative assessments in the past.
- ☐ Prepare questions to ask the interview panel (e.g., "How does the district support new teachers?").

Demonstrate Teaching Competencies
- ☐ Be ready to discuss specific teaching strategies, including how you engage diverse learners.
- ☐ Share examples of how you integrate SEL, DEI, and academic standards into your lessons.
- ☐ Bring examples of formative or summative assessments you have used and explain how you adjust instruction based on data.

Understand Key Standards
- ☐ Review and understand the relevant state or national standards (e.g., SEL benchmarks, academic content standards).
- ☐ Know how to explain how you will apply these standards to support students' success.

Follow Up After the Interview
- ☐ Send a personalized thank-you email to the interviewers within 24 hours.
- ☐ Reaffirm your interest in the position and briefly highlight what makes you an excellent fit for the role.

Prepare for Success if Hired
- ☐ Organize your teaching materials (e.g., lesson plans, classroom setup).
- ☐ Connect with other teachers or mentors for advice on starting strong in your new role.

Stay Resilient and Reflective
- ☐ Ask for feedback and identify areas for improvement if you do not get the job.
- ☐ Stay motivated by continuing to build your skills (e.g., attend workshops, volunteer for new opportunities).
- ☐ Breathe and stay true to yourself!

References

Dweck, C. S. (2007). *Mindset: The new psychology of success*. Random House.

Goldhaber, D., Strunk, K. O., Brown, N., Naito, N., & Wolff, M. (2020). Teacher staffing challenges in California: Examining the uniqueness of rural school districts. *AERA Open, 6*(3). **https://doi.org/10.1177/2332858420951833**

Thornton, L., & Lambert, D. (2024, July 30). *Can high school teacher academies address the shortage? Programs point to yes*. CapRadio. **www.capradio.org/articles/2024/07/30/can-high-school-teacher-academies-address-the-shortage-programs-point-to-yes/**

Chapter 2
Navigating the Early Years

Emily Wells and James O'Brien

The transition from being a student to becoming a teacher comes with many challenges. Starting off a career as an educator is a transformative period, which can feel overwhelming. The goal of this chapter is to outline a comprehensive guide that can set the foundations for a fulfilling and impactful career in education.

This chapter offers insight and practical strategies to help new teachers successfully navigate the challenges and opportunities of the early years in the social studies classroom. In this chapter, you will find information on managing initial classroom experiences with vast information on building community and classroom management. This chapter also focuses on effective communication and actionable techniques for managing early experiences as an educator.

Central to this journey is the art of relationship building, whether it is with students, parents/guardians, or colleagues. This chapter emphasizes the importance of collaboration within the school community, recognizing that a supportive, interconnected environment is crucial for both personal and professional growth. As we work to teach our social studies students the importance of civic engagement, it is important that we model and explicitly teach them the skills within our school community that they will need in order to act as responsible citizens both inside and outside of the classroom.

Classroom Community

This section discusses how to establish a classroom community rooted in high expectations and feelings of safety, how to maintain a sense of community throughout the year, and how to repair issues that occur within the classroom as they arise. The takeaway from this section should be that classroom management is not reactive; it is a byproduct of meticulous planning and proactive thinking. By investing class time at the start of the year to establish a strong sense of community, you will have more time to focus on content as the year progresses, rather than having to reteach expectations when issues with behavior arise later in the year.

Maslow Before Bloom

The goal of educators should always be to deliver high-quality instruction that pushes students to be better people, thinkers, readers, and writers. Maslow (1943) would describe this as self-actualization or the desire to be the best version of themselves. It is important to realize that in order to create an environment that is academically rigorous for all students, you must first ask what you are doing to meet the non-academic needs of your students (see Figure 2.1).

Figure 2.1 *Maslow's Hierarchy of Needs*

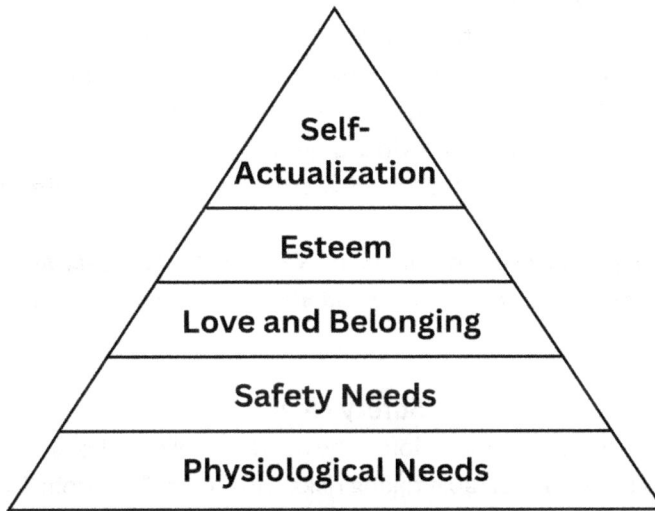

Physiological Needs

First, Maslow addresses physiological needs. If students are worried about things like food, water, shelter, sleep, and clothing, they cannot be worried about the content of a class. This may seem like something that falls outside of the responsibilities of a classroom teacher; however, there are some very basic steps that can be taken in order to help meet students' physiological needs. One easy step is setting up a "What I Need" (WIN) station in the room. In the back of the classroom, there can be a closet or bin stocked with snacks, clothes, lotion, travel-size toiletries, hair products, and menstrual care items. The teacher should want students to know that when they enter the room, the teacher has taken steps to meet their most basic needs. This is the first step in building trust between students and the teacher, which is one of the most important pillars of an effective classroom community. It may sound like a big ask to go out and purchase a closet full of materials, and it is. It would be remiss to say that educators should further drain their personal bank accounts to meet these needs for their students, so consider the following ideas to help meet these needs.

Strong teachers would thrive in the days of hunting and gathering. In order to stock their WIN bin, they can reach out to community partners and be an advocate for their students in need. Over the summer, they can visit missions and religious institutions with food and clothing pantries. These organizations are typically happy to donate new or gently used items to the classroom community. Oftentimes, the health office at a school will have personal care items for students that the teacher can ask to include in their classroom. If the teacher struggles to find these resources in the building, they can pay a visit to a community healthcare clinic. These are great resources to supply these products, or at the very least, they can offer insight into other organizations to contact. In short, do not put it on yourself to meet every student's needs, but do your best to advocate for your students and find outlets that can also offer assistance.

Once the teacher has stocked their WIN bin, they should explain the system to the class. Explain what resources are available for students and how they should access these resources. The teacher should be sure to explain that this bin is stocked by the teacher for students who are in need and that students should be mindful about what resources they take. The teacher should remind students to take what they need but use what they take, as this is a shared resource for all students. Students should know that, if there is an emergent need, they can take from the closet without question, but the expectation is that they check in with the teacher before accessing this resource. It can be uncomfortable to ask for some of these items in a large setting, so make sure students know when the teacher will be available so that students can come access the WIN bin privately during this time.

Teacher Tip: *A possible time for access to the WIN bin can be during the first five minutes of the lunch period, but ensure you check with your administration so this does not disrupt school procedures.*

Safety Needs

The next step on the road to self-actualization is the need to feel safe. For students to grow academically, they need to be comfortable taking risks within the classroom. Moreover, teachers must take great care to create this safe environment for students. This idea will be further developed in the next section, but the base of this work falls within the safety parameters set within the classroom. Teachers, especially new teachers, should take time to think about the steps they have taken to create, and more importantly maintain, a safe environment for all students. There are countless ways to set and maintain expectations, and what works for one teacher may not be as effective for another. Therefore, there are core principles that all teachers should keep in mind when developing the expectations for their classroom.

First, expectations should be clear, versatile, and limited in number. By limiting the number of expectations, the core values of your classroom community are clearly defined, and students are able to understand why certain things are, or are not, acceptable in the classroom. The teacher should think of two to three core principles for their classroom, such as, "Be safe and try hard." Framing expectations in this light allows students to think through the "why" for their actions in the classroom and can make it much easier to address undesirable behaviors in a way that maintains the teacher's role as a facilitator of the classroom community, rather than forcing the teacher to be a compliance officer in the room. When behaviors are addressed or corrections have to be made, they are tied back to the core principle of safety, which in turn creates an environment that is clearly putting safety at the forefront. This reinforcement allows all students in the room to predict that, when something is unsafe in any way, it will be addressed in a way that highlights the importance of safety. Maslow references the need for predictability regarding safety, and the ability to address concern in the room through this lens fosters that predictability.

Second, expectations should be discussed with the class in a way that allows students to take ownership of these expectations. During the first week of school, the teacher should clearly lay out their core principles and have groups develop profiles of students who meet these expectations. The question is simple, "What does a safe student look, sound, or feel like in a classroom?" Typically, students latch onto physical safety. Their early responses reference a controlled body, keeping their hands to themselves and being at their desk. This is a great entry point into the conversation. The teacher should have students focus on how these ideas might make other students in the room feel and how being physically safe can help the class be successful. Once the community has a firm grasp on physical safety and its importance, the teacher can challenge students to think about the other ways they can remain safe in the classroom.

This is where the conversation can be opened to what students say and how they say it. This is where students might start to phrase their thinking in negative ways. "A safe student doesn't swear," is correct, but the goal is not to create a list of what not to do, so the teacher should challenge students to describe what strong habits are observed from typically safe students. Framing the conversation in this light allows the teacher to model concrete behaviors that are acceptable, while helping students understand how these kinds of behaviors align with the core principles of the classroom. Also, having students develop these profiles helps put the onus of the classroom expectations onto them, as they were the team who laid out what safety should look, sound, and feel like in the room. To offer a reference of what this might sound like in a classroom, here is an example of how the teacher can try to guide students to a place of finding positive behaviors that tie back to the core principles, while modeling academic discourse they will use throughout the year.

Teacher: I appreciate the insight on what a safe student looks like. Now let's think about what a safe student might sound and feel like. What kind of language does a safe student use?

Student: A student doesn't swear.

Teacher: I agree with the idea that the words we use can affect the safety of our community, but I want to challenge you to word that idea in a positive way. What type of language can we expect from a safe student?

Student: A safe student uses kind words.

Teacher: I think that's a very strong example of how a safe student sounds. Can anyone build on that idea by offering an example of how we can be kind to other students in the room who are struggling with an assignment? Let's restate that question when we offer an answer as well.

Student: We can be kind to students who are struggling in class by telling them not to give up or asking them if they need help.

Teacher: That's an interesting idea that I think we should talk more about. Turn and talk with a partner for 30 seconds, tell your partner how offering to help a classmate when they are struggling could help make our community safe. We'll share our strong ideas in 30 seconds.

It is important to remember that teaching about expectations is no different from teaching content. Students need direct instruction on the expectations in the room; they need time to

A Classroom With Purpose: A Guide to Teaching Social Studies Today

develop an understanding of the expectations through discussion, modeling, and think-alouds; and most importantly, they need time to practice these expectations with low-stakes, high engagement activities. The next section discusses how the teacher can incorporate these activities in a way that pushes students closer to the realm of self-actualization.

Love and Belonging

Once safety of the environment has been established, the teacher can begin to focus on the next domain of Maslow's hierarchy of needs: love and belonging. For students to feel comfortable taking risks within the classroom, they need to feel a sense of connection with those around them. Obviously, the teacher cannot make all the students in the room become friends with each other; however, the teacher needs to know that students are comfortable interacting with their peers in class. This section outlines the activities that can be used during the first days of school to help foster connections among students. This section briefly explains each activity, highlights how each activity helps foster connections between students, explains the rationale behind the sequencing of the activities, and offers tips on how to incorporate talking stems to introduce students to the academic language register used throughout the year within the classroom.

First, students need to know the names of all their classmates as soon as possible. Asking another student their name can be an uncomfortable task for a student, and students often miss opportunities to connect with a classmate simply because they do not know how to call them. For this reason, the teacher should spend one of the first days doing a Name Chain with their students. The class should sit in a circle in the middle of the room, and each student should come up with a verb or adjective and accompanying gesture that starts with the same letter as their first name. Once the chain starts, each student must repeat the name, word, and gesture of every student who has gone before them. The goal is to get around the whole circle, remembering the name and information shared by each student in the class (see Figure 2.2).

Figure 2.2 *Name Chain: Student-Facing Instructions*

Name Chain
1. Move into a circle in the middle of the room.
2. Say your name and an action that starts with the same letter.
   "My name is James, and I like to jam."
3. The person on your right repeats your name and action and adds their own.
4. We go around the circle until everyone has gone and we can remember all the names and actions.

This activity is extremely low stakes, gets students used to sharing in front of their peers, and allows each student to hear their classmates' names pronounced correctly numerous times over a single class period. This is a great way to introduce a collaborative structure, circles, in a way that removes the academic or more intense social demands that can be incorporated into circles later. The teacher should ask students what they can do to make sure their classmates feel safe sharing in the circle and continually point out positive behaviors as they work through the activity. The teacher can also include talking stems (see Figure 2.3) to help students effectively communicate

Figure 2.3 *Talking Stems for Students to Support in Statement and Question Making*

Agreement	**Clarification**
I agree with ___ because ___.	Can you repeat what you said about ___?
I like what ___ said because ___.	How does that support the idea that ___?
Disagreement	**Extension**
I disagree with ___ because ___.	When I heard ___, it made me think that ___.
I can see that ___; however, I disagree with ___.	Now I'm wondering if ___.
	Can you tell me more about ___?

Note. Adapted from *Instructional Tools to Address the Complex Language Demands of Academic Interaction*, by K. Kinsella, February 3, 2017, Idaho Association for Bilingual Education Annual Conference, Boise, Idaho, United States.

with their peers during the Name Chain. By taking these steps, the activity moves beyond a simple introduction and serves as a means for students to become acclimated with the routines and expectations of the class.

The next day, the class can start with a challenge to see if anyone can remember all the names learned previously. This refresher is a great way to set up the next activity, Collect a Classmate. For this activity, students are given a worksheet that resembles a bingo card, with the simple goal of collecting a different classmate's name for each statement. The teacher can get creative with what they include in this activity, but the purpose is that each statement helps students discover a connection with a different classmate. By the end of the activity, students should have a visual representation of at least one commonality that they have with each member of the class. Establishing these connections early allows students to pursue relationships with peers who they may not have known very well before and spurs conversations that help establish a community rooted in connection between students.

This activity involves movement and gives the teacher an opportunity to teach their expectations once again. Before sending students off to work, it is important to review the importance of safety, both physical and social. It is important not only to spend time going over what a safe student looks like while moving around a classroom but also to challenge students to think about how they can approach their classmates in a way that will make them comfortable to share with them. It is helpful to model strong interpersonal communication here; students need to see and hear what the activity should be like. The teacher should take time to talk about tone, body language, and greetings. It may sound simple, but students are still working to develop healthy communication, and this is a fantastic opportunity to teach that skill.

Once students have begun to communicate and build connections, the teacher needs to push them further into the collaborative structures used within the classroom. The Deserted Island Survival game is a classic team-building activity, where students have found themselves and a group of classmates on a sinking ship. They have enough time to grab four items from a predetermined list and swim to a nearby island, and the group must come up with a plan detailing how they will use these items to survive on the island. See Figure 2.4 for more detailed instructions and printouts to use in class. We encourage you to incorporate this activity into your classroom, as it is typically a favorite activity among students.

Figure 2.4 *Deserted Island Worksheet, Challenge Cards, and Activity Overview*

Group members: _____
Directions:
As your ship is going down, you see these items around you.
Your group has enough time to grab a total of four items. Write
the items you have selected and your reason for selecting
them on the right side of this page.

lantern	hiking boots	toilet paper	knife
axe	lighter	bug spray	pot
blow-up raft	mirror	water filter	tent
fishing rod	first aid kit	flare gun	sun block

Write your four items here, and explain why you decided to
take them:

Item 1: _____

Reasoning: _____

_____

Item 2: _____

Reasoning: _____

_____

Item 3: _____

Reasoning: _____

_____

Item 4: _____

Reasoning: _____

_____

There are several tribes on your island. Some of them are very kind and willing to help. Others take visitors as a threat that they need to protect themselves from.	You cannot see any clear threats on the island! However, every 12 hours a tropical storm blows through and destroys any shelters that have been set up.	Three years ago, a group of 5th graders was also stranded on the island. It seems like they have established a community on the island.	Your island is very nice; however, it is sinking ½ an inch each day. You can tell that it is 30 inches above sea level.
You're on King Kong Island! There is a massive gorilla that inhabits your island, and he does NOT trust humans.	The island is very nice during the day, but it reaches a temperature of -10 degrees Fahrenheit at night.	Welcome to Big Bird Island! Mutant eagles live in the trees, and you see them scoop up a wild boar as you get there! They are hungry and big enough to scoop up a person.	Pirates hid their treasure on this island a year ago, and they have come back to take it. They cannot find it and cannot be convinced that you did not hide it from them.

Activity overview

Introduction:
In this activity, students use their critical thinking and problem-solving skills to survive being trapped on a desert island.

Procedure:
Set the scene by drawing a boat on the board. The teacher can set the stage by letting the class know that their group has won a free cruise! Have students start by saying what they are looking forward to doing on their trip. Then, draw a huge wave crashing over the boat. Tell students that the ship has capsized.

After this, the teacher can divide students into groups of three or four and hand out the worksheet. The teacher should tell students that there is an island nearby that they can swim to and that they have time to grab four items from the worksheet to help them survive. On the worksheet, students need to write which items they have selected and explain why they picked those items. After they have selected their items, the teacher can give students the chance to explain their choices to the class.

At this point, the teacher should hand out a different challenge card to each group. This card details a unique challenge that awaits their group on the island. After they have selected a challenge card, each group will take time to develop a plan on how they will survive on the island using the four items to help them.

Once groups have shared, the teacher can give them a survival score from one to three. The teacher can explain that there is also an element of luck when it comes to survival and roll a die to see what each group's luck score will be. Add together each group's survival and luck scores for their final survival grade.

Scores:
6+: Thriving! Congrats on your new, enjoyable island life.
4–5: Surviving. It's pretty difficult on the island. You're hoping to get rescued, but you can make it until you are found.
Under 3: You tried your best, but your survival skills were not up to the task. Sadly, you did not make it off the island.

Students are excited to engage with this critical thinking activity and collaborate on their survival plans. The teacher should take time to review procedures for working in groups, with a particular focus on productive disagreement. Before the activity, the teacher should introduce new talking stems on disagreeing with ideas. Students need to remember that the purpose of the activity is to work effectively with their classmates and that the way they voice their disagreement can greatly impact their group. The teacher needs to review how tone can impact feelings of safety in the group and model how to effectively use newly introduced talking stems. In short, the teacher needs to remind students that what they say is only part of communication and how they say those words also impacts how their ideas will be received. As groups work, the teacher should point out positive communication and offer praise for students who are using the talking stems effectively.

After giving students the chance to practice their team-building skills, the teacher can challenge them to further develop these strong communication strategies with the Cup Stacking game (see Figure 2.5). Students will have to work collaboratively to arrange plastic cups into different formations using a rubber band with strands of twine tied off in different directions. Students can only touch one of the strings, and together they must find a way to stretch the rubber band over the cup, pick it up, move it, and place it in the correct formation on the table. In order to do this effectively, students must offer clear directions to their peers and work in unison to reach the desired results.

In this culminating activity, students have the chance to practice the skills that they have developed through all the community-building activities they have completed to this point. The teacher should remind students to use the talking stems that have been practiced and have the class stop to observe groups who are exhibiting strong communication during the activity. Once students are able to see their peers finding success using the skills they have learned throughout the first few days, student buy-in continually increases, and the result is a community that is continually practicing healthy communication that promotes the feeling of safety.

A Classroom With Purpose: A Guide to Teaching Social Studies Today

Figure 2.5 *Cup Stacking Game*

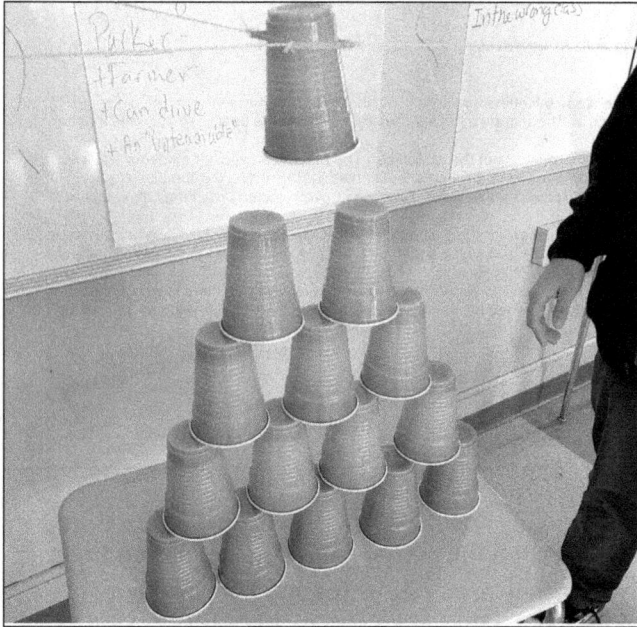

Esteem & Self-Actualization

By establishing a classroom community centered around Maslow's first three domains, students can begin to access the upper two levels. It is important to remember that in order to reach the level of self-actualization, students' esteem needs must be met. In order for this to happen, students must feel esteem for themselves as well as acceptance or value from others. In order for students to work within these levels, which is what we strive for, it is important for the teacher to maintain the expectations and sense of community that they have established throughout the year. The teacher needs to celebrate moments that showcase this sense of community and give students the opportunity to celebrate moments of growth within the classroom.

At the end of a project or unit, the teacher should give students the chance to reflect on their work and the skills they have developed in the given learning segment. The teacher can have students select an assignment they are proud of and explain what they think stands out in that assignment. This gives students the opportunity to look back on weeks of work that they have completed in order to better understand a concept. Allowing students the space to reflect on the learning that has taken place is extremely impactful, as it gives them the opportunity to uncover growth they may not have seen as they were in the act of learning. When students begin to notice tangible changes in their reading and writing work, their confidence within the classroom will grow. By fostering these reflective moments that focus on growth, the teacher is helping the student identify themselves as a capable learner, which in turn helps fulfill their esteem needs.

Maintaining Community & High Expectations

Once the teacher has done the work to establish a community rooted in safety, it is vital that they continually hold students to this expectation. With the polarization of the world today as well as

A Classroom With Purpose: A Guide to Teaching Social Studies Today

the tougher demands of the content taught in social studies classes, it is crucial for the teacher to establish a strong classroom community to allow difficult conversations to take place in a safe and meaningful way. Students will rise to meet the expectations set in the classroom, as long as these expectations remain consistent. There should be a limited number of very structured rules, and students should be held accountable for their actions every time the expectation is not met. Doing this avoids power struggles related to compliance.

When the teacher observes a behavior that impacts the classroom community, they can clearly state the observed behavior of concern, remind the student of the expectation, and offer them assistance to realign with the expectation. This structure does not allow room for the student to question the validity of a classroom rule or call into question the consistency of expectations within the room, which are hallmarks of power struggles in the classroom. By saying, "I see you're turned around talking to a classmate. When a student is being safe and trying hard, they should be facing the person who is speaking. Please move to this desk to help your focus," the teacher has addressed the behavior in a way that helps the student find success within the classroom, rather than simply pointing out how they were out of compliance.

It is important for the teacher to remember that they should be teaching behavior with the same importance and rigor that they teach content. Scaffolds for behavior are just as important as their academic counterparts, as they often serve as a bridge to academic successes.

The same way that the teacher can anticipate certain academic needs from students, they can also prepare for specific behavioral needs. The teacher will have hyperactive students who struggle to maintain focus while tracking the speaker. Flexible seating options like a wobble cushion or chair bands on desks can help these students meet the classroom expectations, while also meeting their need to move. Having a few quiet fidget toys can offer students the stimulation they need, rather than tapping their pencil on a desk. Some students will become overstimulated in the classroom or just need a moment alone to reset. Some teachers keep an empty envelope with a "very important document" in their desk. When a student needs a break, the teacher simply asks the student to deliver the envelope to someone close by, as long as the receiver has agreed to be part of this plan. The student gets to take a short break to reset, has been trusted by the teacher to complete an important task, and is a helpful member of the classroom community. In short, the teacher needs to ensure that they have taken steps to make their expectations accessible for all learners.

Teacher Tip: *Contact the administration to see if there are allocated funds for sensory items to meet students' needs.*

Restoration of Community

Just as teachers should think about how they want to address smaller concerns in their classroom, it is important for new teachers to think about how they want to address larger concerns as they arise throughout the year so that they can maintain community without damaging relationships with individual students. Safety needs to remain nonnegotiable, and even with meticulous planning, the teacher will encounter situations that warrant more action than simply addressing a behavior during the class period. It is safe to assume that a student will use harmful language toward a classmate at some point in the year. In most cases, it is appropriate for the teacher to follow their building's procedures to have this student spend the rest of the class period in a designated cool down area.

Once the community has been damaged, the teacher needs to have a clear procedure in place to restore community rather than simply punishing negative behaviors.

First, the teacher needs to think about how this procedure will have students take accountability for the action. Rather than assigning a detention, the teacher could hold a restorative conversation with the student. The purpose of this conversation should be for students to identify what factors led to the negative decision, recognize how their decision was not aligned with the core principles of the class, and reflect on how this decision impacted the safety of the room. These conversations take practice on the teacher's end, and it can be helpful to ask for assistance from a teacher or faculty member who has been trained on restorative practice until the teacher feels comfortable facilitating these conversations on their own. Most restorative practitioners are passionate about this work and will likely be excited to help.

After having time to reflect on the decision, the student needs to take steps to help restore community. In many cases, this takes the form of offering a written or verbal apology to the person or parties impacted by the decision. If the student used harmful language towards a classmate, the teacher should find time outside of class for the student to offer an apology and explain what the student will do to avoid situations like this in the future. This step assures that both parties can reenter the class feeling safe and comfortable moving forward.

Finally, the student needs to take steps to ensure that this incident will not impact their academic success. The teacher should contact home regarding the incident, explain the steps that are being taken and offer times when the student can complete the work they might have missed in a given period. This time can be facilitated by the teacher before or after school, during a free period, or as part of a school-wide program that is already in place for work recovery. It is important to mention that any procedure such as this can only be effective if it is supported by building leadership. The teacher should make sure that the administrative team feels comfortable supporting this procedure and that it aligns with the district's code of conduct. New teachers should remember that administrative support is important, but by overseeing this work, the teacher is making it clear that they are the adult who is holding the members of the classroom community accountable.

Building Meaningful Relationships With Adults

An essential skill in the classroom is the ability to develop, build, and maintain relationships. In the world of education, cultivating meaningful connections extends beyond students to include a network of adults who will play important roles in the teacher's professional journey. This section shifts the focus to building relationships with the adults who contribute to success as an educator.

Establishing strong relationships with parents/guardians and colleagues is essential. Effective collaboration and communication with these groups not only supports an educator's professional growth but also creates a foundation for positive student behavior, improved academic performance, and valuable insights that can enhance teaching practice.

This section explores the art of building meaningful relationships with adults, specifically parents/guardians and colleagues. We share many strategies that have been found to be successful and will benefit new teachers within the field.

Parents and Guardians

Building relationships with parents/guardians can often feel like a delicate balancing act. It is essential to keep them informed and aware of their child's educational journey while maintaining boundaries to preserve the educator's authority in the classroom. Determining the appropriate level of communication—what is too much or too little involvement—can be a complex and overwhelming challenge.

Establishing a connection with parents/guardians early in the school year sets the stage for effective communication throughout the school year. Starting with an introduction—whether through a letter, class website, school communication app, syllabus signature (see Figure 2.6), or mass email—creates an open channel for communication and establishes a foundation for collaboration. This introduction should also include clear guidelines for communication. Consider the following questions: What methods should parents/guardians use to contact the teacher? Is email effective, or does the district have a preferred communication platform? Clearly outlining these expectations ensures that the communication line developed is accessible with purpose.

Teacher Tip: Before creating your syllabus, check with your department to see if there is a premade syllabus guide you should follow with necessary information to include.

Balancing the demands of reaching out to parents/guardians as well as other responsibilities can be a struggle for new teachers. Finding time to make calls can feel like a difficult puzzle, and starting conversations with adults can often make a new teacher nervous. Over time, we have found that building a routine for communication helped us. Scheduling regular contact and finding positive reasons to reach out can not only assist confidence but also help in strengthening the teacher's relationships with families.

When addressing classroom concerns with parents, the "sandwich method" has been found to be effective. This approach begins with positive feedback, transitions into discussing areas of concern, and concludes with another positive note to reinforce the student's achievements. This structure helps the teacher stay organized in conversations and reduces anxiety they could feel when having difficult conversations.

However, not all communication with parents/guardians should center on challenges within the classroom. One of the most impactful decisions a teacher can make is dedicating time to share purely positive news about student successes and achievements. Parents/guardians deeply appreciate hearing about their child's progress and accomplishments, and these positive conversations will foster trust in the educator's teaching.

While most guardians are eager to stay informed about their child's education, it is important to strike a balance between welcoming their involvement and maintaining professional boundaries. Establishing a clear and consistent system of communication from the start helps ensure that both parents/guardians and the teacher feel supported and aligned in the shared goal of student success.

Colleagues

The relationships constructed with colleagues play a pivotal role in shaping the teacher's professional identity as well as strengthening their effectiveness as an educator. Establishing a support system among workmates not only helps combat the inevitable challenges and fatigue associated with a career in education but also serves as a powerful reminder of the passion and purpose of the teacher's career choice. In the early years as an educator, there are several groups

Figure 2.6 *Sample Brochure Syllabus*

GRADEBOOK BREAKDOWN

Your graded work will fall into either the assessment or practice category. Both carry a 50% weight on your grade. Not all assignments will be graded.

Sample Assessments (50%)	Sample Practice (50%)
Unit Tests	Bell Ringers/Do Now's
Essays	In Class Assignments
Presentations	Homework
Projects	Document Analysis

Homework
- Will be assigned on occasion in order to advance your knowledge of the course material and to help prepare you for upcoming lessons.
- You may be expected to finish assignments you began in class

Test & Assignment Corrections
- All assignments are eligible to be corrected.
  - The goal is for you to learn, which is not always possible on the first try!
- Assignments are eligible for correction up to one week after it is handed back.

Late Work
- You are expected to turn in work on time, however I understand that things happen. Late work will be accepted and not penalized.
- If something happens resulting in you needing a deadline extension, please reach out to me and let me know!

FAST FACTS ABOUT MS. WELLS

→ Graduated from SUNY Oneonta
→ 115 lbs dog named Bear
→ Yankees fan
→ Favorite topic to teach is WWII or the Cold War
→ Last book read: *The Making of a Racist* by Charles B. Dew

I acknowledge that I have read the entire 7/8 Accelerated Social Studies syllabus. I understand the content, and I know how to contact Ms. Wells if I have any questions or concerns.

Student name:
_____

Student signature:
_____

Parent/guardian name:
_____

Parent/guardian signature:
_____

WELCOME TO U.S. HISTORY

Ms. Wells
She/Her
Email@organization.org

COURSE DESCRIPTION

7/8 Accelerated Social Studies is an exploration of US History from the pre-Columbian era through the modern era. We will be using the Discovery Techbook, along with other supplemental resources to help understand the complex history of the United States.

The accelerated course compresses two years of study into one; and as a result, we will be moving at a rapid pace throughout the year.

You will also be assigned a fair amount of writing assignments. You will be given plenty of notice to complete these assignments. Time management will be one of the many skills we work on this year!

EXPECTATIONS

Be Here
→ Be present in the moment! We are covering exciting material and it is important for you to be aware of what is going on.

Be Safe
→ What you do impacts those around you, be conscientious of the choices you make!

Be Responsible
→ Make good choices, no cheating or plagiarism.

Set Goals
→ Strive to better yourself as a student this year. Always work on improving yourself as both a student and a young adult.

REQUIRED MATERIALS
- Charged chromebook
- Binder
- Agenda
- Writing utensils

WHAT TO EXPECT

1. You are expected to stay organized!

2. You are welcome to get extra help during my conference periods, or before or after school by appointment. Email me to set an appointment up.

3. You earn your grade. If you put the time in and do your best on assignments, tests, writing assignments and projects, you will be successful in Social Studies.

4. Grades will be updated frequently in the portal. If you have a question about a grade, ASK!

5. Class participation and discussion are imperative in a successful social studies class. You are encouraged to communicate your thoughts and ideas on what we are learning. I wont to hear from *you*!

6. When we work in groups or in partners, you are expected to fully participate and work respectfully with your peers.

7. Attendance is *extremely* important. Please make every effort to come to class, and if you are absent, you are responsible to make up the work.

8. Most importantly, expect to learn something new and expand your knowledge of U.S. History.

Note. Here is a sample brochure syllabus that would be sent home with students. This syllabus requires both parent/guardian and student signatures. In this syllabus, the teacher's email is also included so that early steps have been taken to develop relationships.

of colleagues that can be considered particularly invaluable in enriching one's teaching practice: veteran teachers, fellow new teachers, educators within the same content area, and administrators.

Veteran colleagues are an invaluable resource for building both professional knowledge and confidence as an educator. With their extensive experience, they offer insights that range from practical tips—like finding the best copy machine—to more complex topics such as documentation, union guidelines, and the tenure process. Developing strong relationships with these educators can provide not only guidance but also support in navigating the challenges teachers face early in their teaching career. Their assistance can be instrumental in the establishment of the teacher's identity as an educator.

Connecting with fellow new teachers who share similar experiences is equally as important. Much like personal friendships, which are often formed around shared experiences, professional relationships with those at a similar stage can help build resilience and camaraderie. These colleagues can provide a sounding board for challenges, a source of encouragement on tough days, and a space to celebrate victories. Having someone who understands your perspective and can assist with problem-solving will be a vital part of your developed support system.

Another important group of colleagues to build relationships with are those teaching in the same content area or subject. Collaborating with these peers offers the teacher numerous opportunities to share resources, assist in lesson planning, and gain insight into curriculum pacing, teaching hard topics, and addressing student needs. Their experience can help reduce the teacher's workload and stress, especially as they navigate an early career. These colleagues are often eager to share their expertise, and over time, the teacher will find themself in the position to pay it forward to a new educator.

Navigating the complexities of a new work environment can be challenging for an early-career teacher. Gaining insight into the operations and decisions that shape the learning environment helps teachers make choices that best serve their students and the school community. Maintaining an open communication with administrators promotes mutual understanding, allowing them to recognize the educator's efforts in cultivating a positive classroom culture and forming responsible citizens. Consistent and transparent dialogue also allows administrators to speak knowledgeably about the teacher's practice when necessary.

Professional Development—A Life of Learning

Life is a continuous journey of learning. From the early years spent absorbing knowledge in an academic setting to post-secondary education, each stage of learning builds on the last. However, the learning journey should not end with graduation but should continue to grow and blossom within a career in education. When entering the classroom as an educator, it is crucial to embrace the idea that growth and learning are ongoing. This mindset is essential for becoming a well-rounded and effective social studies educator.

Being an educator is synonymous with a lifetime of learning. Each day presents new opportunities to gain new insights—whether from colleagues, students, or the world around them. Actively seeking and embracing these opportunities is vital for professional and personal growth.

In the field of education, professional development plays a central role in supporting the teacher's journey. Professional development serves as an avenue for educators to refine skills, adopt new practices, and expand their knowledge base. It offers the chance to explore new ideas, improve instructional strategies, and ultimately enhance student learning. Engaging in professional development ensures that the teacher will continue to grow in their career and that they are invested in their practice.

Not One-Size-Fits-All

While professional development offers valuable opportunities to enhance teachers' skills and knowledge, not every session will align with their specific needs or teaching style—and that is perfectly fine. Just as educators emphasize the importance of differentiating instruction to meet the diverse needs of students, teachers must also recognize that every educator is unique. Each teacher will bring ideas, strategies, and approaches to the classroom, and not all professional development will be applicable to their practice.

Professional development can be compared to a trip to the grocery store. When shopping, a person does not expect to buy every item on the shelves. Instead, they select the products that meet their needs. Similarly, during a professional development session, the teacher will not take away every idea of strategy presented. Instead, they will identify the concepts that are most relevant to their classroom, such as a new "do now" activity that enhances student engagement or a new collaborative strategy that promotes deeper thinking. Even if educators leave a professional development session with one takeaway to improve their practice, the session can be considered a success.

The key to approaching professional development is having an open mind and a willingness to learn. By selecting what works best for them, teachers can continuously grow while staying true to their practices and their approach to teaching.

Finding the Right Fit

Not every professional development session will be worth your while. For example, as a middle school social studies teacher, attending a session geared towards kindergarten teachers may have little relevance. Identifying professional development opportunities that suit your goals and can help expand your teaching toolbox can be challenging, but having a clear focus and strategy can make this mission achievable.

When searching for professional development, a teacher should start by identifying the specific skill or knowledge they want to take away. Is the educator looking to integrate new pieces of technology into their classroom? Does the teacher want to deepen their knowledge on a particular topic? By narrowing the focus, the educator can streamline their search for sessions that connect to their interests and goals.

Because of how accessible technology is, it is easier now than ever to find professional development opportunities. Numerous organizations provide a wide range of virtual sessions for educators. The National Council for the Social Studies is an excellent resource. Their "Professional Learning" section offers dozens of opportunities tailored to various topics and teaching levels. Additionally, many states have social studies councils that provide more localized professional development opportunities, which connect the educator to nearby and relevant materials.

School districts also often host their own professional development sessions. Once employed in a district, exploring its website can provide insight into the professional development opportunities available for employees. These sessions will also reflect on the district's priorities, practices, and strategies, helping the teacher align their practice to the district's missions. Using search terms like "professional development" or "professional learning" can help refine the search and discover relevant sessions.

By mindfully selecting professional development opportunities that cater to specific needs and goals, teachers can make the most of their career while continuously growing as an educator.

Concluding Thoughts

The transition from student to teacher is an exciting but challenging journey. This journey requires adaptability, patience, and a commitment to continuous learning. This chapter has aimed to provide new educators with a solid foundation for navigating the complexities of their early years in the classroom. By focusing on the essentials of classroom management, building community, and developing effective communication, new teachers are better equipped to manage the demands of their career with confidence and competence.

In your early career as a social studies teacher, it is also essential to remember that it takes time to hone your practice. Resiliency is an artform within the world of education, and it is necessary to practice it. Things will not always go right the first time, but it is important to remember that going back and putting work into your practice will in turn make you a better educator, benefitting the teacher, students, and school community.

Central to this journey is the practice of relationship building, whether with students, parents/guardians, or colleagues. It is essential that teachers recognize that the success of any educator is deeply intertwined with the support and collaboration of the school community. By embracing these principles, new teachers can lay the foundations for a fulfilling and impactful career, one that not only supports their professional growth but also enhances the learning experiences of their students.

Checklist for Navigating the Early Years

☐ Take time in the beginning of the school year to establish a routine to help your teaching of social studies down the road.

☐ Follow through on your routines and expectations to ensure that they do not become lost.

☐ Take time before the school year starts to collect resources to stock your WIN bin.

☐ Put in the time and effort to build meaningful relationships with other adults, this should include, but is not limited to, other teachers, administrators, and parents/guardians.

☐ Investigate professional development opportunities that are worthwhile to you and the honing of your practice.

References

Maslow, A. H. (1943). A theory of human motivation. *Psychological Review, 50*(4), 370–396.

Kinsella, K. (2017, February 3). *Instructional Tools to Address the Complex Language Demands of Academic Interaction* [Conference session]. Idaho Association for Bilingual Education Annual Conference, Boise, Idaho, United States. **https://idahoassocbilingualed.com/wp-content/uploads/2017/10/K.-Keynote-Slides-color.pdf**

Chapter 3
Teaching for Tomorrow: Social Studies as a Path to an Engaged Citizenry

Kristi Fragnoli, Timothy D. Potts, and Paul Gold

It is always a memorable day for a new teacher. As you walk through the classroom door for the first time, an overwhelming feeling suddenly rushes over you. Do you truly feel ready to be the captain of your own ship? What will your students be like? Will they like you? And most importantly, what will you be teaching daily?

Some students will ask you, "Why are we learning this? This has happened so long ago, and I just don't care." Other students may not ask out loud but will still try to tune you out. Within this chapter, we discuss what constitutes social studies as a discipline, examine the strands of social studies, and explore how these strands create a unique dance of standards, politics, and assessment that is essential for teachers to consider as they plan. Beyond that, we show you how to motivate and inspire students to care and to have empathy while addressing standard requirements, controversial topics, and assessment demands. The key approach to student motivation is to promote civic engagement, historical understanding, and critical consciousness in the social studies curriculum. This is no small mission—but it is possible. By embracing the knowledge of the social studies discipline and the coursework that led you to become a social studies teacher, you can create incredible learning experiences as an educator who cultivates empathy, integrity, knowledge, and intellectual curiosity among students.

Definition of Social Studies

When you take a moment to ask yourself, "What is social studies?" it can be surprisingly difficult to craft a concise answer. The subject feels fluid, like trying to hold slime in your hands—you think you have contained it, but parts of it spill and stretch beyond your grasp. Social studies often serves as a so-called catch-all discipline, acting as the thread that connects and integrates interdisciplinary learning across schools. You are tasked to "teach social studies" based on your degree and certification. What does that mean? According to the National Council for the Social Studies (NCSS, n.d.), "social studies is the study of individuals, communities, systems, and their interactions across time and place that prepares students for local, national, and global civic life" (para. 1). The NCSS definition explains that by exploring the past, engaging with the present, and learning to influence the future, social studies equips students with the skills for lifelong participation in civil discussions and active involvement in their communities. How lucky are we to be charged with such a significant and impactful mission? Our roles as social studies educators do not stop here; we are also responsible for weaving the various strands of social studies content into the classroom. We are truly charged with a significant task when it comes to assisting and shaping young minds.

Strands of Social Studies

The definition of social studies demonstrates how the discipline goes much further than studying history. While many social studies teachers have a passion and love for historical content, social studies in itself is a conglomerate of multiple social science disciplines. According to NCSS (n.d.),

> Social studies can include, but is not limited to, disciplines and courses such as:
> - **History**, including local and state history, United States history, world history and global studies, African American history, and women's history as well as other courses about the history of specific groups, regions, and eras;
> - **Geography**, including physical, environmental, cultural, and human geography as well as courses related to the application of geographic tools (i.e., GPS and GIS);
> - **Economics**, including general economics, macroeconomics, microeconomics, and international economics;
> - **Government and Citizenship**, including civics, citizenship education, political science, local, state, tribal, and United States government, international relations, comparative government, and law and legal studies;
> - **Social Sciences,** including psychology, sociology, anthropology, archaeology, gender studies, LGBTQ+ studies, and religious studies;
> - **Ethnic Studies**, including African American studies, Asian American and Pacific Islander studies, Indigenous studies, and Latin American studies;
> - **Human Rights and Social Justice**, including human rights education, social justice issues, international organizations, and genocide studies;
> - **Financial Literacy**, including personal finance (NCSS recognizes financial literacy as an important course for students, but financial literacy is distinct from and is not a replacement for economics and economic education); and
> - **Contemporary Issues**, including courses in current events and the study of one or more social studies topics in current contexts. (para. 6)

Wow, that is impressive! You would have to be a genius to be an expert in all of these areas. To teach all of these strands, the expertise of a social studies teacher has to be broad and inclusive. A social studies teacher has one of the most extensively powerful disciplines, which requires educators to be experts in a slew of ancillary courses. You may be asked to teach psychology, sociology, anthropology, economics, geography, or a multitude of electives. The larger the district, the more course options with many more details. These classes are typically coveted by the veteran teachers. Sometimes, seniority comes with the ability to pick and claim courses that align with specific areas of expertise and interest. What is important to remember is that each of these courses offers an excellent opportunity for teachers to explore, discuss, and create projects and activities that push student skills beyond standardized testing. Within some of these courses, students discover deep personal interests, future career choices, and fantastic lifelong transferable skills.

How to Promote Civic Engagement and Active Citizenship

We have mentioned key roles of the social studies teachers as they go beyond teaching "just history." One key role is to help learners acquire the skills needed to "work together to create a just world" (NCSS, n.d., para. 2). NCSS (n.d.) states, "social studies prepares learners for a lifelong practice of civil discourse and civic engagement in their communities" (para. 2). If this is one of our missions as social studies teachers, then a teacher must have a solid grasp of the skills necessary to be an active citizen—those who participate in civil discourse and civic engagement within communities. Social studies plays a crucial role in preparing future citizens by equipping them with the knowledge, skills, and attitudes necessary to participate effectively in society as active citizens. As a social studies teacher, you are responsible for filling your lessons with opportunities to model and develop these skills. The discipline of social studies, if taught appropriately, has the ability to achieve these skills and more:

Critical Thinking: Students are asked to examine and make informed decisions, present findings, and defend ideas and thoughts by engaging with case studies and real-world scenarios.

Global Perspective: The discipline of social studies is based on a global perspective fostering an appreciation for diversity among individuals.

Ethical Decision-Making: Social studies is filled with experiences exploring ethical and moral responsibility. Students discuss justice and human rights, and the importance of contributing to the welfare of society and acting with integrity (NCSS, 2022).

Interactive Discourse: Social studies help students develop skills in communication and collaboration by articulating their ideas clearly and persuasively through discussions, debates, and presentations.

Lifelong Learning: Social studies can encourage a lifelong interest in learning about the world, fostering curiosity and a desire to stay informed about issues within all strands of social studies, such as social, political, and economic issues, both at home and abroad.

In order to be a truly effective social studies teacher, a growth mindset is essential (Dweck, 2007). If the expectation is that your students must grow in knowledge, effort, skills, and academic discipline, it is critical that you model this in all of your lessons and student interactions. Since the world is always evolving, you must too as a social studies teacher. Through the elements listed above, social studies education equips students with the tools they need to be knowledgeable, thoughtful, insightful, and active participants in their communities and the wider world. Within a PreK–12 social studies classroom, students should develop an understanding of how societies operate and what powerful role students can play.

How Standards and Assessments Guide Teaching

Regardless of where you teach, you will be beholden to a curriculum that will be your guide through the required content for your courses. Teachers have national and state standards as well as district curriculum guides to follow.

i **Teacher Tip:** *New York follows the K–12 Social Studies Framework, which blends the C3 Framework with specific state history* (www.nysed.gov/standards-instruction/social-studies).

California has History-Social Science Content Standards, which emphasize multiple perspectives and cultural literacy (www.cde.ca.gov/be/st/ss/). *Each has a unique approach, with a stronger emphasis on state history.*

We need to look at all district, state, and national curriculum guides through the lens of instruction and assessment. As a social studies educator, you cannot pull these pieces apart. When we look for curriculum guidance, these standards and guides ensure that educators cover essential content and skills. As much as we like to be freelancers in our social studies world, it is essential to make sure we are following our required curriculum guides. Teachers must align their instruction with national and state standards because standardized assessments—whether at the state level (e.g., Regents, STAAR, MCAS) or national level (e.g., NAEP, AP exams)—are based on these standards. This alignment ensures that students are tested on the skills and knowledge deemed essential for their grade level. While teachers cannot ignore the required content, they can explore and add additional topics to their teaching

Figure 3.1 *Layers of Educational Standards in Social Studies*

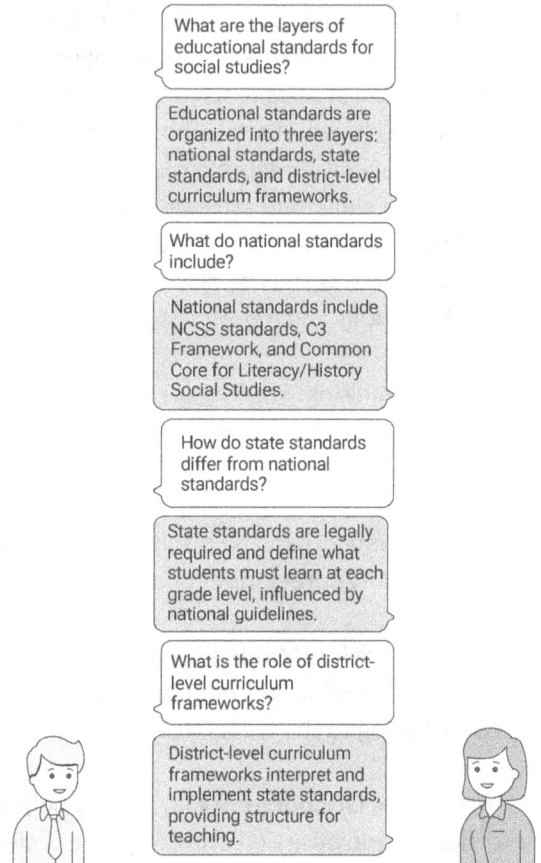

Note. Image generated by Napkin.ai, 2025 (**www.napkin.ai/**), using *Five Key Elements for Developing State Social Studies Standards*, 2023, American Institutes for Research (**www.air.org/resource/qa/five-key-elements-developing-state-social-studies-standards**).

For the most part national standards inform state-mandated standards, which are the main material districts use to build curriculum guides. District curriculum guides are created by teachers within the district. Teachers review state requirements and assessments and develop a framework for instructional units and possible teaching timeframes. Each district's curriculum guide may vary greatly. Some districts will provide a list of concepts, resources, and assessments, while others may give essential or compelling questions. At the school level, teachers take the district's guidelines and turn them into actual lessons. Schools might tweak topics a little, but teachers have the most flexibility when it comes to choosing activities, projects, and assessments that match their students' interests and abilities. Even with this flexibility, everything still refers back to the state and national standards, ensuring students are learning what they need to know.

State-mandated tests are standardized exams that measure how well students are learning in social studies. These tests vary by state and not all states require a gateway exam to pass a grade level in social studies or to graduate. For the states that do, they follow the same format— every student answers the same set of questions and is scored in a way that makes it easy to create item analysis data to better inform instruction. While teachers are required to follow a structured system from state and national requirements, you will still have creative freedom in how you teach and what you incorporate into your classroom each day. Each school year you will form curricular habits whereby your historical knowledge and pedagogical base will grow exponentially. No matter how detailed or potentially vague your district's curriculum guide is, this framework will provide the needed structure and guidance for day-to-day instruction.

Figure 3.2 *Social Studies Standards Hierarchy*

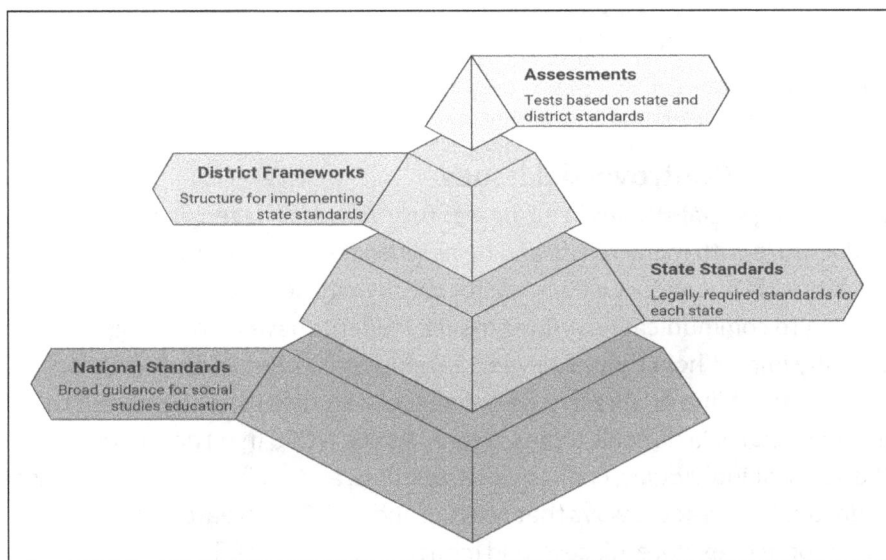

Note. Image generated by Napkin.ai, 2025 (www.napkin.ai/).

While a teacher has the ethical and, in some areas, the legal responsibility to prepare students by teaching material that is aligned with the standards, it is still part of a teacher's role to go beyond that. A key role for the social studies teacher is to teach beyond the classroom and integrate long-lasting, enduring themes or issues that cultivate students to become truly active civil participants. The teacher's role is to teach to the standards, while also incorporating this type of life-long learning. Standardized testing has become a large component of the U.S. education system, helping schools see how well students understand and apply what they have learned.

Teacher Tip: Check out the Education Commission of the States website for a 50-state comparison showing social studies testing requirements (see Figure 3.3; www.ecs.org/50-state-comparison-state-summative-assessments/).

Figure 3.3 *Social Studies Testing Landscape*

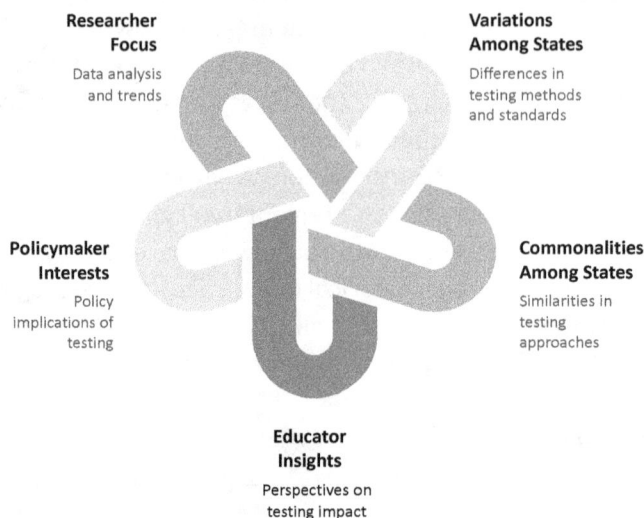

Researcher Focus
Data analysis and trends

Variations Among States
Differences in testing methods and standards

Policymaker Interests
Policy implications of testing

Commonalities Among States
Similarities in testing approaches

Educator Insights
Perspectives on testing impact

Note. Image generated by Napkin.ai, 2025 (**www.napkin.ai/**), using *50-State Comparison: State Summative Assessments*, Education Commission of the States (**www.ecs.org/50-state-comparison-state-summative-assessments/**).

Controversial Issues

Again, it is no mystery that teaching social studies in a 21st-century world is challenging at many levels. Every day is a new adventure with many twists and turns when it comes to curricula. As you start each day, it is not unreasonable to conduct a daily reality check to make sure you are fully aware of what you are planning to communicate to young minds. Students have many things going on in their own lives that greatly impact how they receive social studies content and information. Students may find certain topics troubling or abrasive, so not all social studies teaching is smooth going. As we know, social studies can be a difficult topic to teach. As the NCSS (n.d.) definition states, "social studies is the study of individuals, communities, systems, and their interactions" (para. 1). We know that not all individuals interact in ways that are civil and just. This creates excellent opportunities within the classroom to explore, discuss, and model true discourse. The skill of presenting opinions and listening to others needs to be taught and practiced daily. The social studies classroom is the perfect place! Remember, it is your job to help create active and informed citizens, and acquiring the skill of discourse will play a major role in that.

Teaching discourse skills involves guiding students through the process of engaging in relevant discussions, building logical arguments, supporting claims, and practicing attentive listening. Through proactive instruction and modeling, your students can learn to develop effective oral and written communication skills for diverse scenarios. As social studies teachers, it is your responsibility to help train your students in how to maintain civil and respectful discourse so that no one feels uncomfortable listening to opposing viewpoints. Students need training in how to participate thoughtfully, which will create a learning community that can manage challenges and disagreements confidently. To be clear, all of this takes time, judicious practice, and effort. It is critical to immerse yourself in historical content, current events, political ideology and discourse, and a strong teacher–colleague network to share ideas and thoughts.

Teaching and managing a positive discourse discussion within the classroom is the key to handling topics that might cause discomfort for some students. We are all well aware of the multitude of topics that could fall within this category. Religion, politics, and immigration are just a few of the many required topics we must cover. Social studies teachers need to remind themselves of the NCSS (n.d.) core definition of the discipline: We are not to espouse opinions, but to prepare "students for local, national, and global civic life" (para. 1). Within all the strands of the discipline, students become informed citizens because they develop an understanding of historical events while learning critical thinking skills. In the end, we, as social studies teachers, need to view controversial topics as a key component of our instruction. It is up to us to help students see that diverse perspectives are a positive piece of our society because with dissension and different views come growth and change.

Teacher Tip: Here are some thoughtful tips for teachers navigating controversial discussions: Faculty should inform themselves of all district/Board of Education policies. Read your faculty handbook and any specific department documents related to curricular decisions. Make an appointment with your principal and discuss any questions you might have.

In today's increasingly polarized society, addressing controversial topics within the social studies curriculum is critical and challenging. The truth is, not even the top veteran teachers are fully prepared to tackle every situation that will occur in their classrooms in a highly effective way. As educators, we recognize that each day in the classroom is unique and filled with its own challenges and excitement.

Closing Thoughts

Every school has its own culture, values, and expectations, but no matter where you teach, the classroom will not change. When you close the door and start class, it is a place where students and the teacher feel happy, safe, and comfortable. For many, it might be an escape from social anxiety, peer pressure, and sometimes unkind staff. It can be a sanctuary and a safe space to learn, to exist, to communicate, and to grow. Do not expect to be perfect on your first day, or even in your first year. Plan and prepare, communicate with colleagues, immerse yourself in the school community, and most importantly, know and respect the students in front of you. Our students are entitled to your hard work, efforts, and experiences, and they deserve the best we can offer them. Every day may not be perfect, but kids are intuitive, and they know and respect your time, energy, and efforts. They feed off our passion for teaching social studies and will rise to the various challenges presented to them in class if you create safe and engaging learning spaces for them.

The classroom environment described here is a microcosm of society. As a social studies teacher, you are modeling the skills, knowledge, and habits necessary for a society to grow and continue. Your ultimate role is to prepare students to navigate complex issues with empathy, integrity, research, and intellectual curiosity. This task is difficult, challenging, and extremely rewarding. No other discipline gives students the opportunity to reflect on who they are as a person and how to contribute to what they consider to be a just world.

Checklist for Teaching Social Studies as a Path to Engaged Citizenry

Understand the Role of a Social Studies Teacher
- ☐ Reflect on the significance of teaching social studies
- ☐ Recognize the diverse disciplines within social studies
- ☐ Prepare to answer students' questions about why social studies matters

Master the Strands of Social Studies

Review the key content areas:
- ☐ History
- ☐ Geography
- ☐ Economics
- ☐ Government and Citizenship
- ☐ Social Sciences
- ☐ Global Studies
- ☐ Human Rights and Social Justice
- ☐ Contemporary Issues

Promote Active Citizenship
- ☐ Teach critical thinking and problem-solving skills
- ☐ Foster global awareness
- ☐ Encourage ethical and social responsibility

Align Teaching With Standards and Assessments
- ☐ Identify and follow national, state, and district curriculum standards
- ☐ Prepare students for state-mandated social studies assessments

Handle Controversial Issues in the Classroom
- ☐ Teach students how to engage in civil discourse
- ☐ Model respectful debate and encourage diverse perspectives

References

Dweck, C. S. (2007). *Mindset: The new psychology of success.* Random House.

Napkin.ai. (2025). Napkin.ai [Large language model]. **www.napkin.ai**

National Council for the Social Studies. (n.d.). *Definition of social studies.* **www.socialstudies.org/about/definition-social-studies**

National Council for the Social Studies. (2022, November 30). *NCSS Statement of Professional Ethics.* **www.socialstudies.org/position-statements/ncss-statement-professional-ethics**

Chapter 4
Building Bridges: Crafting Engaging Social Studies Units of Study

Karen Poland and Kristi Fragnoli

i **Teacher Tip:** *Your personal educational philosophy is reflected in your approach to unit and lesson planning.*

As you enter your own classroom, you are in charge of everything! Are you ready? Maybe you are committed to inspiring deep critical thought by embracing culturally responsive teaching. Or perhaps you are inspired to make history real by incorporating a History Lab into your teaching. Or maybe you are just feeling overwhelmed. You are not alone! It takes thought and planning. This chapter is designed to help you structure your teaching goals into well-organized instructional units. You need some structure to organize your teaching throughout the year, and here is how you do it!

Creating Purpose

Designing a social studies curriculum is similar to constructing a bridge: Just as a bridge connects two points, a planned unit connects students' existing knowledge to new content, ideas, skills, and abilities. Both the bridge design and the unit plan serve as blueprints for successful construction. Ultimately, upon completion, this bridge offers students a safe passage toward enhanced comprehension and newfound knowledge. Each year, educators design and construct numerous bridges, as unit plans, that connect to additional units, creating a network of new knowledge linked to students' prior experiences. In this way, educators continually build bridges that enhance learning and foster growth.

Creating a Pacing Guide

To begin the construction of your curriculum for the year, you first need to create a curriculum pacing guide. A pacing guide is a timeline that identifies the number of, and which, main topics (units) you plan to teach, the number of days you plan to spend on each unit, and the order in which you plan to address each topic during the school year. To create your pacing guide, review your school calendar to identify the total number of instructional days. Take into account days when teaching is impossible, such as holidays, standardized testing days, school events, and days that may be shorter than usual due to staff development or school events. This step offers an overview of the total number of instructional days, which are often fewer than expected.

When mapping out units for the year, educators should gather all state standards and assessments, educational materials (e.g., textbooks and resource books), and district curriculum guidelines to determine the topics and content for each unit. Take the time to review the materials to determine the number of units and the required depth and breadth of each unit. Plot each unit length onto the calendar to guarantee enough time within the academic year to teach all required content. By taking this perspective into account, teachers can allocate units within the teaching time while considering which units and topics require more instructional focus. In addition, they can determine which chapters they will use from the textbook, which to skim over or ignore, and which topics might need additional resources and readings.

Let's Give it a Try!

Imagine you are teaching seventh-grade American History. You review the calendar and determine you have 186 planned school days, but when you take into account professional staff days and student conference days, you determine you have 180 instructional days. In addition, after looking over the content and resources, you determine you have 11 units to teach. The following are the unit titles: (a) A Nation Divided, (b) Colonial Developments, (c) Exploration and Exploitation, (d) Injustice and Reform, (e) The Dawn of a Nation, (f) Jacksonian Democracy and American Progress, (g) Historical Inquiry and Geography, (h) The Age of Defiance and Independence, (i) Westward Expansion, (j) The U.S. Constitution in Practice, and (k) Indigenous Peoples. Create your own pacing guide by determining the order in which you will teach the units and the number of days you plan to spend on each unit.

Teacher Tip: Take the time to review the National Council for Social Studies (2013) C3 Framework and compare it with your state's curriculum framework and your school district's curriculum guides. State assessment review books are also a good resource when determining how to spend instructional time.

Now compare your pacing guide with the sample pacing guide in Figure 4.1. Did you start your school year with historical inquiry and geography? This is one possible way of organizing the units for the year, but it could be argued that you might, in an election year, start with the unit The U.S. Constitution in Practice and spend more than the 20 days we allocated.

Either way, this method ensures that you will deliver the content without running out of time. Making the determination of how long to spend on each unit can be based on several factors, including your personal interest in the unit, its ability to promote critical inquiry and creative engagement, student interest, the alignment of the unit to the community within which you teach, the emphasis placed upon the unit in local or state assessments, and your school district and department curricular guides and assessments. The pacing guide gives you a benchmark outline of the unit topics you plan to teach and the number of days you plan to spend on each unit. Think of the pacing guide as the blueprint for your bridge; now it is time to focus on the individual sections—the units of study—that will bring your plan to life. Just as engineers use solid materials to build the bridge, as a teacher, you will need to build solid units of study to design a social studies curriculum.

Figure 4.1 *American History Pacing Guide*

Guiding Questions
What chapters from the textbook, if any, will this unit address?
What chapters or pages will be discarded?

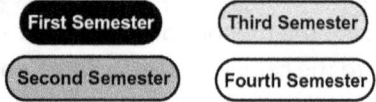

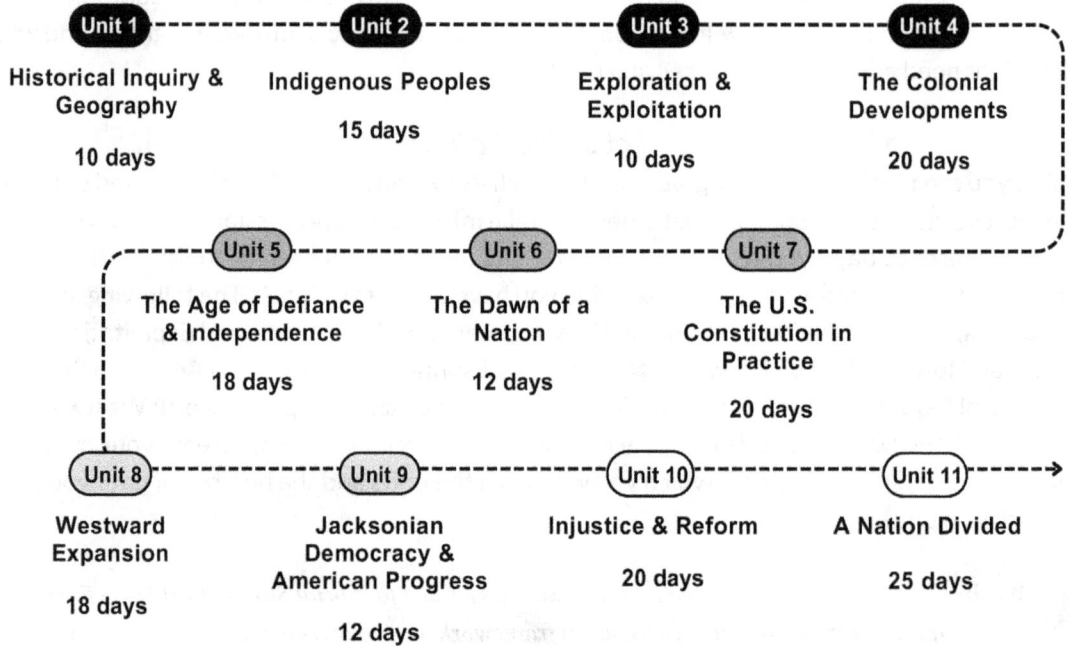

First Semester   Third Semester
Second Semester   Fourth Semester

Unit 1	Unit 2	Unit 3	Unit 4
Historical Inquiry & Geography	Indigenous Peoples	Exploration & Exploitation	The Colonial Developments
10 days	15 days	10 days	20 days

Unit 5	Unit 6	Unit 7
The Age of Defiance & Independence	The Dawn of a Nation	The U.S. Constitution in Practice
18 days	12 days	20 days

Unit 8	Unit 9	Unit 10	Unit 11
Westward Expansion	Jacksonian Democracy & American Progress	Injustice & Reform	A Nation Divided
18 days	12 days	20 days	25 days

Note. For another sample pacing guide, see the 11th Grade U.S. History Curriculum webpage from New Visions for Public Schools (https://curriculum.newvisions.org/social-studies/course/us-history/).

Planning a Unit of Study

It is time to plan your first unit. So, what is a unit of study? Mahood et al. (1991) refer to a *unit* as the organization of curricular topics and content into a focused period of learning for which you can develop specific daily lesson plans. (For more on daily lesson plans, see Chapter 5.) Such units can range anywhere from a few days to a few weeks. This deeper understanding can only occur when a teacher breaks free from reliance on textbooks and develops into a subject-matter expert who understands the material from every angle. In the end, well-thought-out unit planning improves the educational process and increases the significance and impact of learning for students and their engagement with the content.

> **Teacher Tip:** *Physical and digital textbooks are valuable resources for determining the appropriate grade level of difficulty and depth of content. They can guide decisions on how thoroughly to explore topics, such as the number of new vocabulary words to introduce in a specific unit.*

Enduring Understandings

A teacher should approach planning a unit with the end in mind (Covey, 1989/2013). Think: What are five or ten takeaways from the unit you are currently planning? These takeaways should not only align to content and supplemental standards but will also carry over from your unit plan to each individual lesson plan as learning outcomes. Wiggins and McTighe (2005) refer to these as "enduring understandings," emphasizing the deep, transferable concepts that students retain long after instruction. Enduring understandings "articulate what students should 'revisit' over the course of their lifetimes in relationship to the content area" (University of Alaska Fairbanks, n.d., para. 3; Wiggins & McTighe, 2005). To find your enduring understandings, review the standards and ask yourself: What big ideas will frame the unit and help my students attach lasting meaning and importance to the content? Write your ideas as declarative statements and provide an explanation to guide your unit plan.

This approach to unit planning is referred to as the Understanding by Design framework (UbD) by Wiggins and McTighe (2005) and is often referred to as "backward design." The purpose of backward design is to ensure that all instructional activities are aligned with clear, measurable goals that reflect what students should understand and be able to do by the end of the unit.

Let's Give it a Try!

Below are three statements of enduring understandings that could be used in a unit on the American Revolution. Read each statement and rank them with 1 as the most important and 3 as the least important:

- A government's actions impact its citizens, both positively and negatively.
- War has lasting effects and implications for a government and its people.
- Citizens have a voice and choose to exercise their voice in a variety of ways.

Did the content you planned to emphasize in a unit on the American Revolution factor into your ranking? Do you think there is only one way for these to be ranked? All three are important for a unit on the American Revolution, yet these statements could also be applied to different units. For example, the first statement could be applied to a unit about the Great Depression, the second statement could be applied to a unit about World War II, and the third could be applied to a unit about the Civil Rights Movement. The point is that enduring understandings are essential as you plan your unit because they are the pieces of content students keep and hold onto for life.

When planning a unit of study, you need to be thinking about how you envision the unit unfolding, what it might look like in practice, what the students will learn, why and how it applies to their daily life, how they will learn the content, and how they will demonstrate their learning. In addition to enduring understandings, consider the key components in the following sections to help you to envision your unit design.

Teacher Tip: Approaching your unit with enduring understandings will help you to prioritize historical content (e.g., facts, dates, historical figures, events) as a must know or must do as opposed to something that is important to be familiar with.

Learning Goals

As educators, we use a variety of terms such as "enduring understandings," "learning goals," "essential questions," "learning objectives," and "learning outcomes," often interchangeably, but each word has a distinct meaning and purpose (see Figure 4.2). In the context of unit planning, *learning goals* define the specific content and skills students should learn by the end of the unit that guide your planning and help you measure student progress. For example, if you are teaching a unit for Global Studies on World War II, you may want to highlight affective and social goals. Learning goals should take into account students' prior knowledge and current skill development. In addition, they are student focused and are aligned to specific learning standards.

- A *measurable learning outcome* is the combination of a learning objective and learning outcome in one statement. It is a clear, specific statement of what students will be able to demonstrate in terms of knowledge, skills, or values and should be directly accessible because it is linked to activities, assignments, or assessments that provide evidence of student learning (Holden, 2020).
- A *learning objective* is your purpose for creating and teaching the lesson. Ask yourself what you want your students to know (knowledge), do (skills), and feel (values and attitudes) at the end of the lesson. Objectives are verbs tied to Bloom's Taxonomy and are the intended results or consequences you expect of your students as a result of the lesson. Given the focus on your intentions for the lesson, they typically indicate the subject content (e.g., terms, concepts) that the teacher intends to cover.
- In contrast, *learning outcomes* are the achieved results or consequences of instruction. Learning outcomes are the answers or the evidence students can provide or actions the student can take to demonstrate that they have mastered what you have taught. They need to be clear, observable, and measurable. Learning outcomes are more student centered because they describe the actions the learner should take during and after the learning experience.

Figure 4.2 *Educational Terminology*

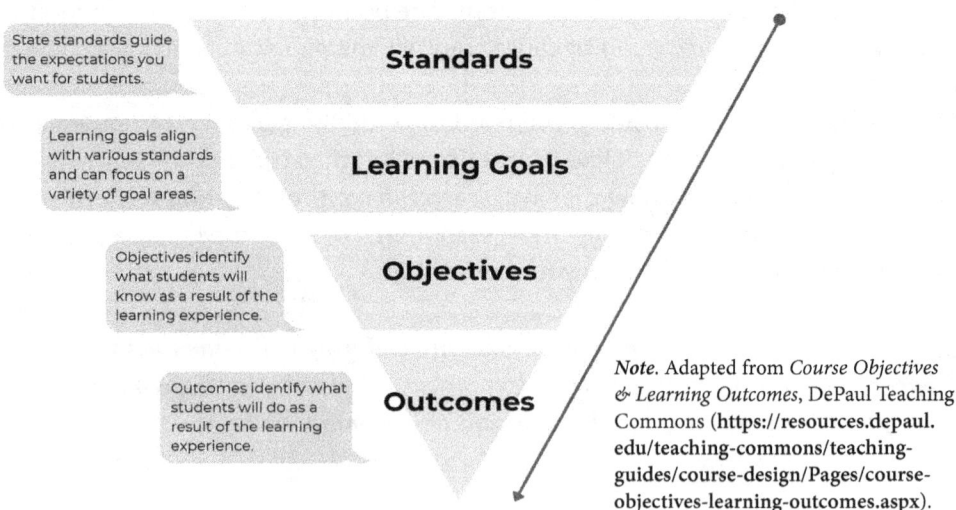

State standards guide the expectations you want for students.

Standards

Learning goals align with various standards and can focus on a variety of goal areas.

Learning Goals

Objectives identify what students will know as a result of the learning experience.

Objectives

Outcomes identify what students will do as a result of the learning experience.

Outcomes

Note. Adapted from *Course Objectives & Learning Outcomes*, DePaul Teaching Commons (**https://resources.depaul. edu/teaching-commons/teaching- guides/course-design/Pages/course- objectives-learning-outcomes.aspx**).

Essential, Compelling, and Supporting Questions

Once you have identified your learning goals, it is time to begin to form your guiding questions, as these will inform your approach to the unit. As Wiggins (2014) explains, all three forms of questioning—essential, compelling, and supporting—become the framework for your unit. Such questions should help focus the unit, providing a central theme around which all lessons and activities are organized.

- *Essential questions* provoke inquiry. They are open-ended questions and not content specific. Rather, they are philosophical and recur over time, meaning you can ask questions regardless of the time period you are studying. These questions promote critical and higher-order thinking and transferability of ideas, and they often lead to additional questions. These questions are timeless. They are applicable today, during the American Revolution, the French Revolution, the Vietnam War, etc. As Wiggins (2014) explains, the best essential questions enable inquiry into particular topics and allow for recurring investigation.
- *Compelling questions* "frame an inquiry" of a social studies unit and topic (Grant et al., 2017, p. 201). They are aligned to the standards, are intellectually rigorous, are relevant to students, seek to foster connections, provoke curiosity, and have academic value. They require students to reflect on a historical issue or concern.
- *Supporting questions* are scaffolded to guide students' thinking and inquiry toward the content they need to investigate and master in order to craft an argumentative answer to essential and compelling questions. Supporting questions are functional and content based.

Table 4.1 compares the use of essential questions, compelling questions, and supporting questions for two different units.

Developing a Content Funnel

Once you have reviewed the standards, crafted learning goals, and developed your guiding questions, it is time to revisit and revise your enduring understandings, if needed. As you review, do these statements capture the essence of your unit plan and what you expect students to walk away remembering about the unit? They are intended to help students apply the knowledge to their lives and remember the material long after they have completed a course. In essence, you are flushing out the purpose, focus, and value of the unit to the rest of the school year and beyond the classroom, creating a content funnel (see Figure 4.3) that stems from an enduring understanding. Now, it is time to develop a content outline.

Table 4.1 *Essential, Compelling, and Supporting Questions for Two Units*

Questions	American Revolution	World War II
Essential Questions	• How do individuals balance the right of the government to govern in the people's best interest with their own personal interest? • How might friendship and trust contribute to conflict?	• What is worth fighting for? • Is war avoidable or justifiable?
Compelling Questions	• Was the American Revolution inevitable? • How did colonists become revolutionaries? • Were all colonists revolutionaries? • Did the American Revolution impact individuals and groups in the same way?	• Could World War II have been avoided? • How did the attack on Pearl Harbor impact American citizens and their view of the war in Europe? • Why was the US on the winning side of World War II? • What moral dilemmas did individuals and governments face during World War II?
Supporting Questions	• Who fought in the American Revolution, both foreign and domestic parties? • What role did the French and Indian War have upon colonial life? • What were the main grievances of the colonists? • Who were the main players in the American Revolution, and how did the conflict impact them? • What is the difference between a colonist and a revolutionary? Were specific colonists labeled revolutionaries? If so, who and why?	• What role did President Roosevelt's speeches play in rallying public support after Pearl Harbor? • How did the attack on Pearl Harbor impact the enlistment rates in the American military? • What were the main arguments used by those who previously opposed American involvement in the war to support the war effort after Pearl Harbor? • How did the United States contribute to ending World War II?

Figure 4.3 *Narrowing Your Focus: A Content Funnel*

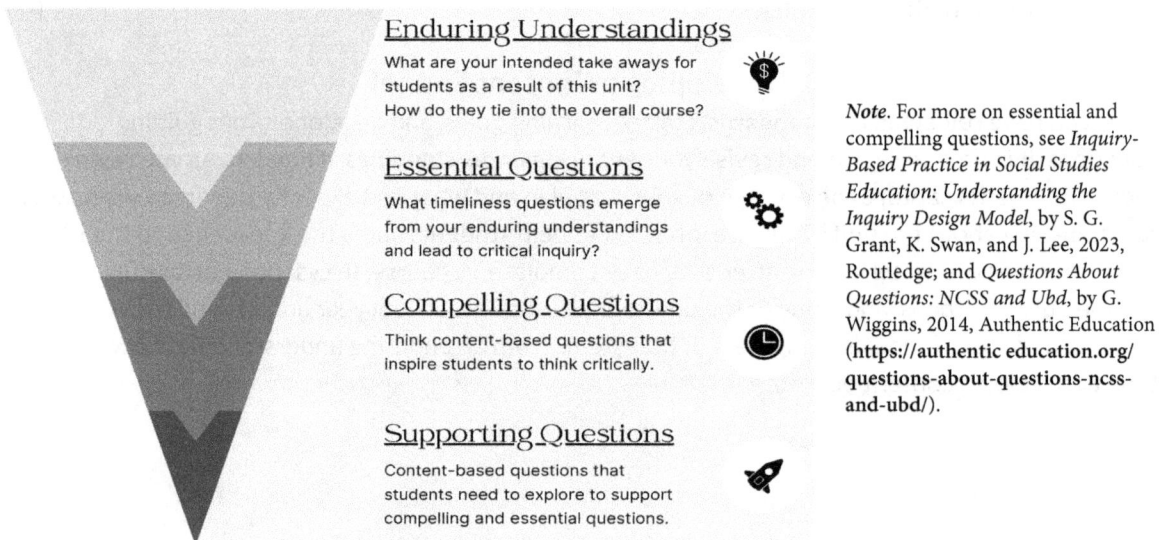

Enduring Understandings
What are your intended take aways for students as a result of this unit? How do they tie into the overall course?

Essential Questions
What timeliness questions emerge from your enduring understandings and lead to critical inquiry?

Compelling Questions
Think content-based questions that inspire students to think critically.

Supporting Questions
Content-based questions that students need to explore to support compelling and essential questions.

Note. For more on essential and compelling questions, see *Inquiry-Based Practice in Social Studies Education: Understanding the Inquiry Design Model*, by S. G. Grant, K. Swan, and J. Lee, 2023, Routledge; and *Questions About Questions: NCSS and Ubd*, by G. Wiggins, 2014, Authentic Education (**https://authentic education.org/questions-about-questions-ncss-and-ubd/**).

Developing a Content Outline

Many teachers struggle at this point in unit planning. Deana, an 11th-grade social studies teacher, is ready for the next step of the planning process. She has developed goals and essential questions for her American Revolution unit, but she has no idea what she will actually be teaching on a day-to-day basis. What does she need to know to decide what is important for her students to learn? She realizes she needs to map out the specific content that will be taught in each lesson. Deana decides she wants to make the American Revolution personal and show her students the human side. Deana researches specific examples: families who were split and families whose members took different sides based on political and economic reasons. Deana writes out all of the content she wants to emphasize for each day of the unit. So, how can she create a content outline to base her lesson plans on? A *content outline* is a framework of the specific content students will learn throughout the unit. All of the names, dates, definitions, explanations, facts, concepts, events, and places will be incorporated into this outline. You must become an expert in the theme or topic of the unit to be able to organize, determine importance, and structure the information according to students' prerequisites and preexisting schemas. Everything you have done so far in organizing your unit comes into play. The content outline serves as a guide for teaching, ensuring that all necessary content is covered and presented in an organized way, allowing for clear understanding, effective lesson planning, and alignment with learning objectives.

Once you have the details of a specific content outline for the unit, you can split and label the information into days of teaching (e.g., day 1 content, day 2 content, etc.). Next, look at each day's content and determine the enduring understanding, or in other words, the day's generalization. At the end of a lesson exploring how political differences tore families apart, Deana might decide her generalization for that day:

> The American Revolution not only split the colonies but also tore families apart, as differing loyalties to the British cause or the Patriot cause created deep divisions within households, reflecting deep divisions over issues of power, allegiance, and the future of the colonies.

As the teacher, you must choreograph the specific content for the day because you want your students to leave with a specific and important generalization.

Organizing a Content Outline

The more confident and knowledgeable you become with the content of the unit, the better equipped you are to organize it effectively and teach it to others. This idea emphasizes the importance of teachers being well prepared and knowledgeable, enabling them to filter and present the most relevant and impactful information to their students. Figure 4.4 shows how a teacher may organize a content outline on the American Revolution. This teacher has decided to view content through the different opinions of war and the ways they may impact relationships.

Figure 4.4 *Sample Content Outline*

Essential Question for the Day of Content:
Can political differences impact personal relationships and family dynamics?

Patriots:
- Advocated for independence from Britain, inspired by Enlightenment ideals like liberty and self-governance.
- Often viewed the Loyalists as traitors to the cause of freedom.

Loyalists:
- Remained loyal to the British Crown, believing in the rule of law and that British governance was essential for stability.
- Loyalists often saw Patriots as rebels or criminals undermining order.

Internal Conflicts:
- Many families had members on both sides, leading to personal betrayals, property disputes, and even imprisonment.
- The Revolution is often seen as a fight between the colonies and Britain, but it also divided neighbors, friends, and families, such as Benjamin Franklin's family

Benjamin Franklin and William Franklin:
- Benjamin Franklin was one of the foremost Patriots who advocated for independence.
- His son, William Franklin, served as the Royal Governor of New Jersey and remained a staunch Loyalist.
- Their relationship deteriorated due to political differences, and they became estranged for life.

Impact on the Family:
- Brothers against Brothers
  - Families with members on both sides often faced intense strain. Some fought on opposite sides in the war, with tragic outcomes.
- Husbands and Wives:
  - In certain cases, marriages faced tension, with one spouse supporting independence and the other remaining loyal to Britain. For example, women like Abigail Adams feared how the conflict would affect their households.
- Notable Divided Families:
  - The De Lancey Family (New York): One of the most prominent Loyalist families, with some family members supporting the British and others becoming Patriots.
  - The Livingston Family (New York): A large and influential family, which was also split by political allegiance, creating long-lasting feuds.

The Loss of Property due to Beliefs:
- Many Loyalists had their property confiscated or were exiled. States passed laws allowing the seizure of Loyalist property, leaving family members penniless.
- Thousands of Loyalists, especially in New York, fled to Canada, the West Indies, or back to Britain after the war, leading to permanent family separations.
- Even some Patriots who stayed behind faced loss of property, imprisonment, or isolation from family members who had become Loyalists.

After the War

- Many families attempted to reconcile, but others remained estranged. The new United States often offered amnesty to Loyalists, but social divides persisted.
- Some family lines continued to carry the scars of the war for generations, with Loyalist descendants feeling alienated from their Patriot relatives.

Generalization: The American Revolution was not just a war for independence—it was a deeply personal conflict that tore families apart, leaving emotional, social, and psychological scars that would last long after the final battles were fought.

Note. Information for this content outline is from Boonshoft (2016), Braun (2001), and Ketchum (n.d.).

Teacher Tip: *Reach out to colleagues teaching other social studies courses and other content areas, such as English, to make connections to relevant information. The approach to connect can be fun to explore.*

Consider the following when planning the content for each day of the unit:

1. **Understand Student Needs and Abilities.** It is important to know your students. Take into consideration the learning needs, abilities, and backgrounds of students to create content that is accessible as well as challenging.
2. **Adhere to Curriculum Standards.** The content needs to align with district, state, and national curriculum standards since they set the learning objectives and benchmarks.
3. **Make Content Relevant to Students.** Choose content that relates to students' lives and interests to help them see its relevance and application in their lives. Use real-life examples to show students how the content is relevant beyond the classroom.
4. **Balance Depth and Breadth.** Strike a balance between covering a range of topics while ensuring students grasp concepts. As an educator, you cannot include everything; be discerning based on this list of considerations.
5. **Determine Pacing.** Determine how much time should be allocated for each topic while progressing steadily through the curriculum.
6. **Build on Prior Knowledge**. Recognize what knowledge students already possess and structure the content in a way that builds upon their existing understanding. Additionally, organize the content outline so as to scaffold new content.
7. **Embrace Diversity and Inclusion**. The material should represent a variety of viewpoints and be inclusive of all students. This creates an environment of acceptance and appreciation for all.

Viewing Content from a Broader Perspective

It is essential that teachers incorporate differing perspectives and resources into the content to develop a comprehensive content framework that reflects a variety of interests. To effectively prepare and deliver lessons, teachers should consider diverse viewpoints and approaches, ensuring they are all well represented. Teachers need to be flexible and inclusive in their approach.

> **Teacher Tip:** *Remember that resources often represent a particular bias, be it political, economic, or social. It is important to use a variety of resources with a variety of perspectives to ensure that the content you present represents a variety of diverse perspectives.*

Personal Bias

When creating a content outline for a unit, it is important to consult an array of diverse resources and consider multiple perspectives. This approach ensures a comprehensive and inclusive foundation for the unit. By integrating various viewpoints and materials, the outline becomes more balanced and reflective of the world we live in. Another aspect of the teaching journey is to reflect upon one's own personal bias. Teachers must recognize how their beliefs and values could impact content decisions. By acknowledging and addressing their biases, teachers can create a more equitable and inclusive curriculum (Ferlazzo, 2022).

Assessment

While you are creating your content outline, you need to be thinking about how you plan to assess the learning of your students. Assessment is a multifaceted tool teachers use to evaluate student progress, guide student learning, and improve instructional practices because it provides essential insights for future instruction. It is an integral component of the teaching and learning process and is an evaluation tool for teachers. Assessment should occur throughout the lesson, at the end of the lesson, and at the end of the unit.

Summative assessments are used to evaluate and measure student learning at the end of an instructional period or at a clear break in the learning, like at the end of the unit. This would be a way of assessing overall knowledge and understanding of the unit's content and skills. These summative assessments, usually graded assignments, can include unit quizzes, exams, projects, writing assignments, and portfolios that are administered as a culmination of the unit's content. Effective assessment practices gauge students' knowledge and skills and provide valuable feedback to inform future teaching strategies and support student growth.

There are a few important points to remember about the unit assessment:

- The form of assessment you use should reflect what the students learned during the unit. This means you should only include content and skills you spent time on instructing students. This is the content you focused on in lessons, activities, and assignments.
- It is crucial to vary the form or type of assessment you use at the end of each unit. While it is important for students to practice test-type questions, we must go beyond teaching to the test. By allowing students the opportunity to demonstrate their knowledge in multiple ways, such as through project-based assessments, Inquiry Design Modules, or portfolios, you can foster a more innovative and adaptable learning environment.
- Unit assessments should be viewed as more than a grade. All assessments should be used as diagnostic tools. Just like in the medical field, educators should test, read the results, diagnose, and treat students based on their individual needs.
- Teachers need to use quantitative and qualitative data to understand their students' learning. Observing students' interpersonal connections while completing group work

might provide more valuable information than a test score when determining a student's strengths and areas of growth.

Highly effective teachers continually use assessment data to
- inform their instruction to tailor to specific student needs,
- adjust supports based on changing needs, and
- create future learning outcomes based on student needs.

Conclusion

A well-thought-out social studies unit serves as the foundation for engaging and meaningful instruction, enabling students to connect required content and skills to the lives of students. The sample in the appendix demonstrates that the practice of organizing content, setting clear goals, designing measurable learning objectives, and aligning assessments is crucial to the process. Only through the planning process do we, as educators, take the time to make connections and organize learning segments that flow and are based on the importance of enduring understandings. As we plan, it is important to remain flexible and responsive to student needs, allowing their interests and insights to guide the exploration of key ideas.

Checklist for Crafting Engaging Social Studies Units of Study

☐ **Determine Your Teaching Philosophy:** Am I teaching with purpose and aligning lessons with guiding principles?

☐ **Create a Pacing Guide:** Have I created a tentative calendar for the school year that addresses all the key content units and is aligned with necessary resources?

☐ **Begin Planning a Unit of Study:** Have I collected a variety of resources to guide me in planning the unit other than the textbook?

☐ **Determine Your Unit Theme(s):** Have I organized the curricular topics and content into a focused period of learning that is guided by central theme(s) that are relevant?"

☐ **Establish Enduring Understandings of the Unit**: Have I created one or two thought-provoking and relevant takeaways I want students to remember in the future regarding this unit?

☐ **Establish Your Learning Goals**: Have I created varied learning goals that address a variety of goal areas, such as cognitive and career-oriented goals?

☐ **Establish Your Essential Questions:** Have I created one or two timeless, thought-provoking, and relevant questions to guide student exploration into the unit content?

☐ **Establish Your Compelling Questions**: Have I drafted one to four content-based compelling questions for students to explore?

☐ **Establish Your Supporting Questions**: Have I created appropriate supporting questions for students to explore that will provide them with content and evidence to answer the compelling questions?

☐ **Check for a Content Funnel**: Do all my questions and understandings flow from broader essential questions to specific supporting questions, creating a cohesive unit structure?

☐ **Create a Content Outline**: Am I prioritizing the content and chunking it to support the enduring understanding, learning goals, essential questions, and compelling questions for the unit?

☐ **Reflect on Personal Bias**: Have I taken the time to ensure the content is balanced and representative of diverse peoples and viewpoints?

☐ **Develop Assessment Strategies**: Have I considered formative and summative assessments that can be used throughout the unit to assess students' knowledge, skills, and cumulative understanding of the unit?

References

Boonshoft, M. (2016, September 19). *Dispossessing Loyalists and redistributing property in Revolutionary New York.* New York Public Library. **www.nypl.org/blog/2016/09/19/loyalist-property-confiscation**

Braun, K. (2021, March 21). *Divided loyalties: Benjamin and William Franklin.* Jefferson Monticello. **www.monticello.org/exhibits-events/blog/divided-loyalties-benjamin-and-william-franklin**

Covey, S. R. (2013). *The 7 habits of highly effective people: Powerful lessons in personal change.* RosettaBooks. (Original work published 1989)

Ferlazzo, L. (2022, September 29). *18 ways to make social studies class more culturally responsive.* Education Week. **www.edweek.org/teaching-learning/opinion-18-ways-to-make-social-studies-class-more-culturally-responsive/2022/09**

Grant, S. G., Swan, K., & Lee, J. (2017). Questions that compel and support. *Social Education, 81*(4), 200–203.

Holden, J. (2020). *Quick reference guide to developing cognitive learning objectives* (8th ed.). **https://resources.careered.com/LCMSFileSharePreview/Resources/AdobePDF/EDU604_Guide_to_Writing_Objectives.pdf**

Ketchum, R. M. (n.d.). *Divided loyalties: How the American Revolution came to New York.* The Gilder Lehrman Institute of American History. **www.gilderlehrman.org/history-resources/videos/divided-loyalties-how-american-revolution-came-new-york**

Mahood, W., Biemer, L., & Lowe, W. (1991). *Teaching social studies in middle and senior high schools: Decisions! Decisions!* Merrill Press.

University of Alaska Fairbanks Instructional Design Team. (n.d.). *Enduring Understandings: The learning that will stay with you.* UAF Center for Teaching and Learning. **https://ctl.uaf.edu/enduring-understandings/**

Wiggins, G. (2014, December 8). *Questions about questions: NCSS and UbD.* Authentic Education. **https://authenticeducation.org/questions-about-questions-ncss-and-ubd/**

Wiggins, G., & McTighe, J. (2005). *Understanding by design* (2nd ed.). Association for Supervision and Curriculum Development.

Appendix
Unit Plan Sample: American Revolution

Stage 1: Desired Results	
Established Goals (What content standards will this unit address?)	Understand the social, political, and economic factors that led to the war, as well as key figures, battles, and people.
Compelling Question (This is an overarching question that centers all instruction. Students need to experience all lessons to be able to answer the question.)	How did the American colonies succeed in gaining independence from one of the most powerful nations in the world?
Content Knowledge (Include a link here to your Content Outline, like the example in Figure 4.4)	**Summary:** The causes of the American Revolution (e.g., taxation, representation, British policies) **Key Events and Turning Points:** e.g., Boston Tea Party, Declaration of Independence, major battles **Important Figures:** e.g., George Washington, Thomas Jefferson, King George III **Outcomes of the Revolution:** Treaty of Paris, effects on various groups like Loyalists, Patriots, Native Americans
Skills (What specific skills and processes should students be able to use?)	• Analyzing and interpreting primary sources (e.g., the Declaration of Independence, letters from soldiers) • Comparing perspectives (e.g., Loyalist vs. Patriot) • Understanding cause and effect in historical contexts • Developing historical arguments and supporting them with evidence

Stage 2: Evidence	
Summative Assessment (How will students demonstrate their knowledge and skills from this unit as a whole?)	**Project:** Students will create a timeline of key events from the American Revolution, showing the connections between causes, events, and outcomes. This will be accompanied by a written analysis. **Test:** Students will answer and respond to a combination of multiple-choice, short-answer, and essay questions on the causes, key events, and consequences of the American Revolution. **Performance Task:** Students will engage in a classroom debate, taking on roles of historical figures (e.g., British officials, American Patriots, Loyalists) and discussing whether to declare independence.

Stage 3: Instruction			
Day # **Lesson #**	**Focal Learning Objectives/** **Standards**	**Primary Learning Events**	**Assessments**
Day 1 Lesson 1	Students will identify the causes of the American Revolution, focusing on taxation and representation.	*Reading*: Excerpts from "Give Me Liberty" by Patrick Henry *Activity*: Simulation on "No Taxation without Representation"	*Exit Ticket*: What were two causes of colonial unrest that led to revolution?
Day 2 Lesson 2	Students will understand the events leading up to the Boston Massacre and its impact on colonial attitudes.	*Video*: Boston Massacre reenactment *Primary Source*: Paul Revere's engraving of the event *Class Discussion*: Bias in historical sources	*Short-Answer Reflection*: How did the Boston Massacre fuel the Revolution?
Day 3 Lesson 3	Students will explore the significance of the Boston Tea Party as an act of rebellion.	*Reading*: Excerpts from participant diaries *Role-Play Activity*: Boston Tea Party	*Written Response*: What was the message behind the Boston Tea Party?
Day 4 Lesson 4	Students will examine the Declaration of Independence and its key arguments.	*Reading*: Excerpts from the Declaration of Independence *Group Analysis*: Break down key phrases and their meanings	*Quiz*: What are the three main arguments in the Declaration of Independence?
Day 5 Lesson 5	Students will understand the key battles of the American Revolution (e.g., Lexington and Concord, Saratoga, Yorktown).	*Interactive Map Activity*: Major battles of the revolution *Reading*: Battle summaries and primary source letters from soldiers	*Exit Ticket*: What was the turning point of the Revolution, and why?

Chapter 5
Tapping Your Creativity: How to Create Engaging Social Studies Lessons

Karen Poland and Kristi Fragnoli

Whew, you made it through the first week of school as a new teacher, spending the first few days building relationships with students. As you considered your busy plans for the weekend, you decided not to worry about planning each lesson for next week, given you have a unit plan. As you walk into school the next week, you plan to talk about the causes of the American Revolution. But when asked by your mentor to explain the essential concepts, themes, or the historical connections students should be making to other historical events and to the present, you are caught off guard and feel completely unprepared.

Lesson planning is about thinking ahead: deciding what content and skills your students need, how they'll interact with the material, and how you will know if they have learned it. Planning helps you to develop the habit of working through the big questions: *What are the students learning today? How will they experience it? How will I check their understanding?* Without this kind of forethought, lessons can feel scattered, and students may miss important connections. Planning can feel a bit mundane and time-consuming, but it is clearly necessary, as it keeps your teaching purposeful and your students engaged.

Moving from unit planning to lesson planning is about translating the broad goals of a unit into specific daily measurable learning outcomes (MLOs) that guide instruction and the delivery of content. At this point, you probably have several questions about lesson planning: Do I need to write lesson plans even if I have a unit plan? Do I need to write a new lesson plan every day? What role does my plan book or an online planning platform play in my planning? Why are experienced teachers able to create lesson plans so much more quickly than I can? These are all valid questions. In this chapter, we aim to simplify the lesson planning process, addressing these concerns while emphasizing the important role that lesson plan creation plays in your professional growth as a teacher.

Learning and the Lesson Plan

At its core, lesson planning is the foundation for creating meaningful and memorable learning experiences that inspire and engage students in a social studies classroom. Lesson planning is about creating a learning experience, and the lesson plan is the guiding tool teachers use to create the experience (Vermette et al., 2010). Think about it: What does a planned learning experience mean? To answer this question, think about a lesson you remember from when you were in school. Why do you remember that lesson? Responses to this question often highlight the importance of having fun, exploring content, making meaning (metacognition), and feeling a sense of autonomy in learning—all of which are connected to what we know about effective learning. The Social

A Classroom With Purpose: A Guide to Teaching Social Studies Today

Constructivist Learning Theory (SCLT), when viewed through the lenses of Piaget (1969) and Vygotsky (1977), demonstrates the deep theoretical connection between individual cognitive development, metacognitive thinking, and social interaction within the learning environment. Piaget contributes to SCLT because he believes children's cognitive development grows over time. We can see this growth in the developing problem-solving strategies of students. Additionally, Vygotsky emphasized the role of the social environment in learning, particularly through scaffolding and the Zone of Proximal Development (ZPD), where learners develop cognitive and metacognitive skills with guidance from more experienced individuals. He argued that learners flourish through social interactions and guidance from those who are more knowledgeable.

So, what does this mean to you as a teacher and creator of lesson plans? These ideas show that metacognitive thinking develops both individually and through social interaction. In cooperative learning settings, such as peer interactions, learners reflect on and adjust their thinking through discussion and collaboration. Learning is not only an individual process but also a social one, in which students build and refine their knowledge together. Think about those moments when students discuss ideas, challenge each other's thinking, and collaborate to solve problems— this is when learning truly comes alive. By creating lesson plans that encourage meaningful collaboration, you are giving students the chance to explore, build, and refine their understanding together, making learning both impactful and memorable.

The Lesson Plan

Simply put, a lesson plan is an outline of what you plan to teach on a specific day. Lesson plans cover the duration of the class period; they are not a plan for two or three days. Although content, themes, and activities may extend beyond just one class period, the lesson plan is designed to outline what you plan to address in one class period, such as a teacher's logical sequencing of content, instructional activities, checks for understanding, key transitions, and assessments of learning. For example, DeVante planned a class debate that would take four class periods. Does this mean the lesson plan lasts for four days? No, there needs to be a plan for each day. In DeVante's class on the first day, students worked in groups to plan for the debate by collecting sources and making a list of facts to support their argument. On the second day, he reviewed the task the students completed the day prior, assessed the status of group work, and then assigned the task for the second day, which was to organize a list of facts into themes. The third and fourth days were devoted to conducting a class debate. On the first day of the debate, he began the class with the rules for the debate and ended the lesson with a summary of the arguments of both teams. On the last day of the debate, he began the lesson by summarizing the key points made the previous day, reminded students of the debate rules, and ended the lesson with an exit ticket asking students to identify five key points of both sides of the debate.

Each day, DeVante had specific learning targets for the students to work toward and a method for assessing their progress. Although lesson plan templates will vary in their format from one university or school district to another, quality lesson plans have several common and consistent components because they lead to a highly effective learning experience. All lesson plans include measurable learning outcomes, an introduction that is designed to get students engaged, a body of content learning activities that includes essential processing activities, a means of assessing student understanding, closure, and teacher reflection. In DeVante's situation, although the plan for four days was to execute a class debate, he had clear expectations for each day of class. Students were informed of his expectations and were held accountable for meeting the expectations. Following DeVante's lead, let's dive into the essential components of a lesson plan!

Essential Components of a Lesson Plan

As we explore the essential components of a lesson plan, consider how each component can enhance and support your teaching philosophy. A well-crafted lesson plan is not just a checklist—it is a roadmap that connects your goals as a teacher with the meaningful learning experiences you want to create for your students.

Measurable Learning Outcomes

The first essential component of a lesson is the measurable learning outcomes (MLOs) because the lesson activities you embed in your lesson revolve around how to best support students in mastering your MLOs. In other words, the content you plan to cover in the lesson drives how you will present the content. As discussed in Chapter 4, "Building Bridges: Crafting Engaging Social Studies Units of Study," although the terms "objective" and "outcome" are often used interchangeably, they are quite different, and when combined into one sentence, they create an MLO.

An MLO is a clear, specific statement of what students will be able to demonstrate in terms of knowledge, skills, or values and should be directly linked to activities, assignments, and assessments that provide evidence of student learning (Holden, 2020). For each lesson, the MLOs should be scaffolded, using Bloom's (1956) Taxonomy as a guide. In other words, you are breaking down the content into manageable chunks with an MLO for each aspect of the content or skill you want students to know and be able to do.

The ABCD method (Mager, 1962) is a structured approach to writing MLOs that will guide you in scaffolding your content, ensuring clarity and specificity. Each letter stands for a different component of an MLO:

- **Audience**: This identifies who the learning outcome is intended for. Generally, this is the learner or student.
- **Behavior**: This specifies what the learner is expected to be able to do after the learning experience. We use Bloom's verbs to describe the behavior (e.g., "list," "describe," "explain").
- **Condition**: This describes how the learner will demonstrate the knowledge or skill during the lesson. It is the evidence, or assessment, that the student will complete (e.g., Venn diagram, exit ticket, T-Chart).
- **Degree**: This sets the criteria for acceptable performance, defining how well the learner should perform the task. The degree could involve accuracy, speed, or other standards (e.g., "with 100% accuracy," "successfully"; adapted from Kibler & Bassett, 1977).

Recall in the introduction that you planned for students to participate in a debate. However, as it unfolded, you realized students were not prepared as expected. In contrast, DeVante devoted the same number of days to the debate, but his students were much better prepared. The difference is that DeVante created clear MLOs for each lesson, regardless of whether the activity spanned multiple class periods. Take the first day of the debate, for instance, when DeVante focused on having students research their topics. He crafted the following MLOs for the first lesson, framing each MLO with four components: audience, behavior, degree, and condition (see Figure 5.1).

- By the end of the lesson, **students** (audience) will be able to **locate** (behavior) five sources to support their research by writing their five sources in **proper** (degree) APA format on a **reference sheet** (condition).
- By the end of the lesson, **students** (audience) will be able to **describe** (behavior) three facts from each source that support their argument by **accurately** (degree) recording their facts about each reference on **index cards** (behavior).

DeVante developed the following MLOs for the second day:

- By the end of the lesson, **students** (audience) will be able to **categorize** (behavior) their facts into themes by **appropriately** (degree) **sorting their note cards** (condition) into piles for teacher review.
- By the end of the lesson, **students** (audience) will be able to **label** (behavior) each theme by giving it a name and **appropriately** (degree) recording the name on a **graphic organizer** (condition).

By narrowing the focus of what students should know and do, DeVante set up a clear path for success.

Figure 5.1 *Measurable Learning Outcomes*

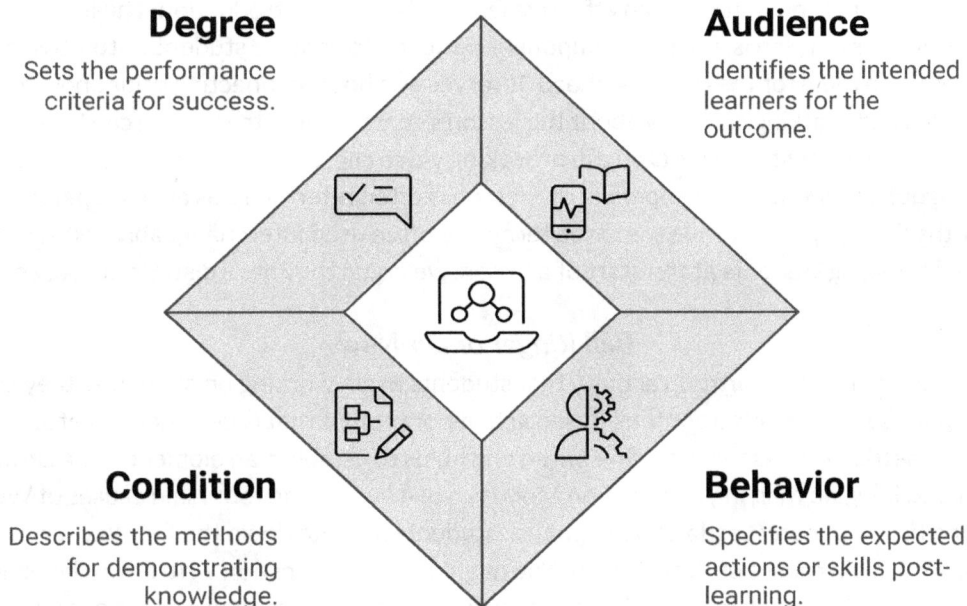

Degree
Sets the performance criteria for success.

Audience
Identifies the intended learners for the outcome.

Condition
Describes the methods for demonstrating knowledge.

Behavior
Specifies the expected actions or skills post-learning.

Note. Image generated by Napkin.ai, 2025 (**www.napkin.ai**), using *Creating Learning Outcomes*, Stanford Teaching Commons (**https://teachingcommons.stanford.edu/teaching-guides/foundations-course-design/course-planning/creating-learning-outcomes**).

Let's Give it a Try

In the following MLO, underline the audience, the behavior, the condition, and the degree. For example: "By the end of the lesson, <u>students</u> (audience) will be able to <u>define</u> (behavior) each theme by providing an <u>appropriate</u> (degree) three-sentence summary on the <u>graphic organizer</u> (condition)."

> By the end of the lesson, students will be able to summarize five key points from each debate side by successfully completing an exit ticket.

As you are drafting MLOs, remember that students need to not only master academic content but also practice and develop interpersonal skills that are crucial for working effectively with others. As Vermette and Kline (2017) explain, this "dual objective" approach encourages a holistic view of education that values both intellectual and affective growth. For example, in addition to content-focused MLOs, DeVante also considered how to support students' social development, especially while working in groups. To address this, he incorporated an MLO that aligned with Bloom's affective domain, focusing on cooperative relationships, further supporting students' growth in collaborative and emotional skills.

Teacher Tip: *For more information on embracing a dual objective framework for instructional design, see* Group Work that Works: Student Collaboration for 21st Century Skills *by P. J. Vermette and C. L. Kline, 2017, Routledge.*

Introduction of the Lesson

The second essential component of an effective lesson plan is the introduction. The introduction, or opening, in a lesson plan is a critical component designed to capture students' attention and mentally prepare them for the learning ahead. It serves as a hook, connecting prior knowledge to new concepts and sparking curiosity about the lesson's content. An introduction can be an intriguing question, a brief demonstration, a thought-provoking video clip, or a short activity that engages students right from the start. The opening of a lesson is often referred to as an anticipatory set, bell ringer, or the Engage phase. While the three terms are often used interchangeably and serve the function of engaging students at the start of a lesson, we argue they have distinct purposes.

Bell Ringer or Do-Now

Usually a brief (5 minute) warm-up activity that students begin working on as soon as they enter the classroom, a bell ringer is a content-based activity or prompt that is designed to get students to focus and settle into class. It is routine based and helps to establish an element of classroom management. Imagine that, in your class on Monday, you covered the four main causes of World War I. For a bell ringer on Tuesday, you might ask students to write down the four key terms used to describe the main causes of World War I. You might have this question written on the board for students to see as they walk into the classroom in order to encourage them to settle in and focus quickly. You might also collect their responses as a means of formative assessment (Marzano, 2007; Wiske, 1998).

Anticipatory Set

Designed to activate prior knowledge, hook students' interest, and set the stage for new learning, the anticipatory set is a creative activity that fosters a higher level of engagement that will spark students' curiosity and may not necessarily be content based. This initial phase not only draws on prior knowledge but also sets a clear purpose for the lesson, helping students understand why the material is important and how it relates to what they already know. An effective anticipatory set creates a positive tone for the lesson and motivates students to dive deeper into the subject matter (Hunter, 1982). For example, students are handed an Oreo cookie as they enter the classroom. The teacher asks students, "Is the outside of the Oreo cookie better than the inside?" After students debate this, the teacher explains the analogy of using the cookie to examine the Middle Ages, explaining that some view it as a period of so-called intellectual darkness while others view it as a time of significant cultural and societal development.

Engage

Stemming from the 5E instructional model (Bybee et al., 2006), the Engage phase is a constructivist approach to lesson planning often promoted in the sciences. The Engage phase is an essential component of an inquiry-based approach to a lesson plan and is designed to help students build their own understanding of new concepts through exploration, questioning, and discovery. The Engage phase aims to spark students' curiosity about the upcoming topic and connect their previous knowledge to the new content. It may involve an interactive activity, a question, or an experiment that elicits students' ideas and misconceptions. This sparks interest and encourages students to ask questions, setting the stage for hands-on exploratory activities (Bybee, 2019). For example, as students enter the classroom, they are provided a card that assigns them to either the De Lancey family or the Livingston family. Each card provides the students with factual information about who their character is and what their interests are. You provide a few prompts for the students that require them to form groups: find your immediate family members, find your extended family members, find the family member who agrees with your position on banking, etc. Finally, the class is divided into Loyalists and Patriots, providing students with a visual to exemplify the divisive impact of the American Revolution upon families.

Let's Give it a Try

As you read the following introductory activities, consider which ones can be used as a bell ringer, an anticipatory set, or an Engage phase activity:

1. The following terms are written on the board in the classroom: "taxation," "colonial resistance," "Boston Tea Party," "loyalists," and "patriots." Students need to select one term and write a brief definition of it.
2. Present students with a selection of songs or music clips (from various genres, modern or historical) that could represent different points of view during the American Revolution. For example, a rebellious, upbeat song might represent Patriot sentiment, while a more somber, orchestral piece could represent Loyalist views. Play the songs and ask students to discuss in small groups which historical event or character they think the song aligns with and why.

3. Students are provided the image in Figure 5.2 from the Library of Congress, which depicts the impact of the closing of Little Rock Schools to avoid integration in the 1960s. Students are asked to make observations, ask questions, and hypothesize about the context, author, or purpose of the image.

Figure 5.2 *Image for Introductory Activity #3*

Note. From *Little Rock, Ark., re: anti-integration story. Classes on TV, after school closings* [Photograph], by T. J. O'Halloran, 1958, Library of Congress, (www.loc.gov/item/2003654356). In the public domain.

Regardless of the introductory activity for your lesson, the introduction is an essential component of a lesson plan. Teachers sometimes dive into the content without an introduction, but students may not be ready to appropriate the new content to their current schemas. Without a proper introduction, students will be lost, will feel unclear as to what their role is during the lesson, and will remain passively disengaged. In addition, it is important to vary how you begin your lesson, so remember to use all three types of introductory activities.

Body of the Lesson

Now, it is time for you to tap into your creative side! The next component of an effective lesson is the body, or instructional segment, of a lesson plan. It contains a variety of teacher-centered and student-centered activities or stages in the learning process. In this component, you need to consider how to effectively introduce the content outlined in the lesson, what thought-provoking questions will foster student engagement, and how to scaffold the material throughout the lesson to build students' understanding. This component is pivotal, as it is a logical and detailed representation (roadmap) of your reasoning for how to present the content to students. It delineates the specific roles and tasks for both the teacher and the students throughout the learning process, guiding each step of instruction. In other words, it is a detailed summary of what the teacher will do and say in the lesson and what the students will be doing during the lesson.

Teacher Tip: *Remember, you cannot have enough details in the body of the lesson plan. When you are teaching and get distracted, use the detailed plan to pick up where you left off seamlessly!*

A well-structured body of the lesson ensures that the lesson flows seamlessly and that all learning objectives are met, ultimately enhancing student comprehension and engagement. By carefully planning this section, you can create a dynamic and effective learning environment that caters to diverse learning needs. It also helps in anticipating potential challenges and allows for adjustments to the teaching approach as needed, increasing the effectiveness of instruction.

Content-Driven Approach

Lesson planning can feel overwhelming due to the many options and countless instructional strategies available. However, it is important to remember that the content you are teaching will shape your lesson plan format and instructional choices. Both the nature of the content and your approach to it will determine how you structure the lesson and what strategies you use to help students understand. In this sense, the endless options of instructional strategies are a blessing. This is where understanding various approaches and strategies can help you make an informed decision about how to write your lesson plan.

If the lesson involves abstract concepts that require critical thinking or problem-solving, such as inquiry or historical analysis, a *constructivist approach* is more suitable. The National Council for the Social Studies (NCSS, 2017) emphasizes that "inquiry is the heart of social studies" (p. viii). In this approach, students actively construct knowledge through exploration, discussion, hands-on activities, and fostering deep understanding. By engaging in an inquiry-based model of instruction, students not only deepen their understanding of social studies concepts but also prepare for informed civic participation. It is through dialogue between students that a deeper understanding is developed.

Teacher Tip: *In the Madeline Hunter (1982) lesson format, the body of the lesson will be characterized as a cycle of direct instruction, modeling, and guided practice, followed by independent practice; whereas, in the 5E model, the body of the lesson would be characterized by Explore, Explain, and Elaborate phases.*

However, for lessons focusing on procedural tasks or foundational skills, such as memorizing facts, definitions, or sequential order of events, a *behaviorist approach* may be more effective. Behaviorist strategies emphasize direct instruction, repetition, and reinforcement to shape learning behavior. A behaviorist approach, often referred to as the direct instruction model, stems from the work of Madeline Hunter (1982). It is a teacher-centered approach in which the teacher presents information to students while at the same time providing processing activities, and then the teacher guides students in their understanding and application of new content in an organized and structured manner.

Let's Give it a Try

Read the following teaching ideas and decide which approach you think they align with. Mark a C next to the ones you believe reflect a *constructivist approach* to lesson planning and a B next to those you believe align with the *behaviorist approach*.

1. Students investigate historical events of the late 1800s and early 1900s by analyzing primary sources like letters, diaries, photographs, and official documents to develop their own interpretations and conclusions regarding the past. Through this analysis, students can define the terms "industrialization," "urbanization," "immigration," "child labor," and "the Great Depression."
2. Students watch a documentary on the Holocaust and complete a question-and-answer worksheet.

Table 5.1 *Two Approaches to Lesson Planning*

Lesson Plan Format	Description	Structure	Use
Behaviorist (Direct Instruction)	This type of lesson plan is linear, often following a direct instruction model where the teacher guides the students through the learning process.	1. Objective 2. Introduction 3. Instruction (teacher-led) 4. Practice (guided and independent) 5. Assessment 6. Closure	Best for content that requires explicit teaching and when introducing new skills or concepts, for learning factual or procedural knowledge
Constructivist	This type of lesson plan encourages students to explore questions and problems, fostering critical thinking and problem-solving skills.	1. Introduction to a question or problem 2. Exploration and investigation by students 3. Analysis of findings 4. Discussion and reflection 5. Application of knowledge	Students make their own meaning and hone the skills of a historian. They learn to corroborate evidence when making an argument or claim, concept formation, and concept attainment.

Table 5.1 is a summary of two lesson plan formats, one that promotes a constructivist approach and the other that promotes a behaviorist approach to lesson planning. As you can see, both approaches to lesson planning can be beneficial for student learning.

Lesson planning helps teachers create a logical sequencing for the exploration of content while incorporating chosen instructional strategies. Regardless of the lesson plan approach, it is essential to vary your instructional strategies to engage all learners, as relying solely on one approach—like lecture or cooperative groups—for several consecutive days can limit student engagement and growth. This can also mean using several different instructional strategies within one lesson, such as combining group activities with visual aids or hands-on tasks with guided practice. By doing so, you ensure that various learning preferences are addressed. This allows you to create a more inclusive and dynamic learning environment.

Content Strategies

Content-based instructional strategies are designed to teach specific academic content or skills. The goal is to deepen students' understanding of the subject matter and develop their understanding of the discipline, in this case, history, geography, economics, civic education, and social studies. The content being taught plays a significant role in determining the type of content-based instructional strategy used. Highlighted in Table 5.2 are a few important strategies to consider when planning a lesson. By thoughtfully aligning instructional strategies with both the content and the diverse needs of learners, educators can create a more inclusive and effective learning environment.

Assessment Within a Lesson Plan

The fourth essential component of a lesson plan is assessment. Assessment is a multifaceted tool that teachers use to evaluate student progress, guide student learning, and improve instructional practices. It provides essential insights for future instruction and is an integral component of the teaching and learning process and an evaluation tool for teachers. With a variety of assessments, teachers can gauge how well the students have grasped the lesson's goals and objectives. When students think of an assessment, they typically think of a grade. As teachers, we need to keep in the forefront of our minds the power and impact each assessment can have for students, not only the importance of the grade but also the purpose it serves in guiding their learning. Assessments include formative and summative assessments, each differing in timing, purpose, and focus, and are administered in both formal and informal ways (Bloom, 1956; Scriven, 1967). Formative assessments happen during the instructional process when learning is occurring as ongoing checks for understanding. Formative assessments can include daily observations, questioning techniques, homework exercises, end-of-lesson summary tasks like exit tickets and beginning-of-lesson bell ringers, one-minute reflections, weekly quizzes, surveys, etc. Although they are designed to inform instruction, they can be graded and used as an evaluative tool, preferably as a low-stakes grade. When used thoughtfully, these assessments act as a bridge between today's teaching and tomorrow's plans, providing valuable insights into what students need next.

Summative assessments, however, are used to evaluate and measure student learning at the end of an instructional period or at a clear break in learning, like at the end of a unit. Summative assessments, which are usually graded assignments, can include unit quizzes, exams, projects, writing assignments, portfolios, notebook checks, etc. Summative assessments are typically a higher-tier grade for the students. Similar to the use of formative assessments, summative assessments not only gauge students' knowledge and skills but also provide feedback to inform future teaching,

Teachers should be mindful of designing assessments that are fair, diverse, and inclusive. Imagine you are teaching an introductory psychology course on stress and discussing how workplace rank affects it. You create a multiple-choice question asking which position—general, sergeant, lieutenant, or corporal—is the most stressful. This assumes students are familiar with these military

Table 5.2 *Content-Based Instructional Strategies*

Content-Based Instructional Strategy	Explanation
Concept Development	Concept development involves helping students distinguish and define a concept by providing both examples ("Yes") and nonexamples ("No") to highlight key attributes. Through these examples and guided discussions, students work towards a shared understanding of the concept. They analyze information, identify patterns, and group related items, forming categories based on similarities and differences. This process enables students to construct their own definition or description of the concept based on the attributes they have identified. See *Concept Formation* by W. Parker, 2018, TeachingHistory.org (**https://teachinghistory.org/teaching-materials/teaching-guides/25184**).
Simulation	This strategy involves creating realistic, interactive scenarios in which students can apply their knowledge and skills to experience, practice, and problem-solve in a controlled environment. Simulations mimic real-world situations or processes, allowing students to take on roles, make decisions, and see the consequences of their actions. For simulation ideas that can bring history alive, see *Simulation as a Teaching Strategy* from The Center for Teaching and Learning, Kent State University (**www.kent.edu/ctl/simulation-teaching-strategy**).
Primary Source Document Analysis	Students examine original documents and artifacts to develop critical thinking and analytical skills. This strategy encourages students to consider multiple perspectives, build arguments based on evidence, and develop a deeper understanding of the event or time period. See *Educator Resources* from the National Archives (**www.archives.gov/education**).
Thematic Description	This strategy organizes teaching and learning around a central theme or topic, integrating various subjects and skills to create a cohesive and immersive educational experience. By focusing on a theme, such as "community" or "revolution," students explore content across different disciplines, making meaningful connections between subjects and content knowledge. See the Smithsonian Learning Lab (**https://learninglab.si.edu/**)
Socratic Method	The strategy uses guided questioning to encourage students to think critically, articulate their thoughts, and examine underlying assumptions. This approach emphasizes dialogue between the teacher and students (or among students), in which the teacher asks open-ended questions that lead students to explore complex ideas and consider multiple perspective. See the Facing History & Ourselves website for steps and rules to help implement an effective Socratic Seminar (**www.facinghistory.org/resource-library/socratic-seminar**).

ranks and their hierarchy. If they know this, they can answer correctly, but without prior knowledge of military titles, their lack of understanding could lead to an incorrect response. This example highlights the importance of being mindful of students' prior knowledge to ensure assessments are fair and accurately measure their understanding of the intended concepts.

Overall, thoughtful assessment practices are crucial for fostering an effective learning environment and enhancing student success. In addition, the assessment(s) you choose to use in a lesson will need to align to your objective. For example, Malik decides he wants students to be able to describe five characteristics of ancient civilizations during the Neolithic era. To do this, he assigns a matching activity. However, the issue is that a matching task does not require students to actually describe anything—it focuses on identifying content rather than engaging in the deeper process of explaining or describing it. Malik has two options to address this. First, he could adjust his objective so that the Bloom's Taxonomy verb aligns better with the matching activity. For instance, instead of using the verb "describe," which involves higher-order thinking, he could use "identify," which is more appropriate. Alternatively, a more effective approach would be to redesign the activity to better meet the original objective. Malik could have students create a newspaper page where they write a headline and a summary for each of the five characteristics of civilizations during the Neolithic era. This task not only aligns with Bloom's level of "describe" but also engages students in higher-order thinking and creativity.

Teacher Tip: *Not every assessment needs to receive a grade. Remember to assess students frequently using different types of assessment.*

Let's take a look at another example. As Tatiana plans her lesson on the American Revolution, she uses a variety of formative assessments to guide her instruction. She first assesses students as they enter her classroom through observation. Do the students appear to be happy, excited, or tired? Do student friendships appear to be intact or stressed? She then begins her lesson with a Fast Five, asking students to list on paper what they believe to be the five main causes of the American Revolution. Once students have completed the Fast Five activity, she plans to collect their responses and give them a participation grade, which will be used as a formative assessment. Then, she has students go through a concept formation lesson that explores influential figures during the American Revolution, such as George Washington. During the exploration, students are tasked with completing a guided note activity, which she reviews as she monitors the students. The guided notes serve as both a formative and summative assessment. They are formative in that she can use them to guide her direction for students and clarify their thinking as they are filling them out. In addition, because she requires the guided notes to be part of a student's online notebook, they are part of a summative assessment at the end of the unit. Finally, as she sums up the lesson, students choose their most admired influential figure and complete a cloze activity for homework, drawing a picture and listing three reasons for their admiration. The cloze activity will be collected and graded the following day. The point is that she has incorporated multiple methods of assessment, both formal and informal, graded and not graded.

Using assessments to inform future instruction is a critical part of planning lessons. Teachers must evaluate whether students have the foundational skills necessary to advance, whether they understood the key concepts presented, and how effectively the lesson built on prior knowledge. The data collected from these assessments can guide lesson planning and target specific skill development (Popham, 2014). By incorporating *assessment for learning*, teachers can use formative assessments to adjust their teaching in real time, ensuring that students are progressing as expected. Reflecting on the outcomes of each lesson informs not only the next day's instruction but also longer-term planning for content and skill acquisition, making assessment an ongoing, essential part of one's teaching practice.

Closure

Now it is time to close your lesson. Many teachers think that as long as you have a lesson assessment, you do not need a closing statement; however, this could not be further from the truth. At the end of the lesson, it is crucial for all students to hear the summary statement from the teacher. This statement includes key concepts, reinforces learning, and links learning to your completed lesson. It helps students consolidate their understanding, connect new knowledge to prior learning, and prepare for future lessons. This brief recap also provides an opportunity for student reflection and feedback.

Teacher Reflection

The last essential component of an effective lesson plan is your personal reflection on the lesson. Teacher reflection is vital for professional growth, as it encourages educators to critically examine their teaching practices and make informed adjustments. Charlotte Danielson and Thomas L. McGreal (2000) underscore the importance of reflection within *Framework for Teaching*, where the authors link reflective practice to ongoing development, particularly in areas like classroom management and differentiated instruction. Both Schön (1983) and Danielson and McGreal (2000) argue that this cycle of reflection and refinement is essential for teachers to advance in their profession, enhance their effectiveness, and better meet the needs of diverse students.

(i) **Teacher Tip:** *As a teacher, you will be frequently evaluated, and a key component will be your ability to reflect honestly on your lessons. Take time to familiarize yourself with the evaluation tool and use reflective questions to assess your teaching before each observation.*

Conclusion

Lesson planning is a critical component of successful teaching and student learning, especially when teaching social studies. Often, teachers become overwhelmed by content and factual information and lose sight of important learning goals, or they defer to the textbook to guide learning. When teachers take the time to create a well-planned lesson, it ensures that students are engaged and their diverse learning needs are met, and it encourages a student's personal ownership of their own learning. Remember, as you progress as a teacher and gain experience with the standards, content, and students, your approach to organizing units and lessons may start to center on a deeper level of historical thinking. This higher level of thinking approach will be explained in the next chapter, Chapter 6, "Investigating History" by Bruce Lesh.

Checklist to Create Engaging Social Studies Lessons

☐ Are your MLOs clear and concise, and are they properly scaffolded? Did you properly narrow down the content to create a focus for the lesson?

☐ Are your MLOs aligned? Are your objective and your outcome in alignment?

☐ Is your introduction appropriately engaging for the lesson? Can you introduce the topic in a more engaging and exciting manner?

☐ Do you identify in your lesson plan the time you anticipate it would take for each aspect of your lesson? Upon reflection, were you on target with your time estimates?

☐ Do you incorporate multiple methods of assessment into your lesson to assess student learning (both formative and summative)?

☐ Do you provide sufficient processing time for students during the lesson to make sense of the content you were presenting?

References

Bloom, B. S. (1956). *Taxonomy of educational objectives: The classification of educational goals.* David McKay Company.

Bybee, R. (2019). Guest editorial: The BSCS 5E instructional model: Personal reflections and contemporary implications. *Science and Children, 51*(8), 10–13.

Bybee, R. W., Taylor, J. A., Gardner, A., Van Scotter, P., Powell, J. C., Westbrook, A., & Landes, N. (2006). *The BSCS 5E instructional model: Origins and effectiveness.* Biological Sciences Curriculum Study.

Danielson, C., & McGreal, T. (2000). *Teacher evaluation to enhance professional practice.* Association of Supervision and Curriculum Development

Himmele, P., & Himmele, W. (2017). *Total participation techniques: Making every student an active learner* (2nd ed.). ASCD.

Holden, J. (2020). *Quick reference guide to developing cognitive learning objectives* (8th ed.).

Hunter, M. (1982). *Mastery teaching: Increasing instructional effectiveness in elementary, secondary schools, colleges and universities.* TIP Publications.

Kagan, S., & Kagan, M. (2009). *Kagan cooperative learning: Structures for learning and collaboration* (2nd ed.). Kagan Publishing.

Kibler, R. J., and Bassett, R. E. (1977). Writing performance objectives. In L. J. Briggs & A. S. Ackerman (Eds.), *Instructional design: Principles and applications* (pp. 49–98). Educational Technology Publications.

Mager, R. F. (1962). *Preparing instructional objectives.* Fearon Publishers.

Marzano, R. (2007). *The art and science of teaching: A comprehensive framework for effective instruction.* Association for Supervision and Curriculum Development.

National Council for the Social Studies. (2017). *The college, career, and civic life (C3) framework for social studies state standards: Guidance for enhancing the rigor of K–12 civics, economic, geography, and history.* **www. socialstudies.org/standards/c3**

Parker, W. (2018). *Concept formation.* Teaching History. **https://teachinghistory.org/teaching-materials/ teaching-guides/25184**

Piaget, J. (1969). *The psychology of the child* (B. Inhelder, Trans.). Basic Books.

Popham, W. J. (2014). *Classroom assessment: What teachers need to know* (7th ed.). Pearson.

Schön, D. A. (1983). *The reflective practitioner: How professionals think in action.* Basic Books.

Scriven, M. (1967). The methodology of evaluation. In R. W. Tyler, R. M. Gagne & M. Scriven (Eds.), *Perspectives of curriculum evaluation* (pp. 39–83). Rand McNally.

Vermette, P., Jones, K., Jones, J., Werner, T., Kline, C., & D'Angelo, J. (2010). A model for planning learning experiences to promote achievement in diverse secondary classrooms. *SRATE Journal, 19*(2), 70–83.

Vermette, P. J., & Kline, C. L. (2017). *Group work that works: Student collaboration for 21st century success.* Routledge. **https://doi.org/10.4324/9781315618364**

Vygotsky, L. (1978). *Mind in society: Development of higher psychological processes.* Harvard University Press.

Wiske, M. S. (Ed.). (1998). *Teaching for understanding: Linking research with practice* (1st ed). Jossey-Bass.

Chapter 6
Investigating History

Bruce A. Lesh

The most significant change I made in my instruction was to stop focusing on answers. That was it. Not grading more efficiently, not increasing positive communication with parents, not incorporating more every student response strategies. Those were all important changes, but none paid the dividends of focusing my instruction on questions instead of answers.

Prior to the change, for every course, unit, and lesson taught, I found myself focused on trying to determine exactly what names, dates, events, places, or people my students needed to know at the end of the day, the end of a month, or the end of the year. The list was insatiable. Fed by the demands of state and/or national standards, district points of emphasis, content culturally relevant to my student community, my own areas of interest, and the never-ending limits to my students' background knowledge, the pressing needs of the list of answers could never be met. Compiling that list was, and is, an exercise in futility. And so, I stopped trying.

Instead of answers, I found student engagement, professional effectiveness, and a renewed passion by switching my focus to questions. It was here, in the formulation of a question to guide instruction, that all the pieces fit together. Questions gave form and function to the list of names, dates, people, events, and ideas. Questions provided a purpose for students to engage with the content. Questions problematized the past in ways that a list of names, dates, people, or ideas could never do. Embracing questions over answers also shifted my instruction. When I was trying to meet the needs of that list of content, my instruction was driven down a rabbit hole of low-level recall, information transfer, and bored students. But instead of focusing my instruction on helping my students prepare for a round of Jeopardy or a game of Trivial Pursuit, I gave them a reason to understand, connect, and utilize the information in order to confront the question that was driving instruction. That one decision made all the difference.

Please, do not construe this decision as turning my class into a content-free, skills-based free-for-all. Not even close. My instruction was always populated by important people, significant events, transformational ideas, and pivotal dates. My students swam in content. But instead of drowning in a pool of facts, names, dates, people, and ideas, the use of questions allowed them to navigate the waters with purpose and direction. It is this interplay between skills and content that is at the heart of investigating history.

ⓘ **Teacher Tip:** *Explore deeper by reading:*
- **Inquiry Design Model: Building Inquiries in Social Studies** *by Kathy Swan, John Lee, and S. G. Grant, 2018, NCSS.*
- **Developing Historical Thinking For All Students: Supporting Historical Inquiry for All Students** *by Bruce Lesh, 2023, Teachers College Press.*

What Is Investigating History?

In a nutshell, investigating history is instruction centered on answering a question by making a claim and supporting it with evidence. Investigating history was designed to counter the prevailing instructional methodology in history and social studies where students are simply told a series of answers without knowing the question being asked. In this instructional approach, we intentionally problematize the past so that the names, dates, events, ideas, and people are used to support a claim, backed by evidence, that in turn address the question being explored.

Think of it this way. If we taught mathematics the same way we often teach social studies, students would come in on Monday and learn the answers to a series of questions. Then, the next day, we would show them the same questions, and they would tell us the answers. If this was the approach to teaching and learning mathematics, no self-respecting math teacher would say that students could do math. But for some reason, in social studies and history, we accept the transmission of a list of information as good instruction.

Instead, high-quality instruction in mathematics finds students learning a series of processes, tools, and approaches about the behavior of numbers in order to solve mathematical problems. High-quality instruction in the social studies and history classrooms should mimic this approach. Instead of pulling a specific number of names, dates, events, and ideas from the insatiable list, telling students about them and then checking to make sure they have memorized them, teachers should ask students to investigate significant questions about the past. Historical investigations align with research on brain science, student engagement, cognition, and learning theory, and it demands a unique combination of skills and content.

The False Dichotomy Between Skills and Content

As illustrated in Figure 6.1, content is central to investigating history, but content alone—just like skills alone—cannot exist in a vacuum. It is the relationship between the two that is opened up through the lens of the questions we pose for students to investigate.

Figure 6.1 *Skills and Content Relationship*

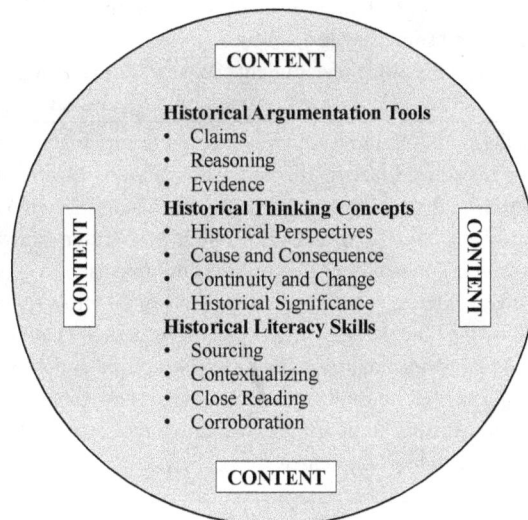

Diagram: A large circle labeled **CONTENT** on the top, bottom, left, and right sides. Inside the circle:

Historical Argumentation Tools
- Claims
- Reasoning
- Evidence

Historical Thinking Concepts
- Historical Perspectives
- Cause and Consequence
- Continuity and Change
- Historical Significance

Historical Literacy Skills
- Sourcing
- Contextualizing
- Close Reading
- Corroboration

A Classroom With Purpose: A Guide to Teaching Social Studies Today

So what does all this mean? In a very loose way, these terms are the ingredients for how to build robust investigations for students. In order for students to investigate the past, they need to blend content and skills so that they are making evidence-based arguments. Too often, as mentioned above, we pick one ingredient over the others: either only content or simply skills. That is not representative of what historians do and does not represent the best practices outlined in nearly a half century of research. Instead, to effectively investigate history, students need to combine the factors enumerated in Figure 6.2.

Finally, investigations should help students to develop a big picture understanding of a time period. They should not serve as the only lens into the Great Depression or the Rise of

Figure 6.2 *Skills and Content Relationship Explained*

Content	This is comprised of the names, dates, events, people, and ideas that populate the portion of history being studied. What comprises this body of knowledge is informed by national and state standards, local priorities, and what is relevant to the location and culture of the school community. Content provides students something to think about, understand, and investigate.
Argumentation About History Skills	Through the creation of narratives, students communicate arguments about the past. In crafting these arguments, students must develop a claim in response to the question being investigated and then analyze, prioritize, and corroborate various pieces of evidence to support their claim. In addition, students test their claims against the claims of others (counterclaims) in order to ensure that the evidence fully supports their argument.
Historical Thinking Concepts	These concepts allow students to provide organization and structure to the past in order to think about how the names, dates, events, people, and ideas work together to become history. There are many more of these concepts, but for the sake of simplicity, I focus my students on the following: • **Historical Perspectives:** Students come to understand that to comprehend history they must understand past decisions and people within the beliefs of the time period they lived and not those of the present. • **Causes and Consequences:** Students come to understand that multiple interrelated factors lead to an event/situation/change and stem from its conclusion. • **Continuity and Change:** Students come to understand that over time some things change and some stay the same. • **Historical Significance:** Students come to understand how we determine what is worth remembering, celebrating, commemorating, and investigating.
Historical Literacy Skills	These skills are particular to the way that historians analyze and synthesize evidence from a variety of historical sources. This requires students to accomplish the following skills: • **Sourcing:** determining who created the historical source, involves identifying the document's creator, when and where it was written, and why it was written. This helps to understand the author's perspective and purpose. • **Contextualizing:** placing an historical source into a specific time and place to determine how that may impact its usefulness as evidence. • **Close Reading:** analyzing the historical source to determine what the creator is saying (or not saying) about the question being investigated. • **Corroborating:** comparing information across multiple sources to determine areas of agreement and disagreement.

Conservatism but instead function as case studies that help students dive deeply and then in turn make a connection to the broader historical narrative.

Teacher Tip: *Do you have a balance of skills and content within your course, or do you give greater emphasis to one or the other?*

Making the Shift

As a teacher new to a social studies classroom, adjusting instruction away from the delivery of information and into having students use evidence to make claims may appear a daunting shift. Research says that most teachers will teach history and social studies in a manner akin to the way they were taught. In addition, research says you were probably taught through some combination of lecture (copying notes from a slideshow), reading a single source (a textbook), coloring in maps, and writing a document-based question. If lucky, you experienced some inquiry instruction during your college coursework. The funny thing is, some of your students, regardless of the grade or course in which they are enrolled, will also come to you with a perception of learning history and social studies aligned more with the idea of gathering information and regurgitating it back than one in which they investigate questions. Students will need to break their own view of schooling to embrace the instructional shifts and manifest the skills needed to successfully investigate the past. So, this is a journey you will undertake together.

The good news is this shift is one that rewards itself with greater student engagement, increased professional satisfaction, and positive learning outcomes. The purpose of this chapter is to outline how to shift instruction so that students are actively investigating the past.

The History Lab Approach

The approach to instruction I adopted back in the 1990s has been labeled "doing history," "historical thinking," "inquiry," "reading like a historian," "the historical problem space," "problematizing history," and numerous other titles. These names are distinctions without a difference. The tie that binds all these methods is students developing their understanding about history by examining significant questions. I called my version of investigating history the *History Lab*. As outlined in Figure 6.3, a history lab consists of a key question, a hook, source work, claim building by linking evidence to the claim, communicating the claim, and assessment.

Figure 6.3 *History Lab Process*

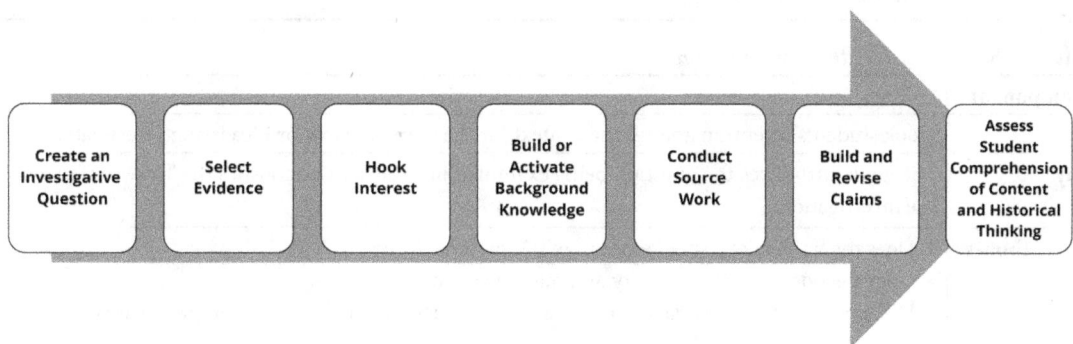

| Create an Investigative Question | Select Evidence | Hook Interest | Build or Activate Background Knowledge | Conduct Source Work | Build and Revise Claims | Assess Student Comprehension of Content and Historical Thinking |

It Is Not a Recipe, But It Helps to Think of It That Way!

Like any recipe, there are key ingredients that must be utilized to create an effective and engaging investigation. Outlined in Tables 6.1–6.7 are the seven steps and considerations that should be made when engaging in an investigation.

Table 6.1 *Step 1: Establish an Investigative Question*

Component	Description
What	Select a question that will drive instruction for a lesson, a series of lessons, or a unit. Question should be linked to one or more of the following disciplinary concepts: • Historical Perspectives • Cause and Consequence • Continuity and Change • Historical Significance
Why	Questions problematize the past and provide a lens through which students can come to understand the reasons events occurred, the behavior of historical actors, the impact of historical ideas, or the significance of major events.
Think Abouts	• Is the question provocative, and does it encourage investigation and discussion? • Is there sufficient evidence to support students' claim development? • Is the question central to the curriculum scope and sequence structuring the course? • Does the question deepen students' understanding of history as an interpretive discipline?

Table 6.2 *Step 2: Select Evidence*

Component	Description
What	Collect a variety of historical sources relevant to the central question that allow students to support a range of historically accurate claims in response to the overarching historical question being investigated.
Why	History and social studies are evidence-based disciplines. Student claims should derive evidence from a wide variety of sources. This also supports broader literacy goals.
Think Abouts	• Have I identified relevant vocabulary and edited the sources for readability? • Do the selected sources allow for the connection of multiple pieces of evidence to different claims in response to the investigative question? • Did I provide sourcing and contextualization information for the sources to assist student analysis? • Did I excerpt the source to ensure that students can access the content but without altering the meaning of the source?

Table 6.3 *Step 3: Initiate the Investigation*

Component	Description
What	Hook students' attention and set the context for the event, person, or idea being investigated.
Why	The hook introduces the question being examined in a way that establishes the "why" or "so what" of the investigation.
Think Abouts	• Does the hook take a small amount of instructional time? • Does the hook initiate curiosity and raise questions? • Did you consider using visuals (e.g., cartoons, images, paintings, etc.) and provocative quotations to serve as hooks?

Table 6.4 *Step 4: Build or Activate Background Knowledge*

Component	Description
What	Provide students with the basic information they need to dive into the question being investigated.
Why	In order for students to dive deeply into an investigative question, they need to have a baseline of knowledge about the time period, event, people, or idea being investigated. Setting context involves helping students to understand the interplay between chronological, spatial, political, economic, and social factors during the time period being studied.
Think Abouts	• What do students actually need to know prior to diving into the investigation? • Did you limit the amount of information so that students have time to conduct the investigation? • Did you place the investigation later in the unit so that the first few lessons in every unit build students' understanding of the time period, personalities, vocabulary, and concepts that were essential knowledge for a deep dive into a topic?

Table 6.5 *Step 5: Source Work*

Component	Description
What	Students examine a variety of historical sources which provide evidence that can be used to develop a claim in response to the overarching question being investigated.
Why	This is at the heart of the work that historians, geographers, economists, and political scientists do. They gather and analyze evidence and then use that evidence to make a claim in response to an investigative question.
Think Abouts	• Did you limit the evidence trail to no more than six sources? • Did you provide information about each source that can assist students with sourcing and contextualizing? • Did you provide a gradual release so that students could hear source analysis being modeled before analyzing their own source(s)?

Table 6.6 *Step 6: Claim Building and Revision*

Component	Description
What	Students work independently or in groups to develop their claim in response to the overarching historical question being investigated. Once they have developed an initial claim and supported it with evidence, allow students to discuss, challenge, and revise claims in response to the arguments and evidence use presented by others.
Why	History is an interpretive discipline, and student engagement increases when there is something to figure out instead of simply being told what they need to know. Claim building is using evidence to support an answer to the overarching question being investigated.
Think Abouts	• Did you model the process for students by thinking aloud how you might construct a claim or use a piece of evidence to support it? • Did you provide students with graphic organizers or tools that aid with the sourcing and contextualizing of documents as well as with corroborating? • Did you instruct students to identify and rank order the sources that most influenced their arguments and why?

Table 6.7 *Step 7: Assess Student Comprehension of the Content and the Historical Thinking*

Component	Description
What	Teachers employ a variety of formative and summative tools to assess student understanding of the core content as well as their ability to support their claims with evidence and utilize a variety of historical literacy skills. In addition, there are opportunities to assess students' ability to source, contextualize, close read, and corroborate sources.
Why	All learning should be assessed to provide feedback for both the teacher and the student.
Think Abouts	• Do your assessments provide feedback on the skills (i.e., sourcing, contextualizing, close reading, and corroborating sources) as well as the use of evidence to support a claim and key content? • Did you consider alternative tools other than a five-paragraph essay? • Does the data generated by your assessment provide feedback that allows you to alter instruction?

Building an investigation takes time, but the benefits far outweigh the costs. Increased student engagement and achievement make the time and effort required to develop an investigation well worth the investment. Once developed, there are considerations about implementation that should be considered so that the transition from disseminating historical information to investigating the past can be navigated safely by both teachers and students.

Table 6.8 *Scaffolding Techniques*

Technique	Purpose	Benefits
Bridging	Identify what students already know about a topic to help link them to the new learning about to occur. Within a History Lab, this means ensuring that the necessary background knowledge is provided before diving deeply into the question being investigated.	This technique allows teachers to build on what students already know and use that knowledge as a stepping-off point for new learning.
Chunking	Break a set of directions, the steps in a lesson, or the elements of a longer-term project into smaller segments. Within a History Lab, teachers can separate the sourcing of a document from the close reading or allow students to consider the first historical source completely before they examine a second or third.	This allows students to focus on discrete parts of the skills being employed or the steps in a full lesson arc and not get lost in the longer term.
Exemplars	Provide students with examples of what each step of a lesson looks like. Previous students' work, videos of class discussions, or the sharing of information from sources are all places within a History Lab where exemplars can be utilized.	Sharing examples of a completed chart or assessment provides students with a target for their efforts. Knowing what their end product should look like can reduce student anxiety, build confidence, and increase the overall quality of their work.
Graphic Organizers	Provide students with graphic organizers (e.g., Venn Diagrams, spider webs, concept maps, sequence charts, etc.) during a History Lab. They can be employed during the analysis of sources, during the corroboration of sources, and/or when students are linking evidence to claims.	These tools help organize thinking, make comparisons, and ensure that students can move back and forth between analyzing evidence and using the evidence to support a claim.
Modeling	Provide clear examples of what is required of students to complete a task, utilize a skill, or express understanding. Immensely helpful modeling strategies for a History Lab would be if a teacher verbalized how they sourced a document or corroborated across multiple sources.	Modeling allows students to see and/or hear how a skill is to be utilized, a process is to be implemented, or a product is to be developed.
Pacing	Adjust how quickly steps in a lesson progress from one step to another to ensure that students are understanding rather than complying. Going slow early, so you can go fast later. This is always helpful as students become familiar with the demands of a History Lab.	By adjusting the pace of a lesson or an element of a lesson, teachers can develop student confidence and capacity with a particular skill or task.
Visual Representation	Visually depict directions, steps in a process, key things to consider, and other elements of a lesson.	Visual representations provide students with something to which they can refer when they need a reminder.

General Advice

Shifting to instruction that is driven by the investigation of questions should not be done overnight. Consider the following as you begin to shift your instructional approach:

Pace Yourself
(This is a Marathon, Not a Sprint!)

If you try to shift your instruction to having a historical investigation every day, both you and your students will burn out quickly. This type of instruction requires more time and thus a higher cognitive load on you to plan and on students to execute. My recommendation is to start slow. For the first year that you engage students in these investigations, plan one per quarter. Then slowly work towards one investigation per unit. This pacing will allow you several years to test drive the instructional approach, to ensure that you do not overwhelm yourself or your students, and to measure the impacts of this approach to teaching and learning.

Manage Anxiety for You and Your Students

Students have been trained to "do school." When confronted with an instructional approach that challenges how they think learning should occur, they can become anxious. In the case of history and social studies instruction, the instructional rhythm has for generations boiled down to students being told what they need to know and parroting back that information. Investigating history upends this rhythm because it demands that students think, analyze, apply, and engage. "Why won't you just tell us the answer!" is a refrain you will hear often as you disrupt the normal instructional rhythm. Help students understand this instructional shift by being transparent with what they need to do and explicit in the skills they need to know to engage in investigations. Break down and model the historical literacy skills and practice them in isolation before students employ them in a full-scale investigation. In addition, scaffold the investigative process by starting with one source and then working students up to six. Also, provide other scaffolds to assist development of student confidence to engage in this work. Table 6.8 illustrates some of the significant scaffolding techniques that can be employed for all students.

Respect the Curriculum Scope and Sequence

All teachers have a scope and sequence to which they must adhere. This scope and sequence outlines the chronology covered, the topics within that chronology, and the order in which material must be taught. Alignment to this scope and sequence could be to meet the demands of district, state, or College Board assessments, to ensure that students have the necessary background information for the next course in a sequence, or to provide students with a history course that gets into the late 20th and early 21st centuries rather than ending with the Cold War! Embracing historical investigations can put pressure on meeting the scope and sequence demands because of the time it requires for students to dive deeply. These deep dives require attentiveness to ensuring that you still meet the scope and sequence requirements. To strike this balance, plan your course backwards. Start with your last unit, knowing the topics and end date that you need to reach, then plan until you get to the first unit. This backwards planning will ensure you do not overteach the first units and that you can meet the demands of your course scope and sequence. In addition, backwards planning enables teachers to identify which investigations are being used in each quarter or unit. This identification then helps with planning so that the investigations—which take more time to implement—do not interfere with the overall demands of the scope and sequence required. This may sound daunting at first, but backwards planning makes a huge difference.

i **Teacher Tip:** *What would happen to the pacing of your course if you planned backwards from the end of the year to the beginning? For more on backward design, see* Understanding by Design *(2nd ed.), by J. McTighe and G. Wiggins, 2005, ASCD.*

An Example

The best way to conceptualize this instructional shift is to see an investigation in action. To help crystallize the things presented in this chapter, I will outline a sample investigation aligned with the investigation development steps outlined in Tables 6.1–6.7.

Step 1: Establish an Investigative Question

The example investigation occurs in my United States History unit on the Vietnam War. The state standard addressed in my district curriculum is "analyzing the evolution, strategies, and turning points of the United States' involvement in Vietnam" (Maryland Department of Education, 2020, p. 16). For me, this broad standard was addressed in a series of lessons. The first lesson focused on the escalation from Truman through Johnson, the second lesson on strategies through Tet, and the final lesson centered on the war under the leadership of President Richard Nixon. With that in mind, I landed on the question: *Is President Nixon trying to "win the war" or bring "peace with honor"?* The impetus for this question stems from the dichotomous way that President Nixon approached the war. He simultaneously escalated the fighting while also dramatically reducing the number of U.S. troops in the country. It is within this contradiction that I found the fulcrum that would drive my students' investigation.

Step 2: Select Evidence

The evidence selected for this investigation was needed to ensure that students could evaluate the actions taken by President Nixon from the vantage point not only of the president and his advisors but also of the anti-war movement and the American public. There was a wealth of sources available online, and sifting through them took some time and some trial and error. Ultimately, for the final version of the investigation, I landed on the six sources in Figure 6.4.

Figure 6.4 *Nixon and the Vietnam War Sources*

Source 1: November 3, 1969, Address to the Nation on the Situation in Southeast Asia by President Nixon (The Miller Center, The University of Virginia)

Source 2: April 30, 1970, Address to the Nation on the Situation in Southeast Asia by President Nixon (The American Presidency Project, University of California, Santa Barbara)

Source 3: Political Cartoons (Primary Source Nexus)
  A. Now, as I was saying four years ago!
  B. Fourth Year of the "Plan To End The War"

Source 4: December 9, 1970, 8:45 PM: Two taped conversations in the White House between President Nixon and Secretary of State Henry Kissinger (National Security Archive)

Source 5: May 1972: Three top-secret eyes-only memos to Mr. Kissinger from President Nixon (Office of the Historian, Department of State)

This source trail provided students with the opportunity to analyze text in the form of private and public communications as well as images. Of particular interest and value were the surreptitiously taped Oval Office conversations and memos that received a top secret clearance and thus were not available to historians or the public while events were transpiring. I edited each of the sources for length, scaffolded to assist student examination, and presented with information to help students source and contextualize it accurately.

Step 3: Initiate the Investigation

My hook for the investigation comes in the form of music. The investigation begins with students listening to the Crosby, Stills, Nash, and Young song "Ohio." While listening and reading the lyrics, students are instructed to draw a picture of what they think is being described. A debrief of student images leads to a discussion of the events that occurred at Kent State and Jackson State universities in May 1970. These protests were in reaction to President Nixon's announcement that he was sending American troops into Cambodia, and this fact dovetails into the activation of background knowledge.

Teacher Tip: *Reminder, you cannot investigate history without some background knowledge of the topic, time period and or geography!*

Step 4: Build or Activate Background Knowledge

Because this investigation occurs later in the Vietnam unit, after a lesson on the anti-war movement and the Tet Offensive, the key background knowledge for students to activate centers on the actions that President Nixon took upon assuming the presidency in January 1969. The building of this knowledge can take many forms: short lecture, a film clip that summarizes these actions, or a student reading. For me, the building and activation of background knowledge was achieved through the review of a student homework sheet. In one column, the sheet provides a brief description of the actions taken: secret bombing of Cambodia, Vietnamization policy, initiation of secret peace talks with North Vietnam, the invasion of Cambodia, the Christmas bombings, and the significant drawdown of American troops. In an adjacent column, students label each action with an up or down arrow to represent the escalation or de-escalation of tensions and write a short sentence explaining their choice. This discussion connects to the song and sets the stage for introducing the investigative question and then beginning the source work.

Step 5: Source Work

Source work can be done in any number of ways. Teachers can model one source, work through a second source with students, and then release them to the rest. Or, a jigsaw method could be employed where each student analyzes one source, then joins a group where all the other sources are represented in order to share information. Regardless of the structure, the focus is on students utilizing the historical literacy skills of sourcing, contextualizing, close reading, and corroborating. After students assess the who, what, when, where, and why of their source(s) and establish the argument being presented, they must determine if each single source is usable in developing a claim about the investigation's overarching question. For example, in the Nixon investigation, the two political cartoons can serve as evidence for claims that President Nixon was attempting to win the war. Once students determine what the evidence is arguing, they can then apply it to their argument or reject it if it does not support their argument. The process of source work often overlaps with claim building.

Step 6: Claim Building and Revision

Claim building—or thesis statement development—and revision is the most dynamic portion of an investigation. It is here that students, either in groups, pairs, or as individuals, begin to corroborate across multiple sources and develop the support for their claim in response to the overarching question. Like source work, this step can occur in a number of different ways. In jigsaw groups, working as a whole class, conferring with a partner, or individually, students assess the usefulness of a source to the question, look for areas of agreement and disagreement across multiple sources, and then align the evidence to their claim. In addition, students will confront alternative claims, alternative prioritization of evidence, and alternative arguments about how evidence supports a claim. Students will either alter their claims and evidence or find stronger support for their argument. This can happen in small paired discussions, full class discussions, responses to the writing of another student, or questions posed to others.

In the Nixon example, the building and revision of student claims often hinges on the relationship between President Nixon's public statements as articulated in his speeches and his thoughts expressed in private. Some students give more weight to the public comments while others invert this and weigh the private statements more. These discussions dominate Step 5. Regardless of the format, this is the dynamic, discussion-based phase of the investigation. It provides students with the opportunity to engage with history through the lens of a question. It is here, in Step 6, that I am again reminded that the most significant change I made in my instruction was to focus my instruction on questions instead of answers.

Step 7: Assess Student Comprehension of the Content and the Historical Thinking

In any lesson, investigations included, there are opportunities for both formal and informal assessments as well as formative and summative ones. Regardless of which is used, the goal is to provide feedback to the teacher and student on progress. The information should both inform instructional decisions for the teacher and help to reinforce or redirect student action.

For the Nixon and Vietnam lesson, I employed several assessments. Informally, I used questioning to assess student understanding of the song and their comprehension of the background information and to check on their ability to source, contextualize, and close read their assigned historical source. In addition, I used a written formative assessment to assess their thinking about corroboration. In five to seven sentences, students responded to one of the following prompts:

> The two pieces of evidence that contradicted the most were ... because ....
> The two pieces of evidence that most complimented one another were ... because ....

As can be seen in Figure 6.5, these quick writes provided me insight into how students were corroborating information across multiple sources.

At the conclusion of the investigation, I used a summative assessment that asked students to rank order their sources from most to least useful in supporting their claim and to explain how the top two sources were most useful in supporting their claim. This can be assessed as students explain their thoughts to me or another peer or in written format. In both the formal and informal instances, the assessments administered provide the teacher with a way to measure student progress in learning, and through the comments provided by the teacher, they also provide guidance to the student. These assessments were quick, short, and easy to score.

Parting Thoughts

Teaching is hard work. There are an infinitesimal number of variables that can impact the development, delivery, and assessment of a lesson, but the one factor that can always derail or deliver a lesson is student engagement. If students are interested, they will work harder, learn more, and manifest fewer distractions. If students are not interested, then all bets are off! The benefits of making the shift to history instruction is one to embrace because of the significant increase in student engagement. As one of my past students said,

> History class in the past has basically been "here is a worksheet, here is a reading, read it and fill out the worksheet." History is pretty straightforward, there is a lot you can't do with it just because it is so factual ... but it is really not enjoyable when all you do is read and take notes on things .... It [investigating the past] is definitely more difficult when you have to interpret and make your own decisions because you have to take into consideration multiple viewpoints and where they are coming from with their information, and their past, and where the information is coming from ... but it's more fun.

History will always be about content, and it should be, but using questions to frame instruction is more authentic to what historians and social scientists do; allows students to practice reading, writing, listening, and communication skills; and in the words of an 11th grader, it is fun—and who doesn't want to teach a subject that kids find fun!

Figure 6.5 *Quick Writes for Assessing Historical Literacy Skills*

> The two sources that most complicated one another were ~~the~~ ~~the~~ Source 2 the Address to the Nation on the Southeast Asia and Source 6, the taped Oval Office conversation between Nixon and the National Security Advisor Henry Kissinger because in ~~the~~ his public speech he promised the Nation ~~that~~ ~~he~~ ~~that~~ that he would try to end the war in Vietnam and get the troops out, and expand the war in Cambodia in order to win the war in Vietnam with peace and he said he will continue to make every possible effor to end this war through negotiation. This source was public that complimented ~~the~~ his private conversation with Kissinger where he says the troops absolutely have to get out of there - and give the war to the Vietnamese

> The two sources that most contradicted one another were the taped conversation between Nixon and Kissinger on December 9, 1970 and another taped conversation between Nixon and Kissinger on March 11, 1971 because they say completely different options for what Nixon wants to do with the war. The first conversation on December 9, had Nixon wanting to put the entire US Air Force in Vietnam and he says "no limitation on mileage and there is no limitation on budget." Nixon also wanted this memo to be top secret and kept from the public. The second memo shows Nixon on the complete opposite side of what he said before. He believed that the troops need to "get the hell out of there" and it is inevitable that fighting will still go on between the N. and S. Vietnamese. Nixon ~~at~~ at the time believed that there was no point of pushing further and the US needed to leave as soon as possible

A Classroom With Purpose: A Guide to Teaching Social Studies Today

Checklist for Investigating History

My investigation

☐ is aligned with my curricular scope and sequence.
☐ has a question that promotes student curiosity and allows for multiple evidence-based claims.
☐ includes a variety of sources that allow students to develop evidence-based claims in response to the investigative question.
☐ provides students with the background knowledge necessary to engage in the investigation.
☐ has scaffolds built in around vocabulary, length of text, and pacing.
☐ incorporates a variety of assessments that will provide feedback to teacher and student.

Reference

Maryland Department of Education. (2020). *High school United States history framework.* **www.marylandpublic schools.org/about/Documents/DCAA/SocialStudies/HSUS.pdf**

Chapter 7

Dreaming of Resilience, Resistance, and Joy in a Culturally Relevant Social Studies Classroom

John M. Palella

In the fourth grade, I reigned as my classroom's champion daydreamer. I would plunge into imagined worlds, the classroom fading away, as I transformed into a medieval wizard or a roller skater racing against Abraham Lincoln on the rings of Saturn with the mythical Apollo as the referee. I once wrote that scene for a class assignment, prompting my teacher, Mrs. Jovell, to call my mother. "I think John has an unhealthy interest in Greek mythology and Abraham Lincoln," she said, as my mom tried not to laugh while feigning concern. My daydreaming always bothered someone at school. Mrs. Jovell possessed a sixth sense for spotting it. Inevitably, she would clear her throat and say, "John, are you with us?" I would snap back to reality, the classroom full of stifled giggles, my cheeks turning red. My report cards usually contained the cautionary note: "John needs to focus more and daydream less." It became a running joke in my family: "John, pay attention!" But honestly, those daydreams felt so much more interesting than social studies worksheets or the hand-cramping notes that defined our daily routine. Looking back, I realize that my daydreams provided respite from monotonous learning and served as magical portals into new worlds where time and space boundaries melted away. My mom knew I wanted to learn and always tried to satisfy my hunger for stories, adventures, and experiences beyond that fourth-grade classroom. She would say, "You dream all you want, baby."

Now, as teachers, we sometimes catch our students in that same faraway gaze, mentally drifting miles away from the present lesson. And when we see it, we might feel tempted to call them back with the classic, "Are you with us?" But what if, instead of reeling them in, we encouraged them to keep going? What if we harnessed the power of their daydreams and channeled it into their learning? Imagine a classroom where those flights of fancy transform into gateways for deeper engagement, a culturally relevant space that bridges the here-and-now with the then-and-there and invites both the what-ifs and how-cans. What if Mrs. Jovell had asked me what I daydreamed about, how it related to what we learned, or how it might apply to what I wanted to explore further? What if just once, one of my social studies teachers had asked me or my classmates what we dream about doing after high school and how they could help us achieve those dreams? Some teachers may already do this—and if so, thank you! You do more for your students than you might imagine. If not, it is never too late to start. Here, I offer guidance on how to support your students' daydreaming and eventually turn those daydreams into something real through culturally relevant social studies pedagogies.

My daydreams eventually led me to a career of over 20 years as a secondary social studies teacher, college-level history professor, and now a social studies teacher-educator. Currently,

I train teachers, pursuing their own dreams at Brown University, to equip and empower their students in the art of daydreaming. Social studies classrooms should function as spaces where students explore the past, understand the present, and dream of a better future. In these classrooms, students learn to imagine the possibilities of resilience, resistance, and joy, exploring the stories of people who have triumphed over oppression. Through inquiry-driven projects, analysis of diverse narratives, and opportunities to connect their identities to historical contexts, students experience history as a source of inspiration and agency. By weaving in daydreams of what could be, we guide students to see themselves as part of an ongoing story of enacting social change in their communities and beyond. I nurture future teachers who make space for students to explore, imagine, and act, fostering classrooms that cultivate dreams of a brighter, more inclusive world.

Gloria Ladson-Billings's Culturally Relevant Pedagogy (CRP) framework serves as my greatest tool in training social studies teachers who empower their students to dream. Dreaming for the future plays a central role in the CRP framework as Ladson-Billings pioneered it in her book appropriately titled *The Dreamkeepers: Successful Teachers of African American Children* (1994, revised in 2009 and 2022). Ladson-Billings illustrates the ways in which teachers equip and empower students to reach their dreams by connecting successful classroom learning to students' cultural backgrounds, lived experiences, and personal interests. Ladson-Billings followed *Dreamkeepers* with more than 100 publications and countless presentations over the past 30 years, demonstrating time and again that for Black, Brown, Indigenous, and White students alike to achieve their dreams, they must learn in classrooms where their voices, interests, and cultures drive the teacher's curricular and pedagogical choices. Ladson-Billings has taught us repeatedly how to create a culturally relevant classroom through seminal works like "Toward a Theory of Culturally Relevant Pedagogy" (1995b), "But That's Just Good Teaching! The Case for Culturally Relevant Teaching" (1995a), and my favorite, "'Yes, But How Do We Do It?' Practicing Culturally Relevant Pedagogy" (2006).

In commemoration of the 30th anniversary of Culturally Relevant Pedagogy, Gloria Ladson-Billings spoke to the Education Department at Brown University entitled "Yes, But How Do We Do It in 2024?" as part of her larger lecture on "It's Time for a Hard Reset." Meeting one of my heroes was beyond exciting. Not only did my students hear her speak in person, they met her and took selfies with her. Later, she and I chatted over coffee, and her insights inspired me to write this piece. When she left, I realized that of all the "culturally [insert adjective here] classroom" frameworks, CRP remains the least discussed in teacher education programs but is actually the most aligned to social studies curricula. Moreover, it operates as the simplest framework to both understand and apply as it manifests through three student-centered results Ladson-Billings refers to as "the pillars" of CRP: academic achievement, cultural competence, and sociopolitical/critical consciousness (Ladson-Billings, 2023). These three student-centered goals foster a culturally relevant classroom that not only supports students in the art of daydreaming but also equips them to turn their dreams into reality. In the sections below, I outline strategies for achieving these outcomes with students and offer social studies–specific examples for creating a culturally relevant environment. While these are not the only paths to building a culturally relevant classroom, adapting some of these practices will

A Classroom With Purpose: A Guide to Teaching Social Studies Today

inspire dreams of resilience, resistance, and joy in your students as they engage with content and develop the skills that students need for life beyond the classroom.

Academic Achievement Through a Student-Centered Classroom

To build your culturally relevant classroom, you must start with *student academic achievement*, the most broadly accepted of Gloria Ladson Billings's (2023) three pillars of culturally relevant pedagogies. Ladson-Billings prioritizes academic achievement because it aligns with the most basic functions of school: students should get good grades, meet rigorous academic standards, attend college if they want to, secure the job of their dreams, perform civic responsibilities, etc. While few question its function as a desired result, debates over its content and form still ensue. Theoretically, academic achievement translates to an asset-based lens in which teachers believe that their students can achieve their goals and use class time to equip them to do so. Practically speaking, academic achievement equates to students themselves believing that they can achieve any dream as they demonstrate how they will use skills or knowledge from their high school classes to reach those goals. In a culturally relevant classroom, student academic achievement does not translate to or stop at performance on standardized tests. Test prep does not prepare your students to reach their dreams and achieve success in the real world; although you may need to do it, you should teach beyond standardized tests (Ladson-Billings, 2023).

Ladson-Billings champions individual teachers' assessment and measurement of academic achievement over a one-size-fits-all model of doing. Therefore, some critics of CRP lament over her lack of prescriptions for applying the framework (Morris et al., 2008; Young, 2010). Ladson-Billings explains that instead of one uniform method for reaching academic achievement, "culturally relevant teachers measure how much their students grow as learners from when they started in their classes in September until the students leave their classes in June" (Ladson-Billings, 2023). Culturally relevant educators, therefore, reflect on what students learned to do in their class that they could not do before and what they can do with the knowledge and skills after their class. Ladson-Billings, a former history teacher herself, uses the "Age of Exploration" as a universal social studies paradigm. She asks, what serves as a more useful goal in 2024: students reciting the names and dates of the explorers (that they can use their phones to find in 30 seconds anyway) or students debating whether we should even call the period the "Age of Exploration" or the "Age of Conquest?" This latter higher order thinking, which requires them to know some of those explorers' (or conquerors') names anyway, demonstrates a type of intellectual growth akin to academic achievement.

A culturally relevant educator fosters academic achievement by creating a student-centered classroom, where students learn *how* to think, not *what* to think. My pre-service teachers know that when I assess their classrooms for student-centeredness, I grapple with two central tensions: the level of cognitive demand based on Bloom's Taxonomy (they should be aiming for "Evaluate" or "Create") and the balance of thinking done by students versus the teacher. My pre-service teachers may tire of hearing me say, "In a student-centered classroom, you do the thinking and work outside the classroom, and the students do the thinking and work inside the classroom." In other words, the locus of control in a CRP classroom shifts from the teacher to the students, thus promoting autonomy, critical thinking, and a personal connection to the material (Hammond, 2015; Ladson-Billings, 1995b; Paris & Alim, 2017). By encouraging students to take active roles in their learning, such as making choices, setting discussion topics, and co-constructing knowledge, teachers build on their students' academic mindset and unlock their confidence as achievers. If the educator ties learning directly to students' lived experiences, they not only develop ownership and investment, but they also will understand and retain the material (Gay, 2010; Hammond, 2015).

For social studies teachers to create a culturally relevant, student-centered classroom, they should engage their students in Project-Based Learning (PBL). In PBL, students "do" history or the social sciences much like a professional would by actively investigating and interacting with the material rather than passively absorbing information. Just as professional historians or social scientists begin their work, PBL also starts with an essential question that the students explore collaboratively and rigorously with materials that the teacher initially provides and students later find for themselves. Authentic PBL demands that students use their funds of knowledge and lived experiences to solve whatever problem or question teachers lay in front of them (Turk & Brensilver Berman, 2018). Teachers play a critical role in this process by providing targeted feedback, posing questions, and guiding students toward making relevant connections between their learning and their lives. By focusing on the processes of PBL instead of daily deliverance of content, you switch up the power dynamics of the classroom and help students see themselves as active participants in their education, fostering engagement and a deeper sense of ownership over their learning (Turk & Brensilver Berman, 2025).

Diana B. Turk and Stacie Brensilver Berman's (2018) article "Learning Through Doing: A Project-Based Learning Approach to the American Civil Rights Movement" represents that pinnacle of PBL's potential impact on student learning. Students move beyond memorizing dates and names of the Civil Rights Movement as they take on the roles of activists themselves. They engage deeply in debates, identify critical needs of the movement, and imagine themselves as advocates for change (Turk & Brensilver Berman, 2018). Students begin by examining key events, such as the Montgomery Bus Boycott, and delve into the tactics employed by civil rights organizations, like the Southern Christian Leadership Conference (SCLC) and the Student Nonviolent Coordinating Committee (SNCC). This foundational knowledge culminates in a project where students apply the historical content to a modern social issue relevant to their own lives. Through this process, students research their chosen issue, gather evidence, and create materials like pamphlets and presentations to raise awareness within their school and community. All the while, they bring it back to the histories that they learned about civil rights activists, many of whom were their own age. This activity not only reinforces historical knowledge but also "connects to students' lives outside of the classroom," which, as we established here, is crucial to achieving authenticity in PBL (Turk & Brensilver Berman, 2018, p. 36).

Building off their 2018 work, Turk and Brensilver Berman's (2025) *Project Based Learning in Real World U.S. History Classrooms: Engaging Diverse Learners* expands on the art of PBL teaching, equipping teachers with practical strategies to drive student academic achievement. While they focus on U.S. history, the application of this work to all social studies subjects and courses is extensive, offering adaptable frameworks that enrich students' understanding of global cultures, applied theories, and civic engagement. Their PBL units guide students to actively engage with history by solving real-world issues, making learning both rigorous and meaningful. The authors emphasize that PBL "creates an environment where students take charge of their learning, think critically, and deepen their knowledge through hands-on projects" (Turk & Brensilver Berman, 2025,

A Classroom With Purpose: A Guide to Teaching Social Studies Today

p. 48). For educators committed to culturally relevant teaching, this book is a powerful resource to make history come alive in the classroom, help students see themselves as capable learners, and inspire them to achieve at high levels. The authors call teachers to action, challenging them to bring PBL into their classrooms and watch their students thrive. Through PBL, students begin to view their academic success as closely tied to personal growth, social awareness, and a commitment to making a difference in their communities. This approach prepares them to see learning as a lifelong journey, equipping them with the skills to continue as informed and engaged citizens.

Many teachers avoid PBL because they cannot teach as many units in a year as if they engaged in traditional direct instruction. However, Ladson-Billings and I both argue that favoring depth over breadth of instruction leads to greater academic achievement for all students. If we try to teach them everything that happened over the course of humankind, we will create a teacher-centered space where students act as passive learners of history. How else could we cover the Age of Conquest up through COVID-19 in a U.S. history classroom or the Neolithic Era up through the War in Gaza in a world history course? We would have to deliver the who, what, where, when, why, and how every day, which would bore students and teachers alike. Like documentarians, we must make choices, and that is a good thing because it models for students yet another professional path for them to use their social studies education (Swan & Hofer, 2013). Choose topics and themes that both leverage your students' knowledge and experiences and provide them a chance to grow academically, professionally, and personally.

As teachers cultivate a learning environment centered around Project-Based Learning and Culturally Relevant Pedagogy, they empower students far more than with knowledge of historical facts. Teachers equip students with the skills to critically engage with the world, understand their place within it, and have the confidence to change it. When students connect their classroom learning directly to their lives, they grow not only academically but also as agents of change who are resilient, resistant, and joyful in their pursuit of knowledge. Remember, as teachers guide students in exploring both the past and the present, they help them dream with purpose, empowering them to act on those dreams and to see themselves as capable of effecting real change. The units that teachers create, whether they focus on debates, historical inquiries, or community activism, all contribute to a larger vision: one where students leave the classroom not just as learners but as dreamers equipped to transform their ambitions into reality. In the heart of a culturally relevant classroom lies an invitation to every student to act as harbingers of resilience, resistance, and joy to each space that they enter.

Teacher Tip: *Foster academic achievement in your classroom by creating a student-centered learning environment through Project-Based Learning. Start with Diana B. Turk and Stacie Brensilver Berman's 2025 book* Project Based Learning in Real World U.S. History Classrooms: Engaging Diverse Learners *(Routledge).*

Cultural Competence Through Mirrors and Windows

Students will not reach academic achievement without simultaneously developing their own cultural competence, the second pillar of CRP. During her visit to Brown, Ladson-Billings (2023) defined *cultural competence* as a student's ability "to be firmly grounded in one's own culture of origin, and fluent in at least one other culture." In other words, students intellectually value and share their own cultural identities while leveraging their understanding of other students' cultures to build both personal and academic connections. The classroom operates as a so-called cultural lab, where students practice engaging with people different from themselves, thus preparing for interactions beyond high school. Some teachers may discount cultural competence because they teach in homogenous classrooms where students seem similar. However, when we engage students in intersectional identity reflection, they discover how different they are from classmates who may look like them. Moreover, in social studies, we have the unique opportunity to introduce students to identities not represented in their immediate environment through the curricula that we teach. Through history, media literacy, civics, and the other content disciplines, social studies teachers actively develop their students' cultural competence (Love, 2019).

Cultural competence functions as the only component of CRP directly related to diversity. It requires students to explore multiple perspectives on all topics and teachers to provide a classroom environment where students can access and appreciate various cultural experiences. Because of this focus on diversity, critics of CRP falsely equate cultural competence with multiculturalism. While transformative scholars like Banks (2009) and Nieto (2002) have illustrated multiculturalism as a path to inclusivity and understanding among students of different backgrounds, they have also recognized its limitations. Multiculturalism often manifests as an additive approach where teachers include diverse voices but do not meaningfully connect content to students' own lives or identities (Banks, 2009; Nieto, 2002). Unlike the teacher-centered nature of multiculturalism, cultural competence manifests as a student-centered goal where students exhibit "academic excellence" and "cultural integrity" because their "culturally relevant teachers utilize students' culture as a vehicle for learning" (Ladson-Billings, 1995b, p. 160). Cultural competence requires teachers to assess students' growth throughout the year and adjust their practices based on whatever rubric the teacher has set. Culturally relevant teachers design curricula and pedagogical practices based on the identities present in the classroom, paying careful attention to critical identities also not present. Culturally responsive teachers do not just add in diverse figures who will not be relevant to their students' lives.

Students can develop their cultural competence authentically and effectively if their social studies teachers employ the "windows and mirrors" learning strategies. First introduced by Emily Style in 1988 and popularized by Rudine Sims Bishop in 1990, this framework asks teachers to provide students with curricular *mirrors* that reflect their own identities and virtual *windows* that offer views into the lives and perspectives of others. Style (1988/1996) explains that "students need both mirrors and windows in the curriculum, so they can see their own experience honored as well as learn about experiences beyond their own," underscoring the balance between self-affirmation and empathy (p. 35). Rudine Sims Bishop (1990) adds that mirrors allow students to "see a reflection of themselves," validating their cultural identity, while windows offer "a glimpse into someone else's world," fostering openness and connection (p. ix). I think that both speak to Ladson-Billings's (1995b) assertion that by focusing on cultural competence, students view their cultural backgrounds as "assets in the learning process" and "not a means of assimilation" as some critics have asserted (p. 84). Social studies teachers have both the opportunity and responsibility to structure all learning around windows and mirrors. In every unit, lesson, classroom decor, field trip, or allocation of resources, a social studies teacher should ask themselves the following: Which students see themselves in this? Which students learn something new from this? Which students have not yet seen themselves in my classroom? Which students have not had the opportunity to learn about new cultures in my classroom? Windows and mirrors help balance representation of identities in the social studies classroom and hold an educator accountable for ensuring diversity, equity, and inclusion.

Teachers who use windows and mirrors transform their classrooms into spaces with robust immersive cultural exchange, community connections, and multisensory experiences. Ladson-Billings (1995a) shares the example of Gertrude Winston, an inspirational teacher who invited community members into her classroom as artists or craftspeople-in-residence. Parents, grandparents, and local artisans engaged students in interactive show-and-tell sessions featuring relevant cultural artifacts such as local foods, furniture, and art. In one instance, a parent known for her sweet potato pie-making skills led the students through the entire process, teaching them how to prepare the crust, fill it, and bake it to perfection. As the pies baked, she shared stories of family, local history, and transnational foodways, thus connecting the ingredients and recipes to cultural heritage. The experience provided much more than a baking lesson; students gained insight into history, economics, and science through a culturally relevant project that elevated their understanding of their own identities and those of others. Students encountered mirrors that reflected their experiences and windows that offered glimpses into the diverse talents and backgrounds of their peers and community. Ladson-Billings (1995a) notes that in Winston's classroom, students "came to understand the constructed nature of things such as 'art,' 'excellence,' and 'knowledge,'" realizing that their community's knowledge and skills held deep academic and personal value (p. 162). Students who had grown up with similar family stories or traditions could see themselves fully reflected in these experiences, reinforcing a sense of pride in their heritage. Meanwhile, students unfamiliar with sweet potato pie found a new perspective through this window, broadening their understanding of their classmates.

If educators cannot bring in parents or community members into their classrooms, teachers should make the students the artist, craftsperson, historian, or media expert-in-residence. Students can present to their classmates on culturally significant aspects of their lives, such as traditional foods, holiday customs, favorite music, art and symbols from their heritage, sports, and more. Imagine the beautiful classroom environment where instead of reading an irrelevant document that the students have no interest in, students choosing primary sources themselves in the forms of recipes, family stories, and old photographs. Educators can apply the same skills and academic heft needed for PBL to the cultural artifacts that the students themselves choose. In my own student-teachers' classes, I have witnessed the magic of applying the five historical thinking skills of Contextualization, Continuity and Change, Cause and Effect, Through their Eyes, and Why It Matters to a student's recipe for feijoada, an old family photograph, or their favorite childhood song (Mandell & Malone, 2007).

Classrooms rich with the sights, sounds, tastes, and textures of diverse experiences not only develop students' cultural competence but also provide a "homeplace" for students. First coined by bell hooks (1990) and later expanded upon by Bettina Love (2019), a *homeplace* provides students with a beloved classroom space to "thrive, dream, and imagine new futures" in educational settings (p. 123). Students, especially those from historically underrepresented backgrounds, experience validation and affirmation in ways that counteract a social studies environment often dismissive of their experiences. When students share a family recipe or favorite song, decorate the classroom,

A Classroom With Purpose: A Guide to Teaching Social Studies Today

or speak home languages, they transform learning from passive consumption to active, meaningful exchange. Students taste the flavors of history, hear the rhythms of resistance, and connect across cultural boundaries. In this multisensory homeplace, students live each other's culture rather than merely study it, building connections through shared experiences that honor and celebrate all the heritages in the room. Cultural competence, where students learn what it means to belong, empathize, and advocate, transforms the entire environment.

In a culturally relevant social studies classroom, students engage with their identities and those of their peers in a space that celebrates resilience, resistance, and joy. As they explore mirrors that reflect their own stories and windows that reveal the diverse experiences of others, students gain the critical awareness to see themselves as part of a larger narrative. Ladson-Billings's framework reminds us that cultural competence moves beyond appreciating diversity to connecting through commonalities and across differences. Through windows and mirrors, homeplaces, and the celebration of each student's intersectional identities, we build classrooms where academic achievement becomes intertwined with personal growth. Students, equipped with a sense of pride in their heritage and an empathetic understanding of others, dream with purpose. They recognize their resilience, engage in resistance, and celebrate their identities as sources of joy.

Teacher Tip: *Build cultural competence in your students by utilizing a windows-and-mirrors-based curriculum coupled with a homeplace environment. Start with Bettina Love's (2019)* We Want to Do More Than Survive: Abolitionist Teaching and the Pursuit of Educational Freedom *(Beacon Press).*

Sociopolitical/Critical Consciousness as Magical Portals

Once social studies teachers have cultivated a student-centered classroom that promotes academic achievement and fosters cultural competence through mirrors and windows, the next step is to build students' *sociopolitical/critical consciousness*. Ladson-Billings (1995b) defines this third pillar of CRP as "the ability to take a critical stance and challenge the status quo of the current social order" (p. 160). Students have a space to name injustices in their lives and communities, as well as the inequities that affect others nationally and globally. Teachers also provide opportunities to unpack the structural and systemic causes of those injustices so that students do not view them universal or static. Most importantly, students strategize about how to combat those injustices either as themselves or through imagining themselves as characters in various scenarios. For example, Turk and Brensilver Berman's (2018) unit on the Civil Rights Movement develops sociopolitical/critical consciousness by having students analyze the choices, actions, writings, and ideas of activists who have shaped social justice movements. Culturally relevant social studies teachers carefully select the people they teach about to intentionally instill senses of agency and responsibility in their students. By exploring people their own age, race, gender, or socioeconomic status, students realize that they have the power to influence change.

Since sociopolitical/critical consciousness requires students to imagine the world they want to live in, teachers should cultivate it through immersive and imaginative experiences that I call *magical portals*. These portals bridge history, media, and creative expression, enabling students to step beyond traditional narratives and into the lives and struggles of people often left out of textbooks. Magical portals bring students face-to-face with the complexities of social issues plaguing people with similar intersectional identities who solve the problems through real-life options. These can manifest through history or historical fiction. No matter which scenario, the magical portal prompts students to see history as a dynamic, living guide. As one of my graduate students recently described them, magical portals are "time machines in the classroom that not only transport students to the past but help them reshape the future when they step out of it" (Gorte, 2023).

By immersing students in oral histories, images, music, or artifacts, students do not just learn facts, they connect with past struggles and envision pathways for change in their own communities. Magical portals invite students to explore critical historical events and engage in what Robin D. G. Kelley (2002) and Bettina Love (2019) call "freedom dreaming." This concept refers to the act of imagining a better, more equitable world and believing that change is possible through calculated and planned action (Kelley, 2002; Love, 2019). Through a multisensory approach of carefully curated stories and texts, students evaluate how people historically resisted oppression, thus gaining inspiration for building a more just future (Love, 2019). Moreover, students map out resilience, resistance, and joy as they reimagine or rewrite (even re-right) historical injustices. Saidiya Hartman's (2008) theory of "critical fabulation" further deepens this process by encouraging students to engage with the silences in history, piecing together the lives that traditional narratives often omit. Hartman describes critical fabulation as an effort to "elaborate the kinds of lives obscured by history's silence" (p. 11). In social studies, this means encouraging students to look beyond standard primary sources and consider creative expressions such as speculative fiction, oral histories, and multimedia content. By questioning which stories are told and why, students engage in the kind of critical inquiry that drives sociopolitical/critical consciousness.

Teachers can start by modeling this approach and then invite students to create their own magical portals, allowing them to see history through a critical lens. One example of a magical portal that serves as both a teacher- and student-facing resource is Malinda Lo's (2021) novel *Last Night at the Telegraph Club*. This story brings to life the world of queer Asian American women during the McCarthy era, a period marked by intense xenophobia and homophobia. Lo's protagonist, Lily Hu, navigates her identity as a young LGBTQ+ Chinese American amid a landscape of fear and discrimination. Through a blend of historical fiction, primary sources, oral histories, and contemporary media, Lo creates a vivid portal into a past that resonates with issues affecting students today. For queer and Asian American students, *Last Night at the Telegraph Club* serves as a mirror, affirming their identities and experiences. For other students, it provides a window, fostering empathy and understanding. Engaging with such texts allows students to consider why certain narratives have been erased from mainstream history, deepening their critical awareness.

While *Last Night at the Telegraph Club* provides a magical portal into a critical historical moment both relevant and overlooked, the text also serves as an opportunity to develop students' media literacy skills. Students need measurable and applicable skills to navigate the magical portals you provide, thus building their sociopolitical/critical consciousness. Media literacy hones those skills. Renee Hobbs (2021), the leading figure in media literacy education, defines it as "an ever-changing set of knowledge, skills, and habits of mind required for full participation in a contemporary media-saturated world" (p. 4). Media literacy teaches students to understand media messaging; analyze and critique its content, function, and form; and most importantly create new media. Media literacy does not rest at using media as supplementary teaching tools. Students learn to question the sources of information they encounter, understand the power dynamics behind media messages, and develop a deeper awareness of how media shapes public perception. In the social studies classroom, this approach enables students to examine media portrayals of historical events, social movements, and marginalized voices, developing the sociopolitical/critical consciousness necessary for informed decision-making.

Renee Hobbs, Pam Steager, and the Media Education Lab (2020) have revolutionized how educators engage students in media literacy through the Media Literacy Smartphone, a hands-on teaching tool that resembles a smartphone. On one side, students have access to the Five Questions of Media Literacy:

1. Who is the author, and what is the purpose?
2. What techniques are used to attract and hold your attention?
3. What lifestyles, values, and points of view are represented?
4. How might different people interpret the message?
5. What is omitted from this message? (Hobbs & Steager, 2020)

The other side features analysis "apps" that help students decode and evaluate media messages. This innovative format aligns with students' daily realities, bridging abstract media literacy principles with their practical application in a relatable and engaging way. Using the Media Literacy Smartphone, students can approach Lo's work, and any magical portal, not only as a historical narrative but also as a construct that reflects choices in storytelling, representation, and omission. Students survey the text for facts and narrative but also for perspective and point of view.

Media literacy, like creating a student-centered classroom, trains students in *how* to think instead of *what* to think. As Hobbs (2021) emphasizes, media literacy is "a learning process that involves inquiry," and it empowers educators and students alike to leap over the lower levels of Bloom's Taxonomy (p. 5). In fact, Hobbs has revolutionized Bloom's Taxonomy by putting "Create" at the center of her taxonomy of student learning. In the media literacy hierarchy of cognitive function, students continue beyond "Create" with "Critique" and "Reflect." "Critique" and "Reflect" comprise the intellectual crux of sociopolitical/critical consciousness. When I asked Ladson-Billings (2023) where she envisioned media literacy in classrooms, she explained that it helps students challenge power structures as students learn to critique both content and the systems that produce it. She also advocated for students using social media in social studies classrooms. By guiding students through the process of creating social media posts, teachers empower them to articulate their perspectives, advocate for social issues, and contribute meaningfully to public discourse. Social media thus becomes a platform for civic engagement, where students can actively participate in shaping the narratives that define their world.

To use multimedia content as magical portals, teachers should thoughtfully select and integrate diverse digital resources that capture students' interest while presenting authentic narratives. Documentaries, podcasts, and digital storytelling can offer rich, nuanced perspectives that traditional texts often lack. Teachers should guide students through these resources with reflective questions, facilitated discussions, and critical analysis. By connecting historical events to contemporary social, political, and cultural challenges, multimedia resources foster a more profound understanding of content. For example, a documentary on the Civil Rights Movement may inspire students to draw connections between past struggles and present-day social justice issues, equipping them with both historical context and a sense of agency.

Fostering sociopolitical consciousness with magical portals and media literacy allows students to dream and act with purpose. In this culturally relevant social studies classroom, students not only explore history but also experience it as a call to action. They learn to connect academic content to their lives, envisioning a world where resilience, resistance, and joy define their journeys. Through the lens of media literacy, they acquire the tools to deconstruct narratives, challenge biases, and contribute to cultural transformations. With these tools, students leave the classroom not just as learners but as dreamers and changemakers, equipped to turn their aspirations for a more just world into actionable realities.

Teacher Tip: *Develop your students' sociopolitical/critical consciousness by providing magical portals for studying the past and media literacy for connecting it to the present. Start with Renee Hobbs and Pam Steager's (2020) Media Literacy Smartphone from Media Education Lab (https://mediaeducationlab.com/media-literacy-smartphone).*

Dream-Releasing Through Social Studies Education

Thinking back to my fourth-grade daydreaming, I now see how those moments of imaginative escape planted seeds of curiosity and wonder that would shape my future. While I never did race against Abraham Lincoln on the rings of Saturn with Apollo chasing us, I also never let go of my fascination with them. Imagine my amazement years later, sitting in my first Queer Studies course, when both Abraham Lincoln and Apollo reappeared together in Kenneth R. Dutton's (1995) *The Perfectible Body* as part of a unit on "Common Heroes for LGBTQ+ Youth." That intersection of history, mythology, and identity felt like a full-circle moment. It validated the daydreams my mother had encouraged, even as my classrooms dismissed them. That moment solidified my choice to work in education and to ensure that all students feel seen, heard, and represented in their social studies classes. My mother always saw value in my fantastical stories. She nurtured my creativity, viewing it as a sign of a vibrant imagination that would take me far in life. Not all students, however, have a support system that encourages dreaming, especially when school suppresses it. As educators, we have the power to fill that gap.

Social studies teachers can welcome daydreams into their classrooms and show students how to channel that dreaming into tools for learning and growth. Through academic achievement, cultural competence, and sociopolitical/critical consciousness, Gloria Ladson-Billings has spent decades teaching us how to be "dream-keepers" for students. However, by incorporating student-centered teaching, mirrors and windows, and magical portals, we can also become "dream-releasers." We can teach students to use their dreams as vehicles for success, whether they aspire to reshape history, reimagine their communities, or simply find their place in the world. By connecting students' identities and lived experiences to the lessons of history, geography, economics, and civics, culturally relevant teaching empowers them to envision a better world and equips them with the tools to achieve it.

The framework of Culturally Relevant Pedagogy, at its heart, equips students to dream with purpose. It substantiates the power of their imaginations, like mine as a fourth grader, in transforming their worlds around them. When we connect imaginations, identities, and academic success, we show students that their dreams lead to success as opposed to hindering it. Moreover, by focusing on resilience, resistance, and joy, we affirm the potential of every student to become someone who both dreams of change and actively creates it. Therein lies the ability to turn their magical portals into bridges that connect their dreams to actionable realities. In doing so, we invite them to become the architects of their own futures, just as I once dreamed mine into existence.

Yes, But How Can We Do it in the Four Major Social Studies Disciplines?

History

To explore the American home front during World War II, use Rosie the Riveter as a dynamic entry point into understanding propaganda, women's activism, and the impact of representation. Begin with resources like *The Life and Times of Rosie the Riveter* (Field, 1980), the American Social History Project's (2010) active viewing activity of Field's film, and PBS's (2021) *Rosie the Riveter Isn't Who You Think She Is* and guide students to analyze these sources through the Five Questions of Media Literacy. Encourage them to reflect on Rosie's dual role as both an icon of empowerment and a tool of wartime propaganda. Introduce texts that highlight Black, Latina, Asian, and LGBTQ+ "Rosies" who contributed to the war effort, and invite students to redraw or reimagine Rosie to include these perspectives. This creative rebranding not only deepens cultural competence by reflecting mirrors and windows but also serves as a magical portal into understanding how media shapes narratives. Culminate with a gallery walk where students present and critique each other's representations. Cultivate resilience, resistance, and joy as students connect their work to contemporary women's rights issues in social media posts, creating real-world links to college or career interests, such as media, history, or gender studies. This project-based approach nurtures student-centered learning and academic achievement, encouraging students to see themselves as both historians and changemakers.

Geography

Present historical and modern maps as influential media artifacts, each shaped by the perspectives of those who created them. Use the Library of Congress's (n.d.) virtual exhibit, *Propaganda Maps to Strike Fear, Inform, and Mobilize*, and challenge students to apply media literacy skills to deconstruct maps as propaganda. Connect this to social media by exploring how modern visuals influence opinions and behaviors. This magical portal activity encourages students to examine maps critically, understanding them as tools that convey selective narratives and promote imperial or national agendas while often omitting marginalized perspectives. Ask students to reclaim the mapmaking process and create maps of their own neighborhoods focusing on where they find their resilience, resistance, and joy in their communities. Students can then present them as part of a class discussion or media project. This exercise in sociopolitical/critical consciousness not only enhances students' understanding of geography but also empowers them to analyze and create visual information in ways that reflect their agency and responsibility. As students evaluate and create maps, they experience joy and resilience, actively engaging in student-centered, project-based learning that connects their analysis to both their academic success and their personal lives.

Economics

Engage students in the intersection of economics, cybersecurity, and media literacy through the lesson *Cybersecurity and Economics: Social Media and You* from EconEdLink (2023). In this project, students learn cost–benefit analysis by reflecting on their own social media use, critically assessing the personal and social costs and benefits of their digital engagement. This activity transforms their social media experience into a mirror, window, and magical portal that connects challenging economic principles to their daily lives. As they consider their digital footprints, students link economic literacy with personal responsibility, viewing their digital presence as part of a larger decision-making process. For assessment, students can write a college application essay on their growth as responsible digital citizens, create public service announcements (PSAs) on social media's economic and ethical impact, or develop business promotion plans that leverage social media responsibly. This culturally relevant approach fosters resilience and joy by allowing students to see their learning directly impact their personal and future goals. Students flex academic achievement as they simultaneously meet national, state, and professional standards and workshop their college application essays in authentic and reflexive ways.

Civics

Use the topic of fake news and misinformation to explore the responsibilities of informed citizenship. Start with case studies on misinformation campaigns during election cycles, public health crises, or social movements, utilizing resources from media literacy organizations like Media Education Lab, Common Sense Media, or MediaSmarts. Encourage students to evaluate these sources using the Five Questions of Media Literacy, building their skills to detect bias, intent, and omission. To deepen engagement, introduce a magical portal by having students create counternarratives that address the effects of misinformation on marginalized communities. Through creative projects such as fact-based op-eds, infographics, or short videos, students develop sociopolitical consciousness and cultural competence as they highlight how misinformation impacts public trust and civic engagement. For a culminating activity, students can design a digital campaign on responsible media consumption, crafting social media posts or PSAs that promote critical awareness and responsible media habits. This project not only builds student-centered, project-based skills but also fosters joy and resilience as students take ownership of their roles as informed citizens, prepared to resist misinformation and advocate for truth and inclusion.

Checklist for a Culturally Relevant Social Studies Classroom

Academic Achievement

☐ Students grow in both skills and content knowledge in your classroom as they meet academic, professional, and personal goals.

☐ You create a student-centered classroom where students do the work and the thinking.

☐ Students engage in Project-Based Learning. See Diana B. Turk and Stacie Brensilver Berman (2025) *Project Based Learning in Real World U.S. History Classrooms: Engaging Diverse Learners* (Routledge).

Cultural Competence

☐ Students value and share their own cultures and lived experiences in class as they learn from students whose cultures and lived experiences differ from their own.

☐ You provide curricular "mirrors" so that students see themselves in the learning, and "windows" so that they learn about people different from themselves in the curriculum.

☐ Students create a "homeplace." See Bettina Love (2019) *We Want to Do More Than Survive: Abolitionist Teaching and the Pursuit of Educational Freedom* (Beacon Press).

Sociopolitical/Critical Consciousness

☐ Students question power structures and inequities as they imagine a world where they feel seen, heard, and included.

☐ You provide "magical portals" for students to brainstorm how to strategize and make that dream world into a reality.

☐ Students develop their media literacy skills. See Renee Hobbs (2021) *Media Literacy in Action: Questioning the Media* (Rowman & Littlefield).

References

American Social History Project. (2010). *Active viewing: The life and times of Rosie the Riveter*. SHEC: Resources for Teachers. **https://shec.ashp.cuny.edu/items/show/1369**

Banks, J. A. (2009). Diversity and citizenship education in multicultural nations. *Multicultural Education Review,* 1(1), 1–28. **www.tandfonline.com/doi/abs/10.1080/23770031.2009.11102861**

Bishop, R. S. (1990). Mirrors, windows, and sliding glass doors. *Perspectives, 6*(3), ix–xi.

Dutton, K. R. (1995). *The perfectible body: The Western ideal of male physical development.* Continuum.

EconEdLink. (2023). *Cybersecurity and economics: Social media and you* [Lesson plan]. Council for Economic Education. **https://econedlink.org/resources/cybersecurity-and-economics-social-media-and-you**

Field, C. (Director). (1980). *The life and times of Rosie the Riveter* [Film]. Clarity Films.

Gay, G. (2010). *Culturally responsive teaching: Theory, research, and practice* (2nd ed.). Teachers College Press.

Gorte, J. (2023). *Magical portals in the social studies classroom* [Presentation]. Brown University Capstone Presentations.

Hammond, Z. (2015). *Culturally responsive teaching and the brain: Promoting authentic engagement and rigor among culturally and linguistically diverse students.* Corwin Press.

Hartman, S. (2008). Venus in two acts. *Small Axe: A Caribbean Journal of Criticism, 12*(2), 1–14. **https://doi.org/10.1215/-12-2-1**

Hobbs, R. (2021). *Media literacy in action: Questioning the media.* Rowman & Littlefield.

Hobbs, R., & Steager, P. (2020). *Media literacy smartphone.* Media Education Lab. **https://mediaeducationlab.com/media-literacy-smartphone**

hooks, b. (1990). *Yearning: Race, gender, and cultural politics.* South End Press.

Kelley, R. D. G. (2002). *Freedom dreams: The black radical imagination.* Beacon Press.

Ladson-Billings, G. (1994). *The dreamkeepers: Successful teachers of African American* children. Jossey-Bass.

Ladson-Billings, G. (1995a). But that's just good teaching! The case for culturally relevant pedagogy. *Theory Into Practice, 34*(3), 159–165. **https://doi.org/10.1080/00405849509543675**

Ladson-Billings, G. (1995b). Toward a theory of culturally relevant pedagogy. *American Educational Research Journal, 32*(3), 465–491. **https://doi.org/10.3102/00028312032003465**

Ladson-Billings, G. (2006). "Yes, but how do we do it?" Practicing culturally relevant pedagogy. In J. Landsman & C. W. Lewis (Eds.), *White teachers/diverse classrooms: A guide to building inclusive schools, promoting high expectations, and eliminating racism* (pp. 29–42). Stylus Publishing.

Ladson-Billings, G. (2023). "Yes, but how do we do it in 2024?" Lecture presented at Brown University Education Department, Providence, RI.

Library of Congress. (n.d.). *Propaganda maps to strike fear, inform, and mobilize* [Virtual exhibit]. Library of Congress. **https://blogs.loc.gov/maps/2019/09/propaganda-maps-to-strike-fear-inform-and-mobilize-a-special-collection-in-the-geography-and-map-division**

Lo, M. (2021). *Last night at the Telegraph Club*. Dutton Books.

Love, B. L. (2019). *We want to do more than survive: Abolitionist teaching and the pursuit of educational freedom*. Beacon Press.

Mandell, N., & Malone, B. (2007). *Thinking like a historian: Rethinking history instruction*. Wisconsin Historical Society Press.

Morrison, K. A., Robbins, H. H., & Rose, D. G. (2008). Operationalizing culturally relevant pedagogy: A synthesis of classroom-based research. *Equity & Excellence in Education, 41*(4), 433–452. **https://doi.org/10.1080/10665680802400006**

Nieto, S. (2002). *Language, culture, and teaching: Critical perspectives for a new century*. Lawrence Erlbaum Associates.

Paris, D., & Alim, H. S. (2017). *Culturally sustaining pedagogies: Teaching and learning for justice in a changing world*. Teachers College Press.

PBS. (2021). *Rosie the Riveter isn't who you think she is* [Video]. PBS. **www.pbs.org/americanexperience/features/riveted-history-of-jeans-rosie-riveter**

Style, E. (1996). Curriculum as window and mirror. *Social Science Record, 33*(2), 1–7. (Reprinted from "Curriculum as window and mirror," 1988, *Listening for All Voices*, Oak Knoll School)

Swan, K., & Hofer, M. (2013). *And action: Directing documentaries in the social studies classroom*. Rowman and Littlefield Education.

Turk, D. B., & Brensilver Berman, S. (2018). Learning through doing: A project-based learning approach to the American civil rights movement. *Social Education, 82*(1), 36–41.

Turk, D. B., & Brensilver Berman, S. (2025). *Project based learning in real world U.S. history classrooms: Engaging diverse learners*. Routledge.

Young, E. (2010). Challenges to conceptualizing and actualizing culturally relevant pedagogy: How viable is the theory in classroom practice? *Journal of Teacher Education, 61*(3), 248–260. **https://doi.org/10.1177/0022487109359775**

Chapter 8

Being the Best Social Studies Teacher for Students With IEPs

Darren W. Minarik

As early career social studies educators, what do we really need to know to effectively teach our students with disabilities (SWDs)? The field of social studies has historically struggled with providing research evidence and research-into-practice support for pre-service and early career in-service teachers wanting to better address the needs of SWDs. The last decade has seen some growth in the research and guidance surrounding the intersections between social studies, special education, and disability, but there is still much work to do (Minarik & Lintner, 2024). Most social studies research on SWDs focuses on students with the most prevalent disability labels, such as learning disabilities, and the strategies address the acquisition of basic content knowledge (Ciullo et al., 2020). Studies are limited when looking at higher order thinking and reasoning skills, and few studies examine the effectiveness of strategies for teaching students with more extensive support needs such as autism, intellectual disability, and multiple disabilities (Wehmeyer et al., 2021).

The lack of research is troubling when you consider approximately 7.5 million students in public education receive special education services under the Individuals with Disabilities Education Act (IDEA), and 67% of those students are in the general education classroom for 80% or more of the school day (National Center for Education Statistics, 2024; Office of Special Education Programs, 2024). There is evidence students with disabilities are more likely to be included in social studies instruction with 87% of students with learning disabilities accessing social studies content in the general education classroom; although, nearly half of these students academically performed below their peers without disabilities (Lintner & Kumpiene, 2017). These findings suggest that students with seats in the social studies general education classroom are not experiencing the instruction needed to access and learn the content. The data does not tell us how students with other less prevalent disability categories are included and to what degree they are academically successful. In addition, we know very little about how disability history is incorporated into our PreK–12 social studies curricula and if teaching disability history has a positive impact on addressing perceptions of disability and supporting the inclusion of SWDs in our schools.

The purpose of this chapter is to provide pre-service and early career in-service social studies educators with guidance regarding how to best address the needs of SWDs in their classrooms. For social studies teachers to best meet the academic, social, emotional, and physical needs of SWDs, we need to consider multiple paths for improving our practice and becoming advocates for inclusive education. Before any changes in practice take place, we must reflect on our own implicit and explicit biases and consider the broader culture of how disability is perceived. For this reason, this chapter begins with an examination of disability bias and the ways teachers, schools, and communities perceive disability and SWDs. The next section explores the Individualized Education

Program (IEP), explaining the core elements necessary to effectively meet the needs of SWDs. The IEP serves as the legal protection to ensure SWDs receive an appropriate education in the least restrictive environment.

Understanding the IEP naturally leads to the importance of effective classroom management and addressing the academic, social, emotional, behavioral, and physical needs of SWDs. In this section, social studies educators will learn inclusive practices to structure and manage a classroom for the individual needs of SWDs so that more time is focused on best practice in the planning and delivery of instruction. A focus is placed on understanding the intersections between High-Leverage Practices (HLPs) within special education, social studies inquiry-based instructional methods, and the use of Universal Design for Learning (UDL) and differentiation of instruction. While knowing the best ways to plan and deliver content is critical, the IEP also requires that teachers monitor the progress of SWDs, so how we assess student understanding of content is addressed. Throughout this chapter, educators are provided with checklists and tips to consider when creating an inclusive social studies classroom. The checklist at the end of the chapter summarizes core principles all teachers should consider when trying to create a more inclusive classroom environment. The hope is that after reading this chapter, you will be encouraged to advocate for SWDs in your classrooms and advocate for schoolwide inclusive education.

Understanding Disability Bias

Throughout history, people with disabilities were often stigmatized and devalued for their disability or impairment, experiencing discrimination and oppression because they were seen as profoundly different from the defined normality of that time (Baglieri & Shapiro, 2017; Minarik et al., 2021). Today, negative perceptions and stereotypes about people with disabilities still exist within our schools and communities. Even though teacher preparation programs provide a survey course in special education to examine legal aspects and characteristics of disability, there is little evidence these courses spend time examining perceptions of disability in society and public schooling (Minarik & Blevins, 2017). Focusing on legal aspects and characteristics without unpacking perceptions of disability may result in a less inclusive school environment where more attention is given to the disability label and stereotypes, emphasizing what SWDs cannot do. In less inclusive school environments, teachers and administrators believe students with IEPs, regardless of actual ability, belong primarily in the special education classroom, separated from their peers without disabilities. Disability characteristics and legal considerations are important, but placement decisions should not be based on labels and perceived deficits. More inclusive schools use a strengths-based approach to support the needs of SWDs and recognize how negative perceptions of disability inhibit a student's ability to learn and feel included in the school community.

Language of Disability

One challenge we face as educators is the language used in schools when talking about SWDs. The concern is that the labels given to students with IEPs end up serving as the defining characteristic. This medicalized perception of a student is sometimes referred to as *deficit thinking* or the *medical model of disability*. It is essential for educators to not see students for what is perceived they cannot do, but rather for the strengths they bring to the classroom. A simple way to outwardly change this thinking is to examine how we speak about SWDs. In this chapter, "students with disabilities" is used instead of "disabled students" when communicating about our students with IEPs in the classroom. This is known as person-first language in which the disability is placed after the person in discussion. As an example of person-first language, you would say "my student with a learning disability" rather than "my learning-disabled student" when having a conversation. This is a safe, default approach when talking or writing about SWDs.

Another way to communicate about disability is through using identity-first language. There are advocates in the disability community who prefer placing the disability first in conversation and writing because the disability is just part of the individual. Identity-first language is often used in the Deaf community: Deaf culture embraces hearing loss and the use of American Sign Language as part of who they are as individuals. Similarly, some people with autism use identity-first language, emphasizing the strengths of their self-described neurodivergence. People who use identity-first language highlight the strengths within the person and the disability, not the deficits defined within the label. This sociocultural approach to communicating about disability suggests that, although there is an underlying medical diagnosis, the person is primarily disabled because of social and cultural structures already in place. In other words, the social model of disability recognizes people are more disabled by the barriers society creates around them than by the actual disability characteristics.

When navigating language, consider taking a more inclusive, person-centered approach when communicating about disability. Table 8.1 provides a reminder about the three

Table 8.1 *Three Approaches to Communicating About Disability*

	Person-first	**Identity-first**	**Person-centered**
Definition	Places emphasis on the individual first, separating the person from their disability	Places the disability as an integral part of an individual's identity	Recognizes the individual's unique preferences, interests, strengths, and needs, prioritizing overall well-being
Examples	"I have a student with autism in class." "I have a student with deafness or hearing impairment in class."	"I have an autistic student in class." "I have a Deaf student in class."	"I have a student who benefits from structured learning and needs accommodations to support explicit routines." "I have a student who benefits from visual learning and needs accommodations for hearing."
Usage	Commonly used to emphasize respect for the individual without defining the person by the disability	Commonly used to respect individuals who see their disability as a core aspect of their identity	Commonly used in planning and decision-making processes to empower the individual with a disability
Implications	Suggests that the disability does not define the individual, changing how others might view a person with a disability	Acknowledges that the disability is a significant part of who they are, which is okay. It challenges the prejudice and bias in society.	Recognizes that individuals have diverse identities and require personalized approaches to education and support

A Classroom With Purpose: A Guide to Teaching Social Studies Today

approaches to communicating about disability. Teachers using a person-centered approach find out what the student and family want when talking about the disability. Teachers explain the language they are using and respect the wishes of the person they are talking about. A person-centered approach also means educating yourself about disability language. Within the disability community, terminology changes over time, and it is important for teachers to keep up to date with those changes. For example, "wheelchair bound" is not an appropriate way to describe a student who uses a wheelchair, and it also does not accurately explain the purpose of the wheelchair. Students are not bound to a wheelchair; they are wheelchair users. The wheelchair gives them mobility and freedom, but "bound" implies that the chair represents a restriction and limitation.

Bias in Classroom Practice

Recognizing our own disability biases is essential, though it can be challenging in a society where individuals with disabilities are often undervalued or assumed to contribute less than their nondisabled peers. These misconceptions perpetuate discrimination, prejudice, and bias. Classroom teachers may unintentionally reflect these biases in how they approach teaching students with IEPs compared to their peers without disabilities. Biases can influence our organization and presentation of content, our instructional strategies, our assessment practices, and even the physical layout of our classrooms.

To address potential prejudice and bias, social studies teachers should reflect on the following questions at the start of a new school year:

1. Do I presume competence in all SWDs?
2. When discussing SWDs, do I use language that respects their dignity and personhood?
3. How does the physical setup of my classroom affect the learning and socialization of SWDs?
4. Do the methods I use to share content ensure full access to essential material, regardless of disability label?
5. Do my instructional practices offer all students the opportunity to learn essential content, regardless of disability label?
6. Do my assessment practices provide multiple ways for students to demonstrate their understanding of essential content?

By thoughtfully considering these questions, teachers can work to improve their practices, reduce disability prejudice and bias, and create a more inclusive and supportive learning environment.

Teacher Tip: *Many states have a disability history and awareness week or month and other celebrations of disability awareness each year. Use these times to address disability topics and challenge prejudice, bias, and stereotypes.*

Knowing the IEP

The Individualized Education Program (IEP) supports the academic, social, emotional, and physical success of our SWDs. The IEP is a document that protects the right of SWDs to have a free and appropriate public education in the least restrictive environment (Minarik & Lintner, 2016; U.S. Department of Education, 2004). The IEP process begins when teachers identify a student struggling academically or behaviorally. In response, schools typically have a team who considers the strengths and needs of the student and provides interventions to address those needs. If the interventions fail to help the student, the parent or guardian is asked to provide informed consent so the student can be referred for a special education evaluation. The general education teacher may be asked to serve on an eligibility team to provide and evaluate academic and behavioral data that helps the team determine whether the student qualifies for special education services. If the student is found eligible, an IEP team is formed, consisting of the student's parents or guardians, the student, general and special education teachers, and other relevant specialists. When writing the IEP, the IEP team considers the student's strengths, interests, preferences, and needs in addition to current academic and functional performance data. Measurable annual goals are developed along with other needed services and accommodations, and the IEP team details how progress will be measured and what outcomes are expected.

The general education teacher plays a vital role throughout the IEP process by contributing insights into the student's strengths and challenges and by collaborating with specialists and parents to consider how the student is best supported in the general education classroom. Once an IEP is put in place, the general education teacher collaborates with a special education teacher and other support personnel to implement the IEP by delivering accommodations and modifications, supporting interventions, providing opportunities for specially designed instruction, and monitoring the progress of the student as it relates to the annual goals (Lisanti et al., 2024). A critical role for the general education teacher is to serve as an advocate for SWDs, ensuring their strengths are emphasized and supporting involvement in the IEP process (Minarik et al., 2021). Teachers can do this by getting to know the strengths and needs of the student. Within the IEP, the Present Level of Academic Achievement and Functional Performance (PLAAFP) is the best place to start. A well-written PLAAFP gives you a background of the student and identifies strengths, interests, preferences, and needs. After reading the PLAAFP, you should understand what academic, social, and behavioral supports and interventions are needed for academic and functional success.

Next, explore the listed accommodations and modifications noted in the IEP. *Accommodations* provide access to the content without changing the content students are required to learn. SWDs might have an accommodation requiring graphic organizers to help structure note-taking or writing. Extra time to complete an assessment or more individualized testing support are common accommodations along with reducing the length of an assignment. *Modifications* are a change in the content and what students are expected to learn. Most often, modifications are developed for students with more extensive support needs like those with intellectual disabilities or multiple disabilities. Sometimes the line between accommodation and modification can be blurred. A common example is assessment of student learning. SWDs may have an accommodation to reduce the length of a test. This accommodation can become a modification if the test length reduction results in a SWD not being assessed on the same content as peers without disabilities. If reducing the length of a test compromises your ability to evaluate all the required content, you need to collaborate with the special education teacher to find an alternate accommodation like extended test time or breaking the test into smaller chunks. As a general education teacher, it is crucial to understand the accommodations and modifications listed in the IEP and the ways these will impact your social studies instruction, student learning, and classroom structure.

Finally, take the time to familiarize yourself with the annual goals, even if they are not specifically written for social studies instruction. Goals related to reading, reading comprehension, and written expression can still be relevant. Additionally, goals that focus on executive functioning skills—such as organization, memory recall, motivation, impulse control, and staying on task—are crucial for teachers to support. Understanding the annual goals of students with IEPs helps us become better advocates for SWDs. It also supports teacher planning, ensuring that all students have full access to the curriculum and that their needs are consistently addressed.

Teacher Tip: *Encourage your SWDs to lead a part of their IEP meeting. The resources from I'm Determined* (**www.imdetermined.org**) *support student involvement in the IEP. Students can create a presentation on their strengths, needs, and future goals. Use the Search option in the site and type "Student Involvement in the IEP" to locate all the available resources.*

Moving From the IEP Into Classroom Practice

Although the IEP may seem intimidating, it contains essential information that supports the success of SWDs in the general education classroom. To fully understand IEP requirements and your role in supporting SWDs, collaboration with special education teachers and other support staff is essential for effectively implementing the IEP in your classroom. The IEP serves as an inclusive classroom guide, influencing everything from the physical setup of your classroom and behavior management strategies to your planning, instruction, and assessment practices. Additionally, many strategies and interventions designed to support SWDs can benefit other students. By building your social studies classroom with the needs of SWDs in mind, you can foster a more inclusive environment for all learners.

Classroom Environment and Addressing Behavioral Needs

We often do not think about the classroom environment when supporting the needs of SWDs, but the environment we create can unintentionally "disable" our students. The IEP will share student needs, and some of those needs can be met by changing the classroom environment. Begin by thinking about the physical structure of your classroom. Is it fully accessible for students with mobility, visual, or hearing challenges? How do you have desks, chairs, and electronic equipment arranged? Is there adequate space to move around in the room? How is the lighting in your room, and do all students have good lines of sight? It is also important to consider the acoustics of the room and whether students can hear you and their peers without interference. Look at the poster decorations and bulletin boards in your room and consider how too much decoration or vibrant color might overstimulate a student with autism or overwhelm and distract a student with ADHD. This does not mean social studies teachers should limit their decoration; we just need to consider that how we set up our room might negatively impact some students' learning.

A structured classroom environment with clear routines is essential for student success. Establish consistent rules and positive reinforcement strategies to encourage good behavior while promptly addressing unwanted behaviors. A well-managed classroom is significant for student success. It provides routine and structure to classroom practices and requires consistency and positivity in reinforcing good behaviors while addressing unwanted behaviors. When SWDs experience barriers to learning due to behavior, teachers must identify the ABCs of behavior through observation and data collection.

The process starts by identifying the *antecedent(s)*—the events or triggers that lead to the

A Classroom With Purpose: A Guide to Teaching Social Studies Today

behavior. Next, note the *behavior* itself or the actions that follow the trigger. Finally, observe the *consequence(s)*, which are the positive or negative outcomes that follow the behavior. While this process is typically led by a special education teacher or specialist, general education teachers should also be involved in data collection if the behavior occurs in their classroom. After analysis of the behavioral data, the special education teacher or behavior specialist develops a Behavior Intervention Plan (BIP), a written plan created to provide targeted interventions for improving behavior. The BIP typically involves ongoing data collection to monitor the effectiveness of interventions and track student progress. General education teachers should be involved in the implementation of behavior supports and interventions and can help the special education teacher monitor student progress.

Creating a structured classroom environment with clear routines is essential. By establishing consistent rules and using positive reinforcement strategies, you can encourage good behavior while promptly addressing unwanted behaviors. Understanding and supporting students with a BIP will help you tailor your approach to their specific behavioral needs. The support you provide for SWDs can also be integrated into your typical classroom routines.

(i) **Teacher Tip:** *Have your students help develop expectations for classroom behavior. If you have a student with extensive support needs who needs a good role model, work with your special education teacher to select a student to serve as a peer support.*

Planning and Implementing Instruction

What are the best practices in planning and implementing instruction to ensure an inclusive learning experience for your SWDs? How can you use information from the IEP and incorporate it into your social studies lessons? The Council for Exceptional Children (CEC) asked a group of experts in special education to identify the core practices all teachers should use to effectively teach SWDs. The group identified 22 High-Leverage Practices (HLPs) that fall within the broad categories of collaboration, data-driven planning, academic and behavioral instruction, and intervention (McLeskey et al., 2019). Ciullo & Garwood (2024) examined the HLPs and highlighted six practices social studies teachers should know within instruction: HLPs 12–16 and 18. HLP 12 emphasizes explicit planning of lessons, proper pacing, and organized delivery need to be in place to guarantee learning goals are met. HLP 13 highlights the importance of adapting materials and classroom tasks to help students access content and meet instructional goals. HLP 14 involves having teachers help students learn strategies to support remembering the essential content and then apply those strategies independently when needed. One example in social studies is the use of mnemonics like "HOMES" (Huron, Ontario, Michigan, Erie, Superior) to support content memorization.

HLP 15 discusses the use of scaffolded supports to help students learn. Teachers might model the process of analyzing a primary source photograph using the SEEK (See, Explore, Examine, Know) critical visual history steps. As students gain more experience, they complete analyses without having the steps explicitly provided. The incorporation of explicit instruction is outlined in HLP 16. Explicit instruction involves tapping into prior knowledge, providing examples and nonexamples, developing guided and independent practice opportunities that use detailed directions and steps for completion, and building in formative assessment throughout the lesson. HLP 18 encourages the use of strategies that create opportunities for active student engagement. In a social studies classroom modeling HLP 18, you would see frequent use of cooperative learning and learner-centered activities in which the teacher facilitates the lesson rather than lecturing to students. The subject matter we teach in social studies is substantial and complex, requiring teachers to thoroughly understand their content and be able to break down essential vocabulary, concepts, and big ideas into manageable and understandable pieces of information to support learning. The HLPs highlighted here remind us that SWDs are successful when teachers put time into thinking about how to make their content accessible through explicit planning and instruction, adaptation of materials, and selection of evidence-based research strategies. For additional reference about HLPs, Table 8.2 provides a checklist of these six practices for use when planning lessons. In addition to the six practices just highlighted, a core HLP that all teachers should embrace is HLP 1, collaborating with professionals to increase student success. None of the HLPs can really help our SWDs if we are not collaborating with our special education teachers and support personnel.

Table 8.2 *Lesson Planning Checklist*

High-Leverage Practices (HLPs)	Universal Design for Learning (UDL)	Differentiation
☐ HLP 12: Systematically Design Instruction—Use student data and foundational knowledge to develop lesson objectives and instructional strategies. ☐ HLP 13: Adapt Curriculum Tasks and Materials—Select materials and tasks that meet student needs and determine what content is essential for all learners. ☐ HLP 14: Teach Cognitive and Metacognitive Strategies—Teach students how to organize and remember content with explicit strategies. ☐ HLP 15: Provide Scaffolded Supports—Select temporary visual, verbal, and written supports, gradually removing them when no longer needed. ☐ HLP 16: Use Explicit Instruction—Provide step-by-step instructions that help easily monitor learning goals. ☐ HLP 18: Use Strategies to Promote Active Student Engagement—Develop activities to promote active participation.	☐ Multiple Means of Representation—Use varied materials to present information in different ways. ☐ Multiple Means of Engagement—Offer choices in activities to motivate and engage all students. ☐ Multiple Means of Action and Expression—Provide choices for students to demonstrate understanding. ☐ Flexible Learning Environment—Arrange the classroom to support different learning preferences and promote better collaboration.	☐ Tailored Content—Modify the complexity of materials to match students' reading levels and interests. ☐ Varied Instructional Strategies—Use a mix of direct instruction, group work, and independent tasks to cater to different learning preferences. ☐ Flexible Grouping—Organize students into different groups based on needs, interests, or learning preferences for various activities. ☐ Scaffolding—Provide additional support (e.g., graphic organizers, models) for students who may need it.

Note. For High-Level Practices, see McLeskey et al. (2019) and Ciullo & Garwood (2024). For Universal Design for Learning, see CAST (2024) and Muente (2024). For differentiation, see Tomlinson (2014) and the IRIS module of differentiation from The IRIS Center, Peabody College, Vanderbilt University (https://iris.peabody.vanderbilt.edu/module/di/).

Differentiation and Universal Design for Learning (UDL) are two frameworks for planning and instruction that fit within the six highlighted HLPs. Differentiation is typically a responsive process of creating instruction to meet individual learning needs after the teacher evaluates those individual needs (Jenkins & Murawski, 2024; Tomlinson, 2014). It involves changing how content is delivered, providing options for the process of engaging with content, and allowing students to share their understanding of the content through a variety of products. UDL is a proactive educational framework designed to remove any barriers before students enter the classroom (CAST, 2024; Muente, 2024). While planning, teachers consider multiple ways to represent the content for the students, multiple ways for students to engage with the content, and multiple ways for students to express their understanding of what was taught. This means creating a flexible curriculum that allows all students, including those with disabilities, to access and participate in learning. Table 8.3 is a checklist teachers can add to a lesson planning template to show how the lesson differentiates instruction and meets the principles of UDL. Examples are provided for representation, engagement, and expression.

Now that you have a basic understanding of HLPs, differentiation, and UDL, consider using the checklist in Table 8.2 for planning. Also, ensure you have background information about your SWDs including their strengths, interests, preferences, needs, accommodations, modifications, and any annual goals that might apply to your lessons. Do not forget to collaborate with a teacher in special education who knows your SWDs!

Teacher Tip: *Work with a teacher partner to brainstorm how you already use HLPs, UDL, and differentiation in your classroom practice. Provide examples for each item on the checklist. You will be surprised how much you already do! For additional information and guidance about HLPs, visit the CEEDAR Center's website (*https://ceedar.education.ufl.edu/high-leverage-practices/*).*

Table 8.3 *Universal Design for Learning Lesson Plan Checklist*

Representation Options for presenting content	Engagement Options for engaging student interest	Expression Options for demonstrating student learning	Diversity, Equity, and Inclusion Considerations
☐ artifacts ☐ pictures ☐ graphic organizers ☐ video clips ☐ audio recordings ☐ lab ☐ lecture ☐ other _____ **Differentiate content**	☐ cooperative learning ☐ partner learning ☐ manipulatives ☐ movement ☐ debates ☐ role plays or simulations ☐ other _____ **Differentiate process**	☐ written response ☐ illustrated response ☐ oral response ☐ technological response ☐ model creation or construction ☐ other _____ **Differentiate product**	☐ nature of content includes learners' perspectives, values, & needs (culturally responsive) ☐ lesson supports components of SEL: empathy, resilience, and relationship building ☐ SDI, accommodations, and/or modifications ☐ other _____

Note. Adapted from Minarik & Lintner (2016) and Muente (2024).

Collaboration and Co-Teaching

Regular communication and planning with special education teachers ensures that the IEP goals are met and that your instruction is accessible for SWDs. Under the Individuals with Disabilities Education Improvement Act of 2004, special education teachers are required to provide specially designed instruction (SDI) to support the individual academic needs of SWDs in the general education classroom. SDI is a service in which the special education teacher applies research and evidence-based strategies to adapt content, deliver content, and make content easier to organize and remember in order to meet the learning needs and annual goals of students with IEPs (Beninghof, 2022). The instruction is tailored to the individual needs of a student, but the strategies and interventions may be beneficial for other students in your classroom. If the description of SDI sounds familiar, you have already read above about conceptual frameworks like UDL that easily allow SDI to be implemented within a lesson plan. General education teachers are not expected to develop SDI in their lessons or to implement SDI on their own. SDI is effectively incorporated into lessons through co-planning and co-teaching with a special education teacher who is the strategy specialist. If you have a student who struggles with written expression and you have a writing-intensive assignment in an upcoming unit, that student will need SDI to meet written expression goals in the IEP. It is your responsibility as the general education teacher to collaborate with a special education teacher to make sure you understand how to support and implement SDI in your classroom.

If co-teaching is part of your classroom structure, familiarizing yourself with the various models (e.g., one teach, one assist; one teach, one observe; parallel teaching; station teaching; alternative teaching; team teaching) is important if you want to best utilize having two or more licensed teachers in your classroom. For co-teaching to be successful, make sure you do not rely solely on the one-teach, one-assist model. If you have two licensed teachers in the classroom, neither teacher should be treated like an instructional aide. The most interactive models are station teaching and parallel teaching, and both models reduce student-to-teacher ratios and allow teachers to address more content in a single lesson. Effective co-teaching also requires regular co-planning and co-assessing. When both educators contribute to student learning and assessment, the multiple perspectives enhance learning opportunities for students. Table 8.4 provides a checklist of reminders for when you co-plan, co-teach, and co-assess.

> **Teacher Tip:** *Plan time for reflection with your co-teacher after the lesson to discuss what worked, what did not work, and how to improve for next time. Consider also including opportunities for student feedback on the lesson to inform future planning.*

Using a collaboration checklist allows social studies and special education teachers to create inclusive, engaging, and effective lessons that support all learners. Incorporating IEP information into classroom practice involves a thoughtful approach that includes SDI, differentiation, UDL, collaboration, and effective classroom management.

> **Teacher Tip:** *Make sure you are using inclusive language in your co-taught classroom. SWDs are "our students" not "your students" or "my students." In an effective co-taught classroom, it is hard to know who has an IEP and who is the content area teacher or special educator.*

Creating an Inclusive Social Studies Classroom

Entire books are written about how to support SWDs in the general education classroom, and this chapter only begins to address best practices. However, it serves as a good reminder that SWDs do need specialized attention and the social studies classroom is a great place to fully include our SWDs, especially those with extensive support needs. We know through research that SWDs who are fully included in general education are more likely to seek future education, have a job, and live independently after graduation from high school (Barrett et al., 2020). There are many ways we can promote inclusion in our schools. See the end-of-chapter checklist for ways you can promote inclusive practice in your school and for a reminder of what is needed to create a more inclusive environment for your SWDs.

If you are successfully including SWDs in your classroom, consider sharing your experiences and organizing discussions that highlight the strengths of SWDs and the benefits of inclusion. When teachers share success stories, it can positively influence the culture of a school.

This chapter covers a wide range of information, which may feel overwhelming as you consider

Table 8.4 *Checklist for Collaboration With Special Education*

Co-Planning	Co-Teaching	Co-Assessing
☐ Review IEPs Together—Discuss individual student needs and determine necessary accommodations or modifications.	☐ Co-Instructing Activities—Identify specific roles during instruction to leverage each teacher's strengths.	☐ Shared Assessment—Develop a common rubric for assessing student work, ensuring alignment with IEP goals.
☐ Develop Targeted Strategies—Collaborate on creating instructional strategies that align with both UDL and HLPs while addressing specific IEP goals.	☐ One Teach, One Assist—One teacher leads while the other supports students, keeping them on task. (limited use)	☐ Co-Teaching Models—Utilize the one-teach, one-observe model when collecting formative assessment data.
☐ Feedback Loop—Establish a process for ongoing feedback of student progress and determining the effectiveness of strategies implemented in the lesson.	☐ One Teach, One Observe—One teacher leads while the other collects data.	☐ Multiple Means of Action and Expression—Work together to develop different ways for students to show their understanding of the content.
☐ Joint Planning Sessions—Schedule regular meetings to co-plan lessons, ensuring both teachers contribute to goals and strategies.	☐ Station Teaching—Content is divided into multiple teaching centers within the room and teachers monitor or facilitate the centers.	
	☐ Parallel Teaching—Divide class into two groups that simultaneously learn the same content.	
	☐ Alternative Teaching—Small group is pulled aside for remediation, pre-teaching, or enrichment.	
	☐ Team Teaching—Both teachers equally share all aspects of instruction.	

Note. Adapted from Murawski & Spencer, 2011; Lisanti et al., 2024.

how to fully include SWDs in the classroom. However, as social studies educators, it is our responsibility to welcome all students and strive to create inclusive learning environments. Remember, by consistently applying the strategies outlined in this chapter and reflecting on your practice, you are thinking like an inclusive educator. As teachers, we are never perfect, but the best teachers are always looking for ways to improve. The social studies classroom provides an ideal setting to fully include all students, regardless of disability label. It is our responsibility to foster a more inclusive environment that supports and benefits SWDs, enriching the learning experience for everyone.

Checklist for Inclusive Practice

- ☐ **Integrate Disability Awareness:** Incorporate lessons about disability rights and history to foster understanding and acceptance of students with disabilities (SWDs).
- ☐ **Collaborate with Special Education Colleagues:** Work closely with special education staff to align strategies, support specially designed instruction, and meet IEP goals and student needs.
- ☐ **Involve Paraprofessionals:** Include paraprofessionals in planning and collaboration, ensuring they understand classroom expectations and strategies for supporting SWDs.
- ☐ **Engage Specialists:** Collaborate with related service providers (e.g., speech therapists, occupational therapists, counselors) to support individual student success.
- ☐ **Diversify Teaching Methods:** Use a variety of teaching approaches to accommodate diverse learning styles and needs.
- ☐ **Build UDL Units and Lessons:** Create lessons with multiple means of representation, engagement and expression to make content accessible to all learners.
- ☐ **Foster Positive Classroom Culture:** Establish an environment of respect, collaboration, and understanding that reinforces positive behavior.
- ☐ **Provide Structure:** Use clear expectations and routines to help students feel secure and supported.
- ☐ **Advocate for Resources:** Seek additional resources, such as aides or assistive technology, to help students succeed.
- ☐ **Participate in IEP Meetings:** Be an active advocate in IEP meetings, emphasizing inclusive practices and ensuring implementation of supports.
- ☐ **Communicate with Families:** Maintain open, consistent communication with families to keep them informed and involved.
- ☐ **Stay Informed:** Keep up to date with special education laws, policies, and best practices for inclusion.
- ☐ **Model Inclusivity:** Demonstrate inclusive language, attitudes, and actions in all interactions with students and colleagues.
- ☐ **Celebrate Diversity:** Show that diversity is valued and celebrated within the classroom community.

References

Baglieri, S., & Shapiro, A. (2017). *Disability studies and the inclusive classroom: Critical practices for creating least restrictive attitudes* (2nd ed.). Routledge.

Barrett, C. A., Stevenson, N. A., & Burns, M. K. (2020). Relationship between disability category, time spent in general education and academic achievement. *Educational Studies, 46*(4), 497–512.

Beninghof, A. M. (2022). *Specially designed instruction: Increasing success for students with disabilities.* Routledge.

CAST. (2024). *Universal design for learning guidelines, version 3.0.* **http://udlguidelines.cast.org**

Ciullo, S., Collins, A., Wissinger, D. R., McKenna, J. W., Lo, Y.-L., & Osman, D. (2020). Students with learning disabilities in the social studies: A meta-analysis of intervention research. *Exceptional Children, 86*(4), 393–412. **https://doi.org/10.1177/0014402919893932**

Ciullo, S., & Garwood, J. (2024). Integrating effective special education practices with best practices in social studies. In D. Minarik & T. Lintner (Eds.), *Creating an inclusive social studies classroom for exceptional learners* (pp. 17–41). Information Age.

Jenkins, M. C., & Murawski, W. W. (2024). *Connecting high-leverage practices to student success: Collaboration in inclusive classrooms.* Corwin.

Lintner, T., & Kumpiene, G. (2017). Social studies instruction for students with mild disabilities: An (updated) progress report. *The Journal of Social Studies Research, 41*(4), 303–310. **https://doi.org/10.1016/j.jssr.2017.03.003**

Lisanti, M., Altieri, E., & Douglas, K. (2024). Inclusive social studies through collaboration and co-teaching. In D. Minarik & T. Lintner (Eds.), *Creating an inclusive social studies classroom for exceptional learners* (pp. 45–69). Information Age.

McLeskey, J., Billingsley, B., Brownell, M. T., Maheady, L., & Lewis, T. J. (2019). What are high-leverage practices for special education teachers and why are they important? *Remedial and Special Education, 40*(6), 331–337.

Minarik, D., and Blevins, M. (2017). Going "full retard": Teaching about disability through film. In W. B. Russell, III, & S. Waters (Eds.), *Cinematic social studies: A resource for teaching and learning social studies with film* (pp. 101–128). Information Age.

Minarik, D., Grooten, R., & Lintner, T. (2021). A justice-oriented approach to addressing disability. In R. W. Evans (Ed.), *Handbook on teaching social issues* (2nd ed., pp. 339–348). Information Age.

Minarik, D., & Lintner, T. (2016). *Social studies and exceptional learners.* National Council for the Social Studies.

Minarik, D., & Lintner, T. (2024). The social studies classroom: Advocating for inclusive education. In D. Minarik & T. Lintner (Eds.), *Creating an inclusive social studies classroom for exceptional learners* (pp. 3–16). Information Age.

Muente, K. (2024). Embracing universal design for learning: Planning for inclusive social studies classrooms. In D. Minarik & T. Lintner (Eds.), *Creating an inclusive social studies classroom for exceptional learners* (pp. 97–122). Information Age.

Murawski, W. W., & Spencer, S. (2011). *Collaborate, communicate, and differentiate! How to increase student learning in today's diverse schools.* Corwin.

National Center for Education Statistics. (2024). Students with disabilities. *Condition of education.* U.S. Department of Education, Institute of Education Sciences. **https://nces.ed.gov/programs/coe/indicator/cgg**

Office of Special Education Programs. (2024). *45th annual report to Congress on the implementation of the Individuals with Disabilities Education Act, 2023.* U.S. Department of Educsation, Office of Special Education and Rehabilitative Services. **https://sites.ed.gov/idea/files/45th-arc-for-idea.pdf**

Tomlinson, C. A. (2014). *The differentiated classroom: Responding to the needs of all learners.* ASCD.

U.S. Department of Education. (2004). *Individuals with Disabilities Education Act.* U.S. Department of Education, Office of Planning, Evaluation and Policy Development. **https://sites.ed.gov/idea**

Wehmeyer, M. L., Shogren K. A., & Kurth J. (2021). The state of inclusion with students with intellectual and developmental disabilities in the United States. *Journal of Policy and Practice in Intellectual Disabilities, 18*(1), 36–43. **https://doi.org/10.1111/jppi.12332**

Chapter 9

Just Remember the
Peanut Butter and Jelly Sandwich:
Supporting Multilingual Learners

Aja E. LaDuke

Learning and language are partners. With few exceptions, language is the vehicle by which we get to any learning goal, whether it be social, academic, or functional. For that reason, teachers of all ages, grades, and subject areas need to have an understanding of language development and language diversity in the classroom. Perhaps you were a student in elementary or middle school who came into a new classroom with a home language that was not English—or perhaps you were the student who was assigned as that student's buddy to help them navigate the day, and you did your best to use gestures and nonverbal cues to communicate. Perhaps you were *always* the new student buddy because you entered school already knowing and speaking English plus another language or perhaps two. Whichever student you were, now you are a teacher of all of these students and responsible for their learning in social studies. What are the most important things to know to support students learning history and social studies in the language(s) of instruction in your classroom? How do they apply specifically to planning, instruction, and assessment in this content area given its depth and breadth? This chapter guides you through key concepts and strategies to effectively navigate and celebrate the linguistic diversity represented in your classroom.

Language About Language

A good place to begin is to reflect on the way we think about and describe students who come to our classrooms with languages other than English. The terminology used to refer to students in schools who are learning English has evolved significantly over the years. Initially labeled as "limited English proficient," students have been reassessed and relabeled as "English language learners" (ELLs), "new language learners" (NLLs), and "English learners" (ELs) among others. As education systems began to recognize that language learners are not merely "limited" in their abilities, the term "English language learners" emerged. However, even this new label had its drawbacks. Martínez (2018) argued that "English learner" emphasizes what students do not know rather than what they can do. This perspective can lead educators to view these students as monolithic, framing them primarily as struggling and at risk of failure. Such a view not only normalizes monolingualism but also fails to appreciate the diverse backgrounds and strengths that these multilingual students bring to the classroom. Research has shown that the labels we assign to students can have a profound impact on how they are perceived by teachers, peers, and even themselves (Dudley-Marling & Lucas, 2009; García, 2009). As the classroom teacher, you are setting the tone for all of your students. It is important to resist labels that take a deficit perspective of students or focus only on perceived limitations rather than their many capabilities.

More recently, the field has embraced the terms "emerging bilinguals" or "multilingual learners" as more inclusive, asset-based descriptions. These terms intentionally de-center English and acknowledge the value and rich history and complexities of other languages, and by extension, student cultures and identities. For example, the term "emerging bilingual" shifts the focus towards students' potential and existing abilities. This term recognizes that many students are already proficient in multiple languages and highlights their potential to develop language and literacy in both their home language(s) and in English. It can be helpful to think about your own experiences, victories, and challenges in learning a new language in order to keep an asset-based perspective. Your students may even inspire you to set new goals to learn the languages they speak. How can you model risk-taking and build an environment that celebrates language diversity through your own actions? How might you position your multilingual learners as experts of their own languages—with valuable knowledge to be shared with other students and the school community—even when English is the language of instruction?

Learning about your students' languages means you are learning about *them*, which is another important first step in effectively teaching any group of learners. Getting to know your students and building relationships are cornerstones of good teaching for all ages and subject areas. Be open to letting your multilingual learners surprise you and challenge any assumptions you may carry stemming from media or pervasive narratives about learning gaps that cannot be overcome. By observing students in various contexts and understanding their unique language practices, you can create instructional opportunities that build on students' existing knowledge, skills, and experiences. This chapter will introduce you to ways to plan with language in mind.

Research in K–12 education recognizes the importance of this evolution in terminology as it reflects a shift toward a more asset-focused perspective on language learning. This change in language not only influences how educators view their students but also impacts the strategies and resources they implement in the classroom. By acknowledging students' linguistic backgrounds, educators can create more inclusive environments that value diversity and promote bilingualism. This shift in terminology aligns well with the concept of translanguaging, which emphasizes the importance of utilizing all languages that students possess in the learning process.

Translanguaging

Referring to the dynamic use of multiple languages in communication, translanguaging allows students in schools to draw on their entire linguistic repertoire, rather than being limited to the language of instruction (Daniel et al., 2019). It goes beyond translation or code-switching (Martínez, 2010) in that it involves the integration of languages to make meaning and express thoughts. According to García and Wei (2014), translanguaging is a natural process that bilinguals engage in as they use their languages to navigate their experiences. This practice empowers students by recognizing and valuing their diverse linguistic backgrounds, fostering a sense of agency in their learning. When teachers create opportunities for students to use their home language *with* English, they provide pathways for deeper access to content, allowing students to connect what they are learning to their own lived experiences.

> ⓘ **Teacher Tip:** *While code-switching is the practice of alternating between two or more languages, dialects, or syntactical systems during a conversation (whether purposeful or unintentional, often based on a social setting or context), translanguaging is different.* Translanguaging *highlights the fluidity of language and how languages interconnect, rather than thinking of them exclusively as separate or to only be used one at a time, back and forth. In addition to a practice, translanguaging is considered to be a pedagogical, asset-based approach.*

In this way, translanguaging not only supports language development but also enhances overall learning by making it more relevant and meaningful to students' lives. Implementing translanguaging opportunities can significantly enhance students' comprehension, foster their engagement, and validate their identities as bilingual or multilingual individuals (Cummins et al., 2015; Garcia et al., 2017; García & Wei, 2014; Paris & Alim, 2017).

What Does Translanguaging Look Like in a History/Social Studies Classroom?

In history and social studies, translanguaging can be particularly effective in helping students explore complex concepts and engage with diverse perspectives. By allowing students to discuss historical events or social issues in their home languages, they can better articulate their thoughts and connect their experiences to the curriculum (Rodríguez et al., 2014). For instance, students might discuss the Civil Rights Movement in their home language, drawing parallels to their personal experiences, which enhances their understanding of the material.

Furthermore, translanguaging encourages critical analysis of historical narratives. When students are allowed to explore texts in multiple languages, they can compare different perspectives and interpretations of events, leading to a more nuanced understanding of history (Collins & Cioè-Peña, 2016). This practice helps students develop the skills necessary to engage with diverse viewpoints, a crucial competency in today's global society. Below are a few examples of how you could incorporate translanguaging opportunities into your lessons.

Collaborative Discussions

- **Group Work:** Organize students into small groups and encourage them to discuss social studies concepts in their home languages. This allows students to express their ideas more freely and build confidence in their understanding.
- **Think-Pair-Share:** Let students first think about a question in their home language, then discuss it with a partner before sharing with the larger class.

Writing Opportunities and Supports

- **Buddy Writing:** Pair students with different language proficiencies to write together. For instance, a student fluent in Spanish can write a paragraph in Spanish while their partner translates or responds in English.
- **Journaling:** Encourage students to maintain journals where they can write reflections, summaries, or responses in both their home language and English. This practice supports

language development and content retention.

- **Sentence Frames**: Provide sentence starters or frames in both languages to help students articulate their thoughts. For example, "In my opinion," can be translated as "En mi opinión," to guide discussions.
- **Graphic Organizers**: Use bilingual graphic organizers to help students organize information visually. This tool can assist in comparing and contrasting historical events or social issues.

Assessment and Feedback

- **Presentations**: Allow students to present social studies topics in their home languages, possibly with translations or summaries in English. This can be done through group projects, where students contribute in their preferred languages.
- **Feedback**: Provide constructive feedback that acknowledges the use of multiple languages, emphasizing the value of translanguaging in the learning process.

It may seem daunting and too time-consuming to work these opportunities into each and every lesson. Remember that you do not have to do all of them all of the time. As you become more familiar with your students and with your curriculum, you will be able to see the best matches for translanguaging opportunities and particular lessons. In addition, you are always noting what your students respond to or do not respond to. Perhaps there are certain opportunities that work particularly well to help engage your learners or move them closer to your learning objective. Take note of what works. Even if the opportunities are small in scale, incorporating room for translanguaging in history and social studies will benefit your learners, and not only your multilingual learners. Translanguaging can enhance comprehension, promote inclusivity, and foster a deeper understanding of historical and social concepts among all students (Hernandez Garcia & Schleppegrell, 2021).

The Peanut Butter and Jelly Sandwich: Including Explicit Language Objectives

All of your students, regardless of their language background, are learners of English. Perhaps they are native speakers, but through your instruction, you are guiding them to become proficient speakers, readers, writers, and listeners of English in academic, professional, and disciplinary contexts. Though you are not an English teacher, this work is embedded in what you do, and time spent focused on how language works is never time wasted. In fact, building habits of mind in your instructional planning that take language development into account is a powerful practice that will benefit all of your students (Palmer & Martínez, 2016; Souto-Manning, 2016; Vogel, 2021).

Explicit language objectives are one way to address and support language development in your instruction (Himmel, 2012). You may be familiar with crafting content objectives for your lesson. In other words, noting what students will be able to do in terms of demonstrating their mastery of the history or social studies content as aligned with national or state standards. Take a moment to think about *how* your students are going to demonstrate that they are meeting your content objective. Does it involve reading, writing, speaking, or listening? If so, your content objective has a language expectation or demand embedded within it. In order to achieve the content objective and show evidence of that, students *must* do something with language. By pulling out the specific language objectives that support the content objectives, students of all language backgrounds can benefit from an explanation of how they need to use language to be successful in the lesson. As the teacher, you are showing the students exactly what is expected.

Think about the steps to make a peanut butter and jelly sandwich. How might you describe the steps to someone who had never made one before? You might say something like this:

Step 1: Put the peanut butter on a slice of bread.
Step 2: Put the jelly on another slice of bread.
Step 3: Put the two slices together.

While not incorrect, this description is assuming a lot of the other person. Namely, an assumption is being made about existing background knowledge and experiences. What needs to happen even before Step 1? For starters, the sandwich maker would potentially need to (a) get money; (b) buy peanut butter, jelly, and bread; (c) find a butter knife and a clean surface; (d) open the peanut butter jar; and (e) put peanut butter on the knife. Even here, I have left out a few steps between (a) and (b), such as finding a mode of transportation, going to a grocery store, and deciding what brands to buy. The simple instruction in Step 1 of "Put the peanut butter on a slice of bread" is not wrong, but it keeps Steps (a)–(e) implicit rather than explicit. Step 1 does not provide a complete picture of what needs to be done in order to complete the task at hand.

In this same way, language objectives already exist within your content objectives. As a teacher focused on addressing and supporting language development, you are tasked with extracting your language objectives from your content objectives. Language objectives serve as a roadmap for both educators and students. They provide clarity about what students are expected to learn and achieve concerning language skills in a specific lesson or unit. For example, if the content objective is to analyze a historical event, the corresponding language objective might require students to "discuss the event in small groups, using academic vocabulary, and present their findings to the class." This approach ensures that language development is integrated into content learning, allowing *all* students to practice and apply their language skills in meaningful contexts.

Teacher Tip: Is academic language simply the disciplinary vocabulary of a lesson? NO! Academic language refers to the oral, written, auditory, and visual language proficiency required to learn effectively in schools and academic programs. In other words, it is the language used in classroom lessons, books, tests, and assignments, and it is the language that students are expected to learn and achieve fluency in. Frequently contrasted with "conversational" or "social" language, academic language includes a variety of formal language skills—grammar, punctuation, syntax, discipline-specific terminology, or rhetorical conventions, as well as content-area vocabulary—that allow students to acquire knowledge and academic skills while also successfully navigating school policies, assignments, expectations, and cultural norms (California Commission on Teacher Credentialing, 2024). For example, consider the use of sequence words like "first," "next," "then," and "finally" in teaching about cause and effect or describing a timeline of interrelated events. While not content-specific vocabulary words, they also hold meaning and are important to the comprehension of a text or entire lesson. This is an example of an academic language convention that students are expected to become familiar with and ultimately use in their own writing.

By articulating these objectives, teachers can ensure that all students understand the focus of their learning. When students are aware that they need to use academic language to explain their reasoning or use key terms related to a specific historical event, they can practice and refine these skills as they engage with their peers. This practice not only enhances their language proficiency but also builds confidence in their ability to communicate effectively. Let's look at a few examples in Figure 9.1.

In each of these cases, the language objective gets more specific about *how* the student is going to use language to demonstrate the content objective. This is not unique to multilingual learners as all learners will need to meet the language objective and will benefit from a detailed explanation. Your multilingual learners gain greater access to the content with additional language support strategies, but not exclusively. In all of the examples above, students are expected to use academic language in order to meet the content objective. Academic language does not always come in the form of discipline-specific vocabulary. For example, the middle school example in Figure 9.1 asks students to use transition words, which are not unique to any content area and are certainly a form of academic language in that they provide a framework for an argument to show sequence and/or cause and

Figure 9.1 *Examples of Content and Language Objectives Across Grade Levels*

Upper Elementary Lesson Plan: Understanding Community Roles

NCSS Theme: ❺ INDIVIDUALS, GROUPS, AND INSTITUTIONS

Content Objective:
Students will identify and describe various roles within their community and how these roles contribute to the community's functioning.

Language Objective:
Students will *speak* to a partner using descriptive words to explain at least three community roles and then *listen* to their partner.

Middle School Lesson Plan: The Impact of Historical Events

NCSS Theme: ❷ TIME, CONTINUITY, AND CHANGE

Content Objective:
Students will analyze the effects of a significant historical event on their local community.

Language Objective:
Students will *write* an argument expressing their views on the event's impact using transition words ("first," "next," "then," "finally").

High School Lesson Plan: Analyzing Economic Systems

NCSS Theme: ❼ PRODUCTION, DISTRIBUTION, AND CONSUMPTION

Content Objective:
Students will compare and contrast different economic systems and their effects on society.

Language Objective:
Students will *discuss* and *write* about economic concepts using key terms.

Note. NCSS Themes from *National Curriculum Standards for Social Studies: A Framework for Teaching, Learning, and Assessment*, by National Council for the Social Studies, 2010.

effect. It is important to consider all of the language expectations within a content objective, not only those related to key vocabulary.

History and social studies teachers, particularly in the upper grades, must also recognize the importance of disciplinary literacy, which refers to the specialized knowledge and skills required to read, write, and communicate effectively within a particular field. This includes understanding how historians analyze sources, interpret data, and construct arguments based on evidence. By developing disciplinary literacy, students become more adept at navigating the complexities of history and social studies, preparing them for future academic and professional pursuits, as well as engaging in civic participation (Agarwal-Rangnath, 2013; LaDuke et al., 2016). Explicit language objectives within your lesson planning can help to develop students' disciplinary literacy as well. Attending to how historians use language, for example, will guide students in both their comprehension and production of their own texts.

The inclusion of explicit language objectives also creates an inclusive learning environment. In classrooms where language objectives are consistently part of the planning process and are implemented, students who may struggle with the language of instruction are not being singled out or asked to do something different from their peers. All students are language learners—learning how to use either their home language or a new language in a variety of ways and for a variety of purposes and audiences. This approach recognizes and reinforces the idea that language is a fundamental tool for learning and is embedded in every content area and aspect of education. Additionally, as a new teacher learning to plan with assessment in mind, consider what is expected of students in terms of language. This often helps to make clear what you are looking for from your students in order to say that they have successfully met your content objective. Including language objectives as part of your planning process early on will make it part of your routine and will benefit your students for years to come.

Language Support Strategies

At the risk of overusing the example, language support strategies go with explicit language objectives like peanut butter and jelly. Once you have identified how students need to use language to meet the history or social studies content objectives, what support can you incorporate to help them get there? As previously noted, translanguaging opportunities are powerful tools and can be incorporated into a variety of lessons. In addition, specific support strategies that align with the language objective can be included in your lesson. For example, how can you support students in learning key vocabulary that they may read in a given text or be asked to use in a written response? One language support strategy is pre-teaching vocabulary.

Pre-Teaching Vocabulary

By introducing key terms and concepts before delving into a lesson, teachers can help students build a foundation of understanding. For example, if the lesson focuses on the American Revolution, teachers might introduce essential vocabulary such as "independence," "colonies," "taxation," and "revolution." This can be done through visual aids, such as flashcards or word walls, and by providing definitions and examples in context. Engaging students in discussions about these terms also solidifies their understanding and helps them make connections to prior knowledge.

New vocabulary words can often be connected to a known concept. For example, though a multilingual student may not be familiar with the term "branch" as used to describe a branch of government in English, it is likely that there is an understanding or knowledge of the word when using it to describe the branch of a tree. The core concept of something stemming from a larger body or being connected to a whole can be built upon. This is an asset-based approach that builds on what the student knows and connects a new word—or a familiar word that has a particular meaning in a disciplinary context—to that prior knowledge and better prepares the student for the lesson ahead.

Using Sentence Frames

As noted above, sentence frames can provide an opportunity for translanguaging within a lesson, particularly if they are offered in English as well as other home languages represented in the room. It is worth highlighting sentence frames as a general language support strategy because they provide students with a template to express their ideas and by extension confidence to engage with and also produce academic discourse, both spoken and written. The examples in Figure 9.2 showcase sentence frames that (a) can support students in engaging in academic discourse across content areas, (b) are more specific to history and social studies, and (c) can help students to work with peers and summarize group discussions.

Collaboration and Discussion

In the case of the peer feedback frame, there are both academic implications and benefits to social learning. These frames not only guide students in articulating their thoughts but also foster a collaborative learning environment where students can engage with their peers meaningfully and respectfully. Beyond sentence frames, encouraging students to work together in pairs or small groups is also a language support strategy—and translanguaging opportunity—that can be applied to most lessons. Peer-to-peer interaction helps students learn from one another while also allowing them to practice using language in social contexts. This is greatly beneficial to multilingual learners, but of course it is good practice for all students. Group work can enhance students' confidence in speaking

Figure 9.2 *Sentence Frame Examples for History and Social Studies*

Agreeing/Disagreeing:	Adding Information:	Clarifying Ideas:
I agree with ___ because ___. I disagree with ___ because ___.	Additionally, ___ can be seen in ___. Another important point is ___.	To clarify, I mean ___. In other words, ___.
Making Connections:	Analyzing Texts:	Discussing Historical Events:
This reminds me of ___ because ___. I can relate this to ___ because ___.	The author uses ___ to show ___. A key theme of the text is ___.	One cause of ___ was ___. The impact of ___ on ___ was significant because ___."
Evaluating Perspectives:	Sharing Ideas in Groups:	Peer Feedback:
From the perspective of ___, ___ was important because ___. People might argue that ___ due to ___.	In our group, we discussed ___ and concluded that ___. We decided that ___ is the best approach because ___.	I like how you ___ because ___. Have you considered ___? It might help because ___.

Note. Chart adapted from Sentence Frames and Starters, Colorín Colorado (**www.colorincolorado.org/teaching-ells/ell-classroom-strategy-library/sentence-frames**).

and using academic language, as they have the opportunity to discuss their ideas and clarify their understanding with peers.

Use of Culturally Relevant Texts and Text Sets

Incorporating texts that reflect students' backgrounds and experiences is crucial for creating an inclusive classroom environment. As noted in Bishop's seminal work on texts that serve as mirrors, windows, or sliding glass doors (1990), when students see their identities represented in the material, it enhances their engagement and connection to the learning process. Culturally relevant texts can also help students understand diverse perspectives and foster empathy. Text sets allow educators to provide materials that are appropriately challenging for all students, providing selections that range in text complexity but convey the essential facts or concepts. This ensures that all students can engage with the content and work towards achieving the same learning objectives. By using text sets in conjunction with existing curricular materials, educators can deepen students' understanding of the content and foster greater engagement, making learning more accessible to students across all levels of language proficiency (Henry et al., 2021; LaDuke et al., 2016).

Text sets can include books, articles, videos, multimedia resources, and primary documents. The integration of text sets into curricular programs, especially alongside required history and social studies textbooks, can greatly enhance students' access to content and assist them in meeting learning objectives. Well-curated text sets provide multiple perspectives on a given topic or event, some of which may represent the perspective of the student if they are coming to the lesson with background knowledge or a deeper connection to it. By offering diverse formats and viewpoints, text sets allow students to engage with material in a more meaningful way. For instance, when studying the Civil Rights Movement, a text set might include autobiographies of key figures, scholarly articles analyzing the movement, multimedia presentations, and primary source documents such as letters and speeches.

Sample Text Sets

Tables 9.1–9.4 contain some examples of effective text sets for specific historical topics, along with a brief description of each text included in the sets. Of course, these text sets can be adapted based on students' grade levels and interests, making historical topics more relatable and engaging.

Table 9.1 *Text Set for the American Civil Rights Movement*

Text Type	Text and Description
Primary Source Document	"Letter from Birmingham Jail" by Martin Luther King Jr. This letter provides insight into King's philosophy of nonviolent protest and his views on justice and civil disobedience.
Narrative Nonfiction	*March: Book One* by John Lewis This graphic novel recounts the experiences of John Lewis during the Civil Rights Movement, making the history accessible and engaging.
Biography	*Rosa Parks: My Story* by Rosa Parks Parks's autobiography tells her perspective on her role in the movement and the events surrounding her famous act of resistance.
Poetry	"Still I Rise" by Maya Angelou This poem reflects themes of strength and resilience, resonating with the struggles faced during the Civil Rights Movement.

Table 9.2 *Text Set for the American Revolution*

Text Type	Text and Description
Historical Overview	*A People's History of the American Revolution* by Ray Raphael (selected chapters) This text provides a different perspective on the American Revolution, focusing on the experiences of everyday people.
Primary Source Document	The Declaration of Independence An essential document that outlines the colonies' reasons for seeking independence from British rule.
Biography	*Founding Brothers: The Revolutionary Generation* by Joseph J. Ellis (selected chapters) This book explores the lives of key figures in the Revolution, providing insight into their motivations and relationships.
Fiction	*Rebellion 1776* or *Chains* by Laurie Halse Anderson Both are historical fiction novels that chronicle the experiences of young girls during the American Revolution—one free and one enslaved, both grapple with the loss of family members and taking on new challenges and identities in order to survive.

Table 9.3 *Text Set for the Women's Suffrage Movement*

Text Type	Text and Description
Primary Source Document	Declaration of Sentiments from the Seneca Falls Convention This document outlines the grievances and demands of women seeking equal rights, marking a pivotal moment in the suffrage movement.
Narrative Nonfiction	*Votes for Women: The Fight for Suffrage in the United States* by Winifred Conkling This book provides an engaging and informative overview of the suffrage movement, highlighting key events and figures.
Biography	*My Own Story* by Emmeline Pankhurst Pankhurst's autobiography shares her experiences and the strategies used in the fight for women's suffrage.
Poetry	"Women" by Alice Walker This poem celebrates the strength and resilience of women, connecting to the themes of empowerment in the suffrage movement.

Table 9.4 *Text Sets for the Great Depression*

Text Type	Text and Description
Historical Overview	*The Great Depression: A Diary* by Benjamin Roth This diary provides a firsthand account of the experiences of individuals during the Great Depression, offering personal perspectives on economic hardship.
Primary Source Document	Franklin D. Roosevelt's First Inaugural Address This speech is significant for understanding Roosevelt's response to the crisis and his vision for recovery.
Biography	*The Grapes of Wrath* by John Steinbeck (selected passages) Steinbeck's novel portrays the struggles of a family during the Great Depression, illustrating the broader societal impacts.
Documentary Film	*The Dust Bowl* by Ken Burns This documentary explores the environmental and economic challenges faced during the Great Depression, providing visual and narrative context.

Supporting Newcomers and Including Home Languages

Supporting newcomers in the classroom requires intentional strategies and a commitment to fostering an inclusive environment. Even as a monolingual English-speaking teacher, you can significantly impact the educational experiences of students new to the country (Vogel, 2021). Newcomers often arrive with varying levels of educational background and language proficiency. These students may experience feelings of isolation, confusion, and anxiety as they adjust to a new culture and educational system (Jaffee, 2016). It is crucial for teachers to acknowledge these emotional and social challenges while also addressing academic needs as best they can. The recommendations throughout this chapter to support multilingual learners also apply to newcomers for whom English is brand new. Think of the suggestions below as additions to a list you have already been making while reading this chapter.

Creating a Multilingual Classroom Environment

As a first step, creating a safe and welcoming classroom environment can help newcomers feel more comfortable and encouraged to participate. A supportive and understanding approach not only aids newcomers in their adjustment, but also enriches the entire classroom community, preparing all students for a diverse world. Your students will follow your lead. You may be unsure of how to help your newcomer and feel uneasy or even guilty about not having enough tools in your belt as a new teacher—and that is okay. Ignoring or avoiding your student is not (Kohli & Solórzano, 2012). As long as you are showing that your classroom is a place where your newcomer belongs, your students will follow suit.

One of the simplest ways to create a multilingual classroom environment is to include home languages in signage and labels around the room. You can label classroom objects in multiple languages, particularly the language of the newcomer and any other home languages that your students speak. You can invite students to share words, phrases, or stories from their home languages during class. Home languages are not just a means of communication; they are a vital part of a student's identity and cultural background. When you can acknowledge and integrate these languages into your teaching, you send a powerful message that all languages and cultures are valued. Research shows that young learners who develop their home language skills alongside their second language often perform better academically (Martinez et al., 2008; Pacheco & Miller, 2016; Rodríguez et al., 2014). By respecting and incorporating home languages, teachers can create a more engaging and effective learning environment, providing an opportunity for students to learn from one another and enriching their understanding of different cultures (Noguerón-Liu, 2020; Osorio, 2020).

Utilizing Visual Supports

Another effective strategy for monolingual English teachers, or for multilingual teachers who do not share a language with their newcomer, is to incorporate visual aids into their lessons. Visual aids such as images, charts, and realia can help students understand concepts without relying solely on language. For instance, when teaching a new topic, a teacher can use pictures or diagrams to illustrate key ideas. This approach not only supports language acquisition but also enhances comprehension, allowing newcomers to grasp content alongside their peers. Think of a visual aid as a "text" within a text set, as it is providing an entry point to the content.

Collaborating With Families and Communities

Engaging parents and communities can significantly enhance the support newcomers receive. You can reach out to families to understand their cultural backgrounds, expectations, and challenges. Seek out help from your school and district colleagues. This collaboration can involve organizing community events, inviting parents and family members to share their experiences, and providing resources in multiple languages. These collaborations can help you find the spaces within your content and curricular programs to integrate the funds of knowledge (Moll et al., 2006) represented within your families and wider community while still meeting standards and moving toward learning outcomes. Building a network of support helps newcomers feel connected and valued in the school community.

Utilizing Technology as a Tool

Technology can serve as a powerful resource for supporting newcomers and for multilingual learners in general. Online translation tools, language learning apps, and educational websites can assist students in overcoming language barriers. As with all educational technology tools, be sure to evaluate them and ask around about which ones have been most effective with students. You can also ask your students directly too! Translation apps, in particular, are not completely accurate but can often be the catalyst for learning about nuanced meanings and expressions that are unique to a particular culture. Additionally, as generative artificial intelligence tools continue to grow and advance, these can be a resource as well. Of course, as with any text or teaching resource we bring into our instruction, it is important to consider the source, quality, and potential impact of each one. Remember to consult the educational technology experts in your school or district as well as school leaders regarding any relevant policies.

What Now?

As a new teacher, you are encouraged to try these strategies to fit the unique needs of your classroom to foster a culture of inclusivity and respect for all languages and cultures. By understanding the importance of terminology, creating clear language objectives and incorporating language supports within lesson and unit plans, you can significantly enhance the learning experience for *all* students, particularly those who are multilingual. Ultimately, this approach will help create a more equitable and supportive educational environment for every learner.

Checklist for Supporting Multilingual Learners

☐ Be mindful of terminology and ways of referring to students—intention vs. impact.

☐ Remember that it is the responsibility of teachers to help all students acquire and develop proficiency in English; however, there are ways to do this that do not denigrate students' home languages or mistake a diverse language background as a deficit. It is our responsibility to model this mindset about language for our students.

☐ Be open to learning who your students (and their families) are—and perhaps leaving your comfort zone in order to do so (e.g., trying to speak a new language, etc.).

☐ Consider *all* learners in your classroom as learners of English—speakers of other home languages and native speakers alike.

☐ Think about what you are asking students to do in terms of reading, writing, speaking, and listening to achieve the content objective(s) of your lesson.

☐ Incorporate language support and objectives in instruction consistently to benefit *all* learners.

☐ Remember that *all* teachers, even those who are monolingual English speakers, can support newcomers and the language and literacy development of all students both in English and their respective home languages.

☐ Seek out your colleagues and specialists at your school or within your districts who have expertise in instruction and assessment for bilingual and multilingual learners and translanguaging pedagogy. Ask them what you should be reading or what they have learned from a recent conference. Consider co-teaching opportunities or scheduling a time to observe their teaching.

☐ Think of multilingualism as an asset, not a problem.

☐ Give yourself space and grace to try, fail, and try again! It will be worth it.

References

Agarwal-Rangnath, R. (2013). *Social studies, literacy, and social justice in the common core classroom: A guide for teachers.* Teachers College Press.

Bishop, R. S. (1990). Mirrors, windows, and sliding glass doors. *Perspectives: Choosing and Using Books for the Classroom, 6*(3), ix–xi.

California Commission on Teacher Credentialing (2024). *California teacher performance assessment guide instructional cycle 1, multiple subject, learning about students and planning instruction.* Version 7.0

Collins, B. A., & Cioè-Peña, M. (2016). Declaring freedom: Translanguaging in the social studies classroom to understand complex texts. In O. García & T. Kleyn (Eds.), *Translanguaging with multilingual students* (pp. 118–139). Routledge.

Cummins, J., Hu, S., Markus, P., & Kristiina Montero, M. (2015). Identity texts and academic achievement: Connecting the dots in multilingual school contexts. *TESOL Quarterly, 49*(3), 555–581.

Daniel, S. M., Jiménez, R. T., Pray, L., & Pacheco, M. B. (2019). Scaffolding to make translanguaging a classroom norm. *TESOL Journal, 10*(1), e00361.

Dudley-Marling, C., & Lucas, K. (2009). Pathologizing the language and culture of poor children. *Language Arts, 86*(5), 362–370.

García, O. (2009). Emergent bilinguals and TESOL: What's in a name? *TESOL Quarterly, 43*(2), 322–326.

García, O., Johnson, S. I., & Seltzer, K. (2017). *The translanguaging classroom: Leveraging student bilingualism for learning.* Caslon.

García, O., & Wei, L. (2014). *Translanguaging: Language, bilingualism, and education.* Palgrave Macmillan.

Henry, R., LaDuke, A. E., & Porrata, A. (2021). Using text sets to support the development of biliteracy in "English-only" elementary classrooms. In A. Vandehei-Carter, N. Villanueva, & C. Clark (Eds.), *Multicultural curriculum transformation in literacy and language arts* (pp. 107–123). Lexington Books.

Hernandez Garcia, M., & Schleppegrell, M. J. (2021). Culturally sustaining disciplinary literacy for bi/multilingual learners: Creating a translanguaging social studies classroom. *Journal of Adolescent & Adult Literacy, 64*(4), 449-454.

Himmel, J. (2012). *Language objectives: The key to effective content area instruction for English learners.* Colorín Colorado.

Jaffee, A. T. (2016). Social studies pedagogy for Latino/a newcomer youth: Toward a theory of culturally and linguistically relevant citizenship education. *Theory & Research in Social Education, 44*(2), 147–183.

Kohli, R., & Solórzano, D. G. (2012). Teachers, please learn our names!: Racial microaggressions and the K–12 classroom. *Race Ethnicity and Education, 15*(4), 441–462.

LaDuke, A., Lindner, M., & Yanoff, E. (2016). Content, disciplinary, and critical literacies in the C3 and common core. *Social Studies Research and Practice, 11*(3), 96–111.

Martínez, R. A. (2010). Spanglish as literacy tool: Toward an understanding of the potential role of Spanish-English code-switching in the development of academic literacy. *Research in the Teaching of English, 45*(2), 124–149.

Martínez, R. A. (2018). Beyond the English learner label: Recognizing the richness of bi/multilingual students' linguistic repertoires. *The Reading Teacher, 71*(5), 515–522.

Martínez, R. A., Orellana, M. F., Pacheco, M., & Carbone, P. (2008). Found in translation: Connecting translating experiences to academic writing. *Language Arts, 85*(6), 421–431.

Moll, L., Amanti, C., Neff, D., & González, N. (2006). Funds of knowledge for teaching: Using a qualitative approach to connect homes and classrooms. In N. González, L. C. Moll, & C. Amanti (Eds.), *Funds of knowledge: Theorizing practices in households, communities, and classrooms* (pp. 71–87). Routledge. (Reprinted from "Funds of knowledge for teaching: Using a qualitative approach to connect homes and classrooms," 1992, *Theory Into Practice, 31*[2], 132–141)

National Council for the Social Studies. (2010). *National curriculum standards for social studies: A framework for teaching, learning, and assessment,*

Noguerón-Liu, S. (2020). Expanding the knowledge base in literacy instruction and assessment: Biliteracy and translanguaging perspectives from families, communities, and classrooms. *Reading Research Quarterly, 55*(S1), S307–S318.

Osorio, S. L. (2020). Building culturally and linguistically sustaining spaces for emergent bilinguals: Using read-alouds to promote translanguaging. *The Reading Teacher, 74*(2), 127–135.

Pacheco, M. B., & Miller, M. E. (2016). Making meaning through translanguaging in the literacy classroom. *The Reading Teacher, 69*(5), 533–537.

Palmer, D. K., & Martínez, R. A. (2016). Developing biliteracy: What do teachers really need to know about language? *Language Arts, 93*(5), 379–385.

Paris, D., & Alim, H. S. (Eds.). (2017). *Culturally sustaining pedagogies: Teaching and learning for justice in a changing world.* Teachers College Press.

Rodríguez, D., Carrasquillo, A., & Lee, K. S. (2014). *The bilingual advantage: Promoting academic development, biliteracy, and native language in the classroom.* Teachers College Press.

Souto-Manning, M. (2016). Honoring and building on the rich literacy practices of young bilingual and multilingual learners. *The Reading Teacher, 70*(3), 263–271.

Umansky, I. M. (2016). To be or not to be EL: An examination of the impact of classifying students as English learners. *Educational Evaluation and Policy Analysis, 38*(4), 714–737.

Vogel, S. (2021). *Teaching bilinguals (even if you're not one): A CUNY-NYSIEB Web series.* CUNY-NYS Initiative on Emergent Bilinguals. **www.cuny-nysieb.org/teaching-bilinguals-webseries**

Chapter 10
Transforming Social Studies Through Technology

Ed Finney

Technology has transformed my teaching by allowing me to create engaging, inclusive lessons. When I began my career as a social studies teacher in the mid-1990s, I recognized both the importance and the challenges of technology integration. I was determined and excited to explore how technology could enhance student learning. I believe history should be more than just textbooks and dates; it should prepare students for the advancing, technology-rich world beyond our district. As a new teacher, my goal was to learn how I could maximize the potential of my then-high-tech classroom, which consisted of three Macintosh Performa computers, a VCR, and an overhead projector.

Attending my first National Council for the Social Studies (NCSS) conference in Chicago was eye-opening and a turning point in my career. It connected me with like-minded educators committed to transforming their social studies classrooms. I was immediately hooked, making it my goal to attend NCSS conferences every year. A career highlight was meeting and joining the NCSS Technology Community at the annual conference. They were an incredible group of educators dedicated to advancing social studies education through technology. Becoming an active member of the Technology Community provided access to a supportive network, and I looked forward to our monthly Zoom meetings to "geek out" over technology tools and to plan technology sessions for the annual conference. I would highly recommend any new teacher to become involved with NCSS and state and local social studies councils.

For my district, the pandemic spurred an overnight change from in-person learning on Friday to remote learning on Monday, accelerating the adoption of digital tools and platforms. Tools and resources like Clever, Nearpod, Pear Deck, Seesaw, Canvas, Zoom, Kami, and Google Classroom became essential in the social studies classroom. Technology became central to the remote educational process, not just a supplement. Teachers who were reluctant to integrate technology prior to the pandemic realized they did not have a choice during virtual learning. Even after the return to in-person learning, many of these tools remained integral to the educational foundations of schools. Teachers who may have never considered using technology in the classroom became comfortable with the tools. The pandemic accelerated the rapid increase of schools adopting one-to-one device programs and a well-rounded catalog of educational technology to enhance and facilitate teaching. Many districts decommissioned their computer labs and rolling carts after the pandemic due to the transition to one-to-one devices. Schools allowed students to take computers home for after-school assignments. Change in education has historically been slow, but the need for technology during the pandemic showcased the value of technology integration and accelerated technology adoption.

Professional Development and Networking

As a new or pre-service social studies teacher, it is important to develop an understanding and background knowledge of the various types of technology available to teachers, such as learning management systems (LMS) like Google Classroom or Canvas; interactive tools like Nearpod, EdPuzzle, and Kahoot; and artificial intelligence (AI) tools like SchoolAI and MagicSchool. Most educational technology companies offer free certification programs and professional development on their tools, providing strategies for purposefully integrating technology into your classroom to create engaging learning opportunities. Most certifications and professional development programs take about 30 minutes to an hour to complete. The programs give you deeper insights about the tool and demonstrate strategies to gain valuable skills that can enhance student engagement and learning outcomes. Many of the certification programs offer special perks like beta access to new features, a free account, swag, fun badges to add to your email signature, and possibly the chance to demonstrate the technology at a conference.

The International Society for Technology in Education (ISTE) provides a wealth of information, support, and resources to transform learning experiences and to increase student engagement in social studies through technology. ISTE U is a virtual catalog of professional development courses geared toward strengthening your ability to engage students in lessons promoting critical thinking and digital literacy application. Both self-paced and instructor-led courses are available for a fee. If you or your district is a member of ISTE, you are able to choose a course free of charge. Examples of course topics include accessibility and Universal Design for Learning (UDL), media and literacy, and global collaboration. ISTE offers the chance to earn an internationally recognized ISTE Certified Educator credential. Over about nine months, participants complete 40 hours of learning and then create a portfolio within 6 months to demonstrate their mastery of the standards. The process is rigorous but leads to meaningful growth as an educator.

Both Google and Microsoft offer online training and certifications that are both robust and prestigious and are available at a relatively low cost. Obtaining Google Level 1 Certification typically requires about 10 hours of preparation, followed by a 3-hour exam. The Level 2 certification takes a similar amount of preparation time. The Microsoft Certified Educator (MCE) certification requires approximately 10 hours of preparation and a 1-hour exam. Earning the Google Educator Level 1 and Google Educator Level 2 credentials is an accomplishment that will help you in the classroom and make you stand out during future interviews. Through a similar process, Microsoft offers certification as a Microsoft Educator. Maintaining an updated resume and portfolio of certifications and professional training is important. You earned the certification, so showcase them! Participating in training and certifications can often connect you with a community of educators interested in the tool, offering collaboration opportunities and access to shared resources. Understanding the tools could potentially give you an edge during the interview process and open opportunities for you in your new district. Technology in the arena of education is constantly evolving; it is a professional responsibility to stay current.

Technology has transformed how we learn and collaborate on pedagogy, curriculum, resources, and strategies. Developing an educational social media account focused on your professional interests can be highly beneficial. (See Chapter 11 for tips for educators using social media.) Social media creates the opportunity for ongoing professional development, allowing you to connect and collaborate with educators from around the world, develop a Personal Learning Network

(PLN), share resources and lessons, and stay informed about the latest trends in educational technology. Many educators would be lost without the support of their PLN.

> *i* **Teacher Tip:** *A Personal Learning Network (PLN) is a group of like-minded educators who share and collaborate on topics of mutual interest. PLNs are easy to build through social media by searching for and joining groups like "AI in Education" or "Nearpod in Social Studies." These networks provide valuable insights, and I have gained a wealth of knowledge from my own PLNs.*

Data Privacy and Protection

We have become almost desensitized to the frequent news of data breaches and ransomware attacks. Companies in various industries including telecommunications, healthcare, retail, and even technology have made headlines for data breaches and ransomware attacks, but data breaches are a real threat and concern to school districts too. In 2023, Minneapolis Public Schools had a serious breach that affected more than 100,000 people. Districts store sensitive student data like discipline records, Individualized Education Programs (IEPs), medical history, and family custody information that can be used to steal a student's identity (Cardoza, 2024). It is important for you to protect your students and yourself. It is the role of the teacher to protect a student's personally identifiable information (PII), which is anything that could identify a student, such as a name, email address, physical address, assessment scores, or student work. It is important to follow your state's and district's data policies to protect both you and your students.

Although the massive number of digital tools available can enhance classroom learning, it has inherently increased the number of cyberattacks and data breaches. For this reason, districts should have a list of approved technology tools for use in the classroom that have been vetted by the administration and deemed safe and beneficial for the classroom. On the federal level, laws such as the Family Educational Rights and Privacy Act (FERPA) and the Children's Online Privacy Protection Act (COPPA) have been enacted to help protect students and families. In addition to federal regulations, 40 states currently have their own laws about student data privacy. For instance, you may have noticed web-based games creating a unique username for you. That was done to protect your privacy. If using an online game or program that requires students to add their name, consider randomly giving them a name that corresponds to what you are learning about in class. Or you can keep a deck of playing or sport cards in your desk and hand each student a different card to assign usernames. They can sign in as "Harriet Tubman," "Franklin Delano Roosevelt," "Aaron Judge," or "Ace of Spades."

Data Safety Tips to Consider in the Social Studies Classroom

- Adopt a less-is-more approach when using or assigning technology that requires students and teachers to log in by providing a first and last name. Know your district's data policy and make sure the tool is approved by the district before use.
- Do not enter a student's name or any information that can identify the student when using AI tools like ChatGPT, Claude, or Gemini.
- Have knowledge of your state's data laws. Over 40 states have their own data privacy regulation. For example, New York State Education Law section 2-d requires each district to have a signed data policy agreement with any technology company that collects

PII. The agreement must be posted online for parents to view. The law also creates requirements for how companies must respond to data breaches, ensuring that there are clear protocols for protecting and managing student data.

- It is important to follow your district's technology plan and data policy (if they have one). The district administration and the classroom teacher are responsible for ensuring the educational technology is integrated into the class safely and appropriately and provides opportunities for meaningful learning.
- If you are not sure about using a technology tool that is not approved by your district, ask someone, usually the building principal or director of technology.
- If your district has a list of approved tools, make sure you consult it. Using district-approved tools, taking caution with technology that collects PII, and being aware of state laws will help keep your students' data safe and protect you!

Teacher Tip: *Data Privacy Laws*
- *Family Educational Rights and Privacy Act (FERPA): A federal law that protects the privacy of student education records*
- *Children's Online Privacy Protection Act (COPPA): A federal law that creates requirements for operators of websites or online services directed to children under 13*
- *State laws: Many states have their own regulations regarding student data privacy. For example, New York State Education Law section 2-d requires school districts to have a data policy agreement signed with the technology company.*

SAMR and TEMPEST

Meaningful and impactful technology integration goes far beyond a teacher selecting a tool because it looks fun or is trendy. Effective integration transforms teaching and learning in significant, intentional ways. Ruben R. Puentedura's SAMR model (Substitution, Augmentation, Modification, Redefinition) provides a framework for evaluating how technology either enhances or transforms a lesson.

In addition, I created the TEMPEST model to help teachers design and integrate technology in meaningful, purposeful ways. This strategy was specifically designed to support the creation of engaging, goal-oriented, and standards-aligned lessons. When paired, SAMR and TEMPEST offer educators a comprehensive approach for integrating technology effectively in the classroom. Together, these frameworks empower teachers to integrate technology that transforms their lessons by cultivating creativity, increasing engagement, and preparing students for the 21st century. Incorporating these models assures that the technology integration is not only effective but also meaningful and impactful.

TEMPEST in Social Studies

Engaging students in my social studies classroom has always been at the forefront of my lesson objectives. While technology integration offered a high level of student engagement, I was mindful of the scarce commodity of classroom time and needed to confirm that the lessons were meaningful and purposeful. The TEMPEST model guides teachers in creating effective, innovative lessons that balance engagement with educational value. TEMPEST has become a cornerstone of my teaching, and I frequently share its impact and implementation during professional development sessions and conferences. This model ensures that the selected technology enhances the lesson rather than detracting from learning.

Teachers should understand the SAMR model Substitution, Augmentation, Modification, Redefinition to integrate technology in ways that transform teaching and learning. In the Substitution stage, technology replaces traditional tools without changing the task, such as using Google Docs instead of pen and paper. Augmentation builds on the technology integration in which the technology acts as a direct substitution with improvements, like allowing real-time collaboration on a Google Doc. The Modification stage involves thinking outside the box and redesigning the lesson, such as enabling students to create multimedia presentations with text, images, and hyperlinks using Canva or Google Slides instead of writing a traditional research paper. Finally, at the Redefinition level, technology allows for the creation of entirely new tasks that were previously inconceivable, such as collaborating with students from around the world on a project or creating a Ken Burns-style documentary using Canva, iMovie, or Adobe Express. By moving through these stages, teachers can transition from using technology simply for efficiency or as a gimmick to using it in ways that transcend the learning experience, making it more engaging, collaborative, and transformative. As dynamic and exciting as Redefinition is, not all lessons need to be at this level. Use Redefinition for unit projects, when you are prompting students to solve real-world problems, increasing student engagement, or wanting your students to share their work with an audience.

I first applied TEMPEST to an eighth-grade lesson about the 1920s, transforming a traditional essay assignment into a documentary-style video production focusing on the essential question: "How were the 1920s an era of great change?" Students were provided with a list of possible topics but were encouraged to explore any topic that piqued their interest. Some of the most memorable projects focused on the toaster, football, flappers, jazz, and automobiles. Using artifact analysis sheets adapted from the National Archives, students researched and explored images, radio broadcasts, newspapers, and advertisements to tell the story of their topic. They then crafted their research into a documentary script, including images, sources, and text for approval prior to recording.

For the 1920s project, I selected two easily integrated technology tools: Adobe Express and Canva. Canva offers free premium access to educators through Canva for Education. It is definitely worth checking out! However, I also left the door open for students to use more robust software (with my approval) if they were proficient with it. These tools allowed students to seamlessly incorporate images, video, music, and their own voice narration, resulting in professional-looking video productions. For the video premiere day, we transformed the classroom into a 1920s theater, complete with an excited audience.

The TEMPEST model emphasizes that technology should support and not overshadow the content of the lesson. It ensures that technology integration is purposeful, meaningful, and aligned with educational goals. TEMPEST guides educators in choosing appropriate technology tools that enhance engagement, foster creativity through project-based learning, and support standards while also evaluating whether technology adds value beyond traditional teaching methods. It helps create cutting-edge, relevant lessons that prepare students with real-world skills and enhance their learning experience.

The TEMPEST model helps prepare students for careers and college by ensuring that technology integration in lessons is meaningful, purposeful, skill-driven, and aligned with real-world demands.

By emphasizing transferable academic and life skills, critical thinking, creativity, and digital literacy, TEMPEST cultivates authentic learning experiences that reflect the technology-rich environments of modern workplaces and higher education. It also encourages students to engage and excel in skills and interests they are already proficient in or are eager to explore further. With the rapid adoption of artificial intelligence across industries, a new skill set is emerging. Students must not only understand but also be prepared to use technology and artificial intelligence effectively. By adopting the TEMPEST framework, teachers can ensure that all students are equipped to navigate future challenges with confidence and competence.

TEMPEST, as its name suggests, is a storm brewing against the rising tide of negative perceptions about technology use. It is critical for social studies teachers to differentiate between educational technology and the recreational platforms students engage with, such as Snapchat and Instagram. Teachers can protect the integrity of their lessons by integrating SAMR and TEMPEST and making thoughtful, intentional choices when integrating technology into the social studies classroom (see Figure 10.1 for a checklist). The TEMPEST framework should be aligned to your purpose and goals as an educator. To help implement this framework, the Quick Integration Checklist has been included (see Figure 10.2).

Figure 10.1 *The TEMPEST Checklist*

T.E.M.P.E.S.T.

A Framework for Future-Ready Technology Integration
Use this checklist to guide meaningful tech integration into your lessons and help students build digital skills for tomorrow's careers.

T – Teacher-Driven
Technology use is intentional, purposeful, and led by the teacher.
- ☑ Is the tech chosen with a clear instructional purpose?
- ☑ Does it go beyond simple substitution (e.g., digital worksheet)?
- ☑ Can the goal be met more effectively with traditional methods?
- ☑ Is the tech supporting a need that traditional tools can't address?

E – Educational Goals
Technology supports specific learning outcomes.
- ☑ Does the tech align with curriculum goals and standards?
- ☑ What value does the tech add—efficiency, engagement, differentiation?
- ☑ Does it address a challenge in the lesson (e.g., diverse learners, IEP/504)?
- ☑ Are students learning transferable academic and life skills?

M – Meaningful
Tech use is impactful, equitable, and worth the time.
- ☑ Is the tech necessary to enhance the learning experience?
- ☑ Does it foster collaboration, critical thinking, or independence?
- ☑ Are students applying knowledge in authentic, real-world ways?
- ☑ Are accessibility and inclusivity considered in tool selection?

P – Project-Based Creativity
Students create, collaborate, and innovate.
- ☑ Does the lesson include opportunities for student choice and design?
- ☑ Is there space for exploration, inquiry, or creativity?
- ☑ Are students solving problems or showcasing learning in new ways?
- ☑ Can this reflect tasks they might encounter in future careers?

E – Engaging
Students are active, not passive, in the learning process.
- ☑ Is the technology effective in capturing and maintaining student interest?
- ☑ Does it offer interactive, hands-on, or student-led experiences?
- ☑ Does the lesson provide opportunities for student choice and voice?
- ☑ Are students using tools to express ideas and make connections?

S – Standards-Aligned
Tech tools support academic rigor and accountability.
- ☑ Is the tech aligned with state or national standards (e.g., ISTE)?
- ☑ Is it supporting required content objectives?
- ☑ Is digital citizenship embedded in the activity?

T – Tomorrow-Ready
Prepares students for the digital demands of future jobs.
- ☑ Are students practicing real-world tech skills (e.g., collaboration tools, coding, digital design)?
- ☑ Does the activity build adaptability, creativity, and problem-solving?
- ☑ Are students working in ways that mirror future work environments?
- ☑ Are communication, digital fluency, and ethical tech use modeled?

Ed Finney 2024

Note. TEMPEST Educational Framework Checklist for Instructional Design, by E. Finney, 2024. Copyright 2024 by Ed Finney.

Figure 10.2 *The Quick Start TEMPEST Checklist*

TEMPEST Quick Integration Checklist

A Framework for Future-Ready Technology Integration
Use this checklist to guide meaningful tech integration into your lessons and help students build digital skills for tomorrow's careers.

☑ **Technology Purpose**
- The technology is essential to achieving lesson objectives.
- The tech provides unique learning opportunities not possible with traditional methods.
- The tech help promote higher-order thinking or unique problem-solving opportunities.

☑ **Learning Goals**
- Directly supports curriculum standards
- Enhances student understanding of key concepts
- Measurable learning outcomes identified

☑ **Meaningful Engagement**
- Promotes active student participation
- Encourages critical thinking
- Provides opportunities for creativity and student choice

☑ **Accessibility Check**
- All students can access and use the technology
- Accommodations for different learning needs considered
- Minimal technical barriers

☑ **Standards Alignment**
- Supports curriculum standards
- Aligns with technology integration guidelines
- Supports development of digital literacy and transferable life skills

Teacher Tip: If you cannot confidently check most boxes, reconsider the technology integration.

SAMR Check

☐ Technology substitutes a traditional tool with no change
☐ Technology improves the functionality of a traditional method
☐ Technology redesigns the learning task in a significant way
☐ Technology enables creation of entirely new learning experiences

Ed Finney 2024

Note. TEMPEST Quick Integration Checklist, by E. Finney, 2024. Copyright 2024 by Ed Finney.

Be Prepared for the Unexpected!

Teaching a classroom full of excited students waiting for your directions does not leave much room to troubleshoot unexpected technology issues. Always have a "Plan B" lesson in case the technology fails. Do not panic; take a deep breath and smoothly transition to an alternative activity.

I found it helpful to keep a few folders with interesting and engaging social studies activities and resources on hand (e.g., map activities, document analysis sheets, current event articles, short readings, curriculum-based enrichment activities). These Plan B lesson materials should still offer value for student learning opportunities while also giving you time to solve the technology issue or to transition to a new lesson.

Tips for Ensuring Smooth Technology Integration

- **Check Student Access in Advance:** Try accessing any websites that students need to access on a student device to make sure they are not blocked.
- **Log in to Websites in Advance:** Ensure that all needed websites are working properly and that you do not need to reset a password.
- **Know Your Classroom Technology:** Familiarize yourself with the technology in your room, like the digital display, sound system, and document camera. Practice changing sources on the display, such as changing the sound output from the computer to the digital display or sound bar.
- **Identify Tech Support:** Know who to contact if a technology issue arises. This could be a teacher across the hall, a student in your class, or the IT department.

Remember, all teachers have experienced some sort of technology issue. Do not panic! Showing calm and flexibility will positively model resilience for your students.

i **Teacher Tip:** *Power and internet outages are out of our control, but they happen. Use the checklist and "Plan B" above to reduce the chance for technology issues.*

Artificial Intelligence for Teachers

It will come as no surprise that the demands placed on teachers today have increased greatly, often leading to burnout as teachers leave the profession they once loved. The power of AI can help reduce some of the stress and time spent on routine tasks, allowing you to focus on what truly matters: your students, creating an engaging curriculum, crafting lessons, addressing students' emotional needs, and overall classroom management. Teachers can now ask AI questions about content, suggestions to correct student behavior, ways to increase engagement, and ways to integrate technology. AI can also create simulations, make suggestions on existing lesson plans, grade essays, and provide feedback. The list is endless, and I frequently have one tab that is always open to a Generative AI like ChatGPT. I might need to search for a quick joke or ask a specific question; it is there to help support me.

Making the Most of AI

Individual Learning Spaces. Learning platforms like SchoolAI, Magic School, and Khanmigo allow teachers to create personalized AI learning spaces for their students. SchoolAI and Magic School offer robust access to their platform for free. This is a great opportunity to jump into the sandbox to learn and play before you subscribe. SchoolAI spaces allow students to interact with historical figures, engage with teacher-created topic tutors, or chat with authors and characters. It is important to remind students that the Chatbot is not a real person. Its responses are generated based on what the AI has learned and trained on. Biases and inaccuracies are very possible in the response. For younger students, teachers can utilize SchoolAI in a whole group activity on a digital display board, while older students can access their AI space independently. SchoolAI spaces allow teachers to create unique learning opportunities fostering creativity, critical thinking, and personalized learning experiences.

Grading and Feedback. Programs like Class Companion allow teachers to create writing assignments that provide students with immediate feedback and a grade. Teachers can set the assignment to allow students to resubmit their work based on the feedback. The student can use the feedback to improve their submission, learn from their experience, and know where they need to improve. Teachers gain time and have access to a greater source of data to guide instruction.

Writing Emails. AI can help write emails and tailor the tone to be friendly or encouraging. Responding to a concerned or upset parent is one of the most difficult and time-consuming tasks for new teachers. Teachers can input their draft email or the general message they would like to send and ask AI to write an email in a supportive, serious, or nurturing tone. Remember do not include personal information in your request and always review the AI's responses before sending the final email.

Class Communications. Communicating with parents is an essential and time-consuming part of teaching. Especially for grades PreK–8, parents like to be informed about what is happening in the class. Writing a class newsletter is time-consuming, but AI can help write a newsletter or email. Type notes describing what is going on in your class and school events. The more detailed your input, the more accurate and detailed the response will be. After a recent middle school end-of-the-year meeting, I used ChatGPT to write a class letter for middle school parents and students based on the notes from the meeting. The team was impressed with the quality of the generated content (based on their own notes and information). What started with a reluctant group of teachers transitioned to numerous volunteers willing to use the AI-generated draft to complete the communication. AI provided a great starting point and saved time so that teachers could add personal touches, images, and specific dates and time. The newsletter was emailed home and posted in the LMS by the end of the meeting.

Lesson Planning. Ask AI to critique or improve an existing lesson plan. Many departments lack the time to collaborate, and some departments are made up of only one person. Recently, a high school English teacher used AI to critique an existing lesson. She mentioned to me that, even though she has taught the same novel for 13 years, she learned new ideas and lessons for making her teaching more meaningful.

Your AI Assistant. Keep a tab open with your favorite Generative AI and ask whatever is on your mind. I always have an open tab with an ongoing AI discussion. Do not be afraid to ask for anything. Generative AI can be like PD and mentoring because it is tailored toward your questions and interests. I look at my generative AI chat as a conversation with a friend. Ask away! AI can offer great suggestions for dinner recipes too!

AI in the Classroom: Personalized Learning

One of the most challenging tasks for teachers is differentiating resources to accommodate the diverse abilities and learning styles in the classroom. For example, teachers can upload an article for an eighth-grade social studies class into a text leveler in SchoolAI, Magic School, ChatGPT, or Claude, and ask the AI to rewrite the text at third-grade, fifth-grade, and college levels. With the push of a button, you can adjust the reading level, word count, and complexity so that all students can access the same information at the appropriate level, reducing frustration, decreasing negative behaviors, and increasing both learning and engagement. For example, MagicSchool and SchoolAI both have a built-in text-leveling tool. This tool enables educators to customize text to meet the needs of individual students or groups of students, ensuring that the content is engaging and relevant.

It is common for an eighth-grade social studies class to have some students reading at a second-grade level and others reading at a college level. A class set of resources will not meet the needs of your diverse population. It was not long ago that 504 Plans and IEPs were less common in schools. Today, many students have IEPs and 504 Plans to support their diverse learning needs. AI can efficiently assist teachers in supporting all of their students, designing content individualized for each student. The factory model of education—a philosophy where one teaching method fits all—is outdated and does not work. Today, AI gives teachers the power to teach all students at their individual levels, creating individualized learning for all students efficiently. AI can be the tool to create lessons and resources to meet the students where they are.

Using AI to differentiate lessons will foster a classroom environment focused on equity and equality. Many negative behaviors, discipline referrals, requests to leave the room, and disengagement often stem from a student's frustration with text and tasks that are too difficult. A one-size-fits-all approach does not work in the classroom.

Other Student-Focused AI Ideas

Students can upload their essays and rubrics into tools like ChatGPT for corrections and suggestions on areas of improvement. By using the prompt "proofread and critique," students receive automatic feedback as they work. A student told me using the proofread-and-critique prompt felt like having a teacher sitting next to them throughout the writing process. The list of critiqued suggestions gives students the power to make corrections in the moment. In traditional writing settings, students often write without real-time guidance, submitting their work and waiting days for feedback. This delay can lead to frustration, missed learning opportunities, and a disconnect between the writing and revision processes. As Ray Ravaglia (2023) wrote in *Forbes*,

> [Writing assignments] can be likened to a student shooting free throws but not being told if the ball is going into the basket until the next day. No matter how good the comments are the next day, the student will not be able to make the changes needed to improve without being in the headspace they were in when doing the work. (para. 6)

AI tools bridge this gap by offering instant, personalized support. They empower students to take ownership of their writing, reflect on their choices, and improve their work as they go. Could this be the end of traditional essays? Other student-focused AI ideas include the following:

- Translate documents into a student's home language. Tools like Google Translate, Google Docs, the AI browser extension Brisk along with all Gen AI can easily translate text.
- Students can ask AI to explain or summarize difficult topics.
- Students can generate a list of review questions tailored to their needs.
- Students can upload the assignment and their completed work to ChatGPT and ask the AI to review their responses in order to provide immediate feedback.

AI and Cheating

In many schools, departments such as social studies and English—where essay writing is central—were ready to revolt at the thought of students completing assignments copied directly from AI. Math teachers protested the use of calculators in 1966, and English teachers displayed similar outrage when Google Docs was introduced in 2006, fearing the new technology would undermine basic skills and lead to cheating. Change is an inherent part of the teaching profession, and we are now experiencing a dramatic technological shift. In the 1980s, schools proudly celebrated their typewriter labs, equipped with new IBM Selectrics. In the 1990s, many schools replaced chalkboards with dry erase boards, which were then replaced in the 2000s by interactive smartboards. By the late 2010s, those were being replaced with digital displays. As with all change, there is a learning curve to navigate. Some students will try to cheat with AI, just as they did with other technologies and methods in the past. The question remains: What can we do to address this challenge?

Create AI-Resistant Assignments

Project-Based Learning. Assign projects that encourage students to engage in real-world issues. For example, students might create a multimedia campaign, a service-learning project, a museum exhibit, or a guide for a tour of local history. For more information on Project-Based Learning, see Larmer (2018).

Personal Reflections. Create assignments based on books, topics, or issues. Writing a personal reflection, creating a vlog, or making a podcast will be meaningful and challenging for students to use AI.

Socratic Seminars. Facilitate group discussion centered around open-ended questions. Students must have knowledge of the topic and will need to listen carefully to the comments of others and articulate their own responses. For more details on Socratic seminars, see Filkins (n.d.).

In-Class Assignments. Design in-class assignments that require immediate knowledge and original thinking. In-class writing assignments, presentations, and group work will challenge students to think critically.

Strategies to Monitor AI Use in Social Studies

Understand Your Students' Writing. Know your students' "written voice." We have all read work that does not sound like the student. When reading their completed work, ask yourself if it sounds like them. Is the wording and vocabulary consistent with their typical writing? AI uses similar wording and often uses words like "delve," "tapestry," "elevate," and "leverage." Run your assignment through AI to understand how it creates a response. Use programs like Class Companion to help detect if students pasted answers from AI into their assignment, or require students to use a program with version control, like Google Docs (see Figure 10.3). This can help to determine if the work is AI generated. You should see several edits throughout the document, not just one pasted block of text.

Reinforce Academic Integrity. Emphasize the academic integrity policy of your district and explain the consequences for cheating. Reinforcing this message throughout the year will help students understand the seriousness of the behavior.

Teach Students About Ethical Use of Technology and AI. Teach students how they can use AI tools responsibly. Showcase how AI can be used for tasks such as editing grammar, proofreading, or critiquing their work to enhance their learning. As stated above, reinforce to your students that having AI generate their assignments is cheating and violates the academic integrity policy of your school and discuss what that means.

Share How You Use AI. Explain to your students how you use AI to help prepare engaging lessons and to perform day-to-day tasks. This focuses on appropriate use of AI. Demonstrate scenarios in which human input outperforms AI, such as crafting personal feedback or understanding nuanced classroom dynamics.

Demonstrate the Inaccuracies and Limitations of AI. AI is not perfect and may exhibit biases based on the sources of its training data. It can also provide incorrect answers, making it crucial to teach students the importance of critically evaluating AI-generated outputs. Errors, or "hallucinations," can occur, and a solid understanding of the topic is essential for recognizing bias and inaccuracies. AI cannot replace a student's knowledge and understanding of the topic. The issue arises when students use AI as their first source of learning.

Teaching students to approach AI with a critical mindset ensures they can use it effectively and responsibly. For example, during a recent interaction with AI about American history, the AI downplayed the significance of slavery on America's history and its impact on African Americans. This highlights the need for teachers to help students understand the limitations of AI tools and avoid overreliance or misplaced trust in their accuracy.

Figure 10.3 *Version History in Google Docs*

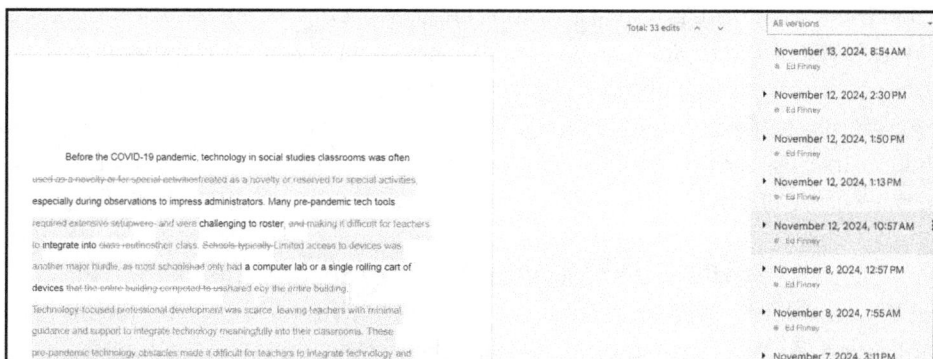

Note. Depending on the assignment, you should see a large list on the right-hand side of the screen. The highlighted text shows changes in the version selected on the right. From Google Docs (**https://docs.google.com**)

A Classroom With Purpose: A Guide to Teaching Social Studies Today

Another student used AI to check his work and noticed that the AI repeatedly marked a question about the Crusades wrong. Instead of accepting the AI's feedback at face value, the student researched the topic and sought clarification from the teacher. This critical engagement with the tool not only deepened the student's understanding of the content but also demonstrated the importance of questioning AI responses. The student demonstrated a true understanding of the topic by questioning the AI.

By fostering a culture of inquiry and critical thinking, teachers can empower students to navigate AI tools effectively while recognizing their limitations.

AI Detectors

Demonstrate to your class how you use AI detectors. The in-class demonstration might deter some from using AI inappropriately. Tools like ZeroGPT and GPTZero are helpful, but they are not perfect. The tools should only be used as a conversation starter about the potential of cheating. Detecting cheating requires detective work using both human intuition and artificial intelligence. Making slight grammar corrections based on AI suggestions can make a fully human-written assignment be flagged as AI generated. Be cautious when using AI detectors as a so-called gotcha tool. However, use the tools to meet with your students and discuss what they did and how they generated the assignments.

What to Do if an AI Detector Shows a Student May Have Cheated

Use AI detection tools as a guide to identify concerns, not as definitive proof of misconduct. Here is what to do if an AI detector flags a student's work as AI generated:

- Start a conversation with the student to understand their perspective.
- Ask the student if they used AI and how it helped them in their process.
- Review the version history of the document, if using a program with version control, together to trace their writing journey and clarify any concerns.
- Ask the student to discuss the assignment. Can they explain their ideas and answer follow-up questions?
- Teach students strategies to use AI responsibly, such as brainstorming ideas or refining drafts, without compromising academic integrity.
- Reflect on your assignment design. Are there ways to make it more AI resistant?

This approach maintains fairness, focuses on learning, and encourages ethical use of AI in academic work.

I recently pasted the complete text of the Declaration of Independence into a popular AI detector, and the results shocked me. According to the AI detector, Thomas Jefferson generated the Declaration of Independence using AI: 98.5%. The high detection of AI could be associated with the famous nature of the document. However, this is an example of what could happen. It is important to use AI detectors to start a conversation with students. Jump into the sandbox, paste items that you wrote into an AI detector, and see the results.

Digital Learning Platforms and Their Role in Social Studies Assignments

Utilizing platforms such as Google Classroom, Schoology, Seesaw, or Canvas to share social studies assignments not only helps streamline learning but also provides families with the ability to apply online translation support when accessing materials. These platforms serve as centralized hubs where educational resources can be stored and accessed by families when working on assignments at home.

Your Learning Management System (LMS) becomes an invaluable tool for managing your curriculum and lesson plans from year to year. Take the time to get to know your LMS well. Many systems, like Canvas, allow you to easily copy a class from the previous year to the current one. This means you can spend your valuable planning time improving your lessons and content instead of rewriting what you have already done. Additionally, an LMS is an effective communication tool, providing a way to easily communicate with families, share updates, and keep everyone involved in the learning process.

Social Media Engagement

Does the district have a social media presence? Many families utilize social media to connect with each other and learn about community events. Posting information on the school's social media can help build relationships and the sense of community for families who are new to the district.

Virtual Events and Workshops

If your district does not already have technology-based workshops for families, offer to help organize them to showcase the support and technology available. Online workshops for families that cover topics like accessing academic support, navigating the school learning management system, using school-supported technology resources and tools, and accessing support resources at home can be beneficial. Virtual conference platforms such as Zoom, Microsoft Teams, and Google Meet provide the opportunity for families to engage with each other and the education team utilizing technology to eliminate the barrier of travel. A great place to start is by sharing access tips with parents at parents' night, during parent conferences, or in classroom newsletters. It is important to keep all stakeholders informed.

Feedback Surveys

Utilize digital surveys, like Google Forms or SurveyMonkey, to gather feedback from families about their experiences and needs. This can help tailor support services and improve engagement with students and families. Teachers can create a multilingual survey of the families concerns, needs, and ideas. This helps clarify and address the major obstacles to learning and wellbeing for the families.

Resource Sharing

Parents are often presented with a plethora of resources from well-meaning teachers. When shared individually, these resources can get lost or buried in an email file. By creating a digital library of resources, including links to community services, academic support services, and cultural events, families can access the resources that they need more readily. Google Sites, Book Creator, and Wakelet are excellent resources for collecting and sharing information with families.

Digital Literacy

Teachers today have the challenge of stuffing 12–16 months of curriculum into a 10-month school year, all while managing growing mandates and increasing emotional needs and demands in the classroom. With these competing priorities, where does digital literacy fit? Who is responsible for teaching digital literacy skills, like typing and navigating digital content? The importance of digital literacy cannot be overlooked. Digital literacy is a vital skill needed for students to understand and navigate the digital world they are immersed in, to evaluate the digital media they encounter daily, and to discern whether a source is factual, reliable, and trustworthy.

Students need the ability to critically assess digital media. Are the sources they find from credible websites with trustworthy URLs (such as those ending in .gov, .edu, or .org)? Is the author listed, and do they have the appropriate qualifications or affiliations? Does the website include citations and references to back up its claims? These evaluation strategies must be taught and reinforced continuously, but this responsibility cannot rest on one teacher or grade level.

Do not be surprised when you spend your weekend designing a TEMPEST-focused lesson only to watch your students peck at the keyboard, searching for a key or punctuation mark as if it were buried treasure. Typing is a skill that is lacking in many, if not most, students today. The challenge lies in finding the time to teach it. While many schools offer programs like Type to Learn to help students become familiar with the keyboard, there is often little time in the day to integrate these programs with consistency. That is why it is important to reinforce keyboarding skills proactively throughout the year, weaving them into lessons whenever possible to build fluency and support digital learning success.

Digital literacy needs to be integrated throughout the school year, starting in kindergarten and continuing through senior year. It is not just about computer skills and using a mouse; it is about teaching students to think critically, whether they are evaluating the reliability of a web source in a high school class or coloring the home row on a drawing of a keyboard in kindergarten. Teachers should understand ISTE standards and state digital fluency standards to ensure students develop the digital skills necessary for future success.

Teaching digital literacy can also be engaging and creative if designed with TEMPEST in mind. For example, using an interactive tool like Book Creator to write a story or essay can transform a meaningful lesson into digital literacy reinforcement while still focusing on the curriculum. I introduce Book Creator to second graders through a hands-on project in which they create a digital book about their favorite person: themselves! They learn to manipulate text, use the device camera, resize images, and add creative elements like backgrounds and thought bubbles. Students become immersed in the project, learning valuable digital skills without even realizing it. Later in the year, I return to the second-grade classroom to support students as they create digital books on research topics they have explored. My goal is to build digital literacy skills, while the classroom teacher's goal is for students to produce shareable, curriculum-aligned digital books.

The key challenge is ensuring that digital literacy is seen as an ongoing, integrated part of education. It should not be treated as an afterthought or the next teacher's issue. It should not be treated as a single lesson but rather embedded throughout the curriculum. Teachers across all subjects must work together to prepare students for the digital world, making sure that they do not just consume information, but engage with it critically and responsibly.

Conclusion

Integrating technology into my social studies classroom transformed the way I teach. It allowed me to design lessons that are not only engaging but also centered on critical thinking and adaptability, skills our students need in today's world. Real-time feedback through technology tools like Nearpod helped me meet students where they were and adjust my instruction accordingly. Simply put, I would not be the educator I am today without the thoughtful integration of technology.

New teachers entering the field are fortunate to have an abundance of digital tools at their fingertips. But remember, do not just use technology for the sake of it. Take the time to understand the tools, reflect on your instructional goals, and then incorporate technology purposefully. Frameworks like SAMR and TEMPEST can guide your thinking and help you craft meaningful, technology-enhanced learning experiences that truly elevate student learning.

Technology also provides us with valuable tools to streamline administrative tasks and support lesson planning and differentiation. See Figure 10.4 for more resources and tools. The time saved can be reinvested into transforming your teaching and enriching the learning experience for your students.

Above all, always remember: It is not about the technology—it is about the learning. Avoid overwhelming your students and their families with too many platforms or apps. Instead, strive for clarity and support. Provide clear instructions and consider sharing brief video tutorials to help students and caregivers navigate the tools confidently. Keep in mind that not all students have reliable internet—or even electricity—at home. Providing flexible learning options and offering class time for digital tasks ensures all learners have access.

This truly is an amazing time to be in education. New teachers have a front-row seat to the rapid transformation of both the classroom and the workforce through technology. It is almost unimaginable to predict what classrooms will look like in the next 10, 20, or 30 years. But one thing is certain: it will be today's and tomorrow's new teachers who guide that evolution and lead the conversation.

Buckle up—and enjoy the ride!

Figure 10.4 *Online Resources and Technology Starter Guide*

General Resources
Digital Inquiry Group, https://inquirygroup.org/history-lessons
Free, research-based resources that help students engage in historical inquiry
Ken Burns in the Classroom, https://pbslearningmedia.org/collection/kenburnsclassroom
Free educational resource by PBS Learning Media that provides access to Ken Burns's documentaries along with curated teaching tools
NCSS Technology Community, https://sites.google.com/view/ncsstechcommunity/tech-tools
Crowdsourced online technology tools and resource list

AI Platforms and Teacher Tools
Canva, www.canva.com
Graphic design tool that allows you and your students to create amazing presentations and projects. Great for making student narrated video presentations.
Common Sense Education, www.commonsense.org/education/digital-citizenship
Free resources to teach students digital citizenship, media literacy, and safe online behavior. It helps teachers integrate responsible technology use into their classrooms, empowering students to make informed decisions in the digital world.
Nearpod, https://nearpod.com and **Pear Deck**, www.peardeck.com
Interactive presentation tools that allow teachers to engage students in real-time through quizzes, polls, and multimedia, fostering active participation and formative assessment during lessons
SchoolAI, https://schoolai.com
An AI platform that engages students with personalized chatbots allowing students to talk to authors, historical features, and characters. School AI also offers powerful AI tools for lesson planning.

Games and Activities
Everfi, https://everfi.com
Free courses for K–12 students including financial literacy, character education, health and wellness, STEM, and career readiness
Flocabulary, www.flocabulary.com
Brief videos using hip-hop songs focusing on tier two and three vocabulary words
Google Earth, http://earth.google.com
An interactive tour around the world using maps and satellites
iCivics, https://vision.icivics.org
Nonprofit organization in the United States that provides educational online games and lesson plans to promote civics education and encourage students to become active citizens.
Kahoot, http://kahoot.com and **Gimkit**, www.gimkit.com
Gamification quiz websites
KidCitizen, www.kidcitizen.net
Interactive game for elementary students focusing on primary source documents
Mission US, www.mission-us.org
Multimedia project that immerses players in U.S. history content through free interactive games
Seterra, www.seterra.com
Over 400 free maps and geography activities
The World From A to Z, http://worldatoz.org
A current events resource that promotes critical thinking and civil discourse

Checklist for Transforming Social Studies Through Technology

Use this checklist to guide meaningful technology integration into your lessons and help students build digital skills for tomorrow's careers.

Technology Purpose
☐ Essential to achieving lesson objectives
☐ Provides unique learning opportunities not possible with traditional methods
☐ Helps promote higher-order thinking or unique problem-solving opportunities

Learning Goals
☐ Directly supports curriculum standards
☐ Enhances student understanding of key concepts
☐ Measurable learning outcomes identified

Meaningful Engagement
☐ Promotes active student participation
☐ Encourages critical thinking
☐ Provides opportunities for creativity and student choice

Accessibility Check
☐ Is accessible by all students
☐ Accommodates different learning needs
☐ Contains minimal technical barriers

Standards Alignment
☐ Supports curriculum standards
☐ Aligns with technology integration guidelines
☐ Supports development of digital literacy skills and transferable life skills

SAMR Check
☐ Technology substitutes a traditional tool with no change.
☐ Technology improves the functionality of a traditional method.
☐ Technology redesigns the learning task in a significant way.
☐ Technology enables creation of entirely new learning experiences.

A Classroom With Purpose: A Guide to Teaching Social Studies Today

References

Cardoza, K. (2024, March 11). *One reason school cyberattacks are on the rise? Schools are easy targets for hackers.* NPR. **www.npr.org/2024/03/11/1236995412/cybersecurity-hackers-schools-ransomware**

Filkins, S. (n.d.) *Strategy guide: Socratic seminars.* ReadWriteThink. National Council of Teachers of English.

Finney, E. (2024a). *TEMPEST Educational Framework Checklist for Instructional Design.*

Finney, E. (2024b). *The TEMPEST Model.*

Finney, E. (2024c). *TEMPEST Quick Integration Checklist.*

Google. (n.d.). *Version history feature in Google Docs* [Screenshot]. **https://docs.google.com**

Microsoft. (2024). Microsoft Designer (version) [Large Language Model].

Napkin. (2024). Napkin AI (version) [Large Language Model]. **www.napkin.ai**

Puentedura, R. R. (2016). *The SAMR Model.* Wikimedia Commons. **https://commons.wikimedia.org/w/index.php?curid=47961924**

Ravaglia, R. (2023, October 5). *Class Companion puts AI to work helping teachers help students.* Forbes. **www.forbes.com/sites/rayravaglia/2023/10/05/class-companion-puts-ai-to-work-helping-teachers-help-students**

ZeroGPT. (n.d.). Detection Results Page [Screenshot]. *ZeroGPT.* **https://zerogpt.com**

Chapter 11
Understanding Ethical and Legal Guidelines for Teachers

Erica Kane

I started my teaching career in public education in the summer of 2004. Then, I was a 24-year-old actor living in New York City, growing restless with odd jobs, inconsistent paychecks, and no healthcare. In the winter of 2003, hoping to find financial security and a potential career pathway with the New York City Department of Education, I applied for and was accepted into the New York City Teaching Fellows program. For two years, I was a full-time graduate student and a full-time high school teacher at a public high school in Lower Manhattan. I was lucky enough to fall in love with the profession, which has since provided me with close to two decades of indelible experiences. In hindsight, while the early years were challenging and life changing, I realized that there were many topics that I did not get to learn about in my graduate program. Through years of experience in the field, as both an educator and a union leader, I have learned firsthand how, in this profession, teachers are held to higher ethical standards. I have learned that the intersection of having a personal life and a professional life as a public employee is complicated. Living life as a private citizen and a public employee can (and will) be easily scrutinized, and that scrutiny is not only centered around perceptions of who we should be as public school educators inside and outside the four walls of our classrooms, but it is also influenced by law.

First Amendment to the United States Constitution

As social studies teachers know, the First Amendment to the Constitution allows citizens of the United States of America the right to express opinions and ideas without fear of government intervention in the form of censorship or punishment. As a fundamental freedom, "Congress shall make no law ... abridging freedom of speech" (United States Courts, n.d., para. 2), and foundationally the purpose of establishing freedom of speech as a constitutional right was to ensure that every citizen has an opportunity to speak and debate on matters of public concern. With that, while the First Amendment prohibits the government from improperly interfering with the freedom of speech, this freedom of speech clause does not define what free speech actually entails. Many Supreme Court cases through the years have helped to define the limitations related to free speech—speech that would not be protected under the First Amendment—and "the Court generally identifies these categories as obscenity, defamation, fraud, incitement, fighting words, true threats, speech integral to criminal conduct, and child pornography" (Killion, 2024, p. 2).

(i) **Teacher Tip:** *Establishing freedom of speech as a Constitutional right was to ensure that every citizen has an opportunity to speak and debate on matters of public concern. As a social studies teacher, how could you turnkey teach this concept to your own students?*

Social studies teachers are well aware of both the freedom of speech and its limitations, often discussing these issues with students—particularly those who believe that freedom of speech is carte blanche, granting them the right to say anything without consequences. Additionally, social studies teachers must be mindful of how they teach their subject matter, particularly controversial topics, as they may face heightened scrutiny due to the current sociopolitical climate. With that, what does freedom of speech look like for a social studies teacher, both inside and outside the classroom? This chapter examines how speech on social media and digital communication platforms can potentially affect the employment of public sector employees, particularly educators.

Relevant Supreme Court Cases and Legal Standards

While there is a preponderance of Supreme Court cases centered around free speech, there are three specific cases that intersect with the educational profession, specifically the public sector. These seminal cases set forth particular guidelines about what protections educators have as public employees, further defining a teacher's working environment.

Tinker v. Des Moines Independent Community School District (1969)

In a landmark Supreme Court ruling, *Tinker v. Des Moines Independent Community School District* (1969) affirmed students' rights to constitutionally protected free speech in a public school setting. Young students—Mary Tinker, her brother, and several of their classmates—planned to wear black armbands to school to protest the Vietnam War. Learning of the students' plans and believing that such action would disrupt the educational environment, the school district preemptively adopted a school board policy prohibiting the wearing of the armbands. If students defied the policy, they faced suspension. Post-policy adoption, students wore the armbands to school and were subsequently suspended. The students and their families filed a lawsuit against the school district, asserting that their First Amendment rights had been violated (American Civil Liberties Union, 2019).

The Supreme Court ruled in favor of Tinker, establishing that

> First Amendment rights, applied in light of the special characteristics of the school environment, are available to teachers and students. It can hardly be argued that either students or teachers shed their constitutional rights to freedom of speech or expression at the schoolhouse gate. (*Tinker v. Des Moines Independent Community School District*, 1969)

The Court determined that wearing armbands was a form of symbolic speech and did not substantially disrupt the educational process and environment, as the school district anticipated.

In sum, *Tinker v. Des Moines* (1969) remains a foundational case in understanding rights and free speech in educational settings, highlighting that expression should be protected if it does not interfere with a school district's broader functioning. This concept will be examined further in this chapter.

Pickering v. Board of Education (1968)

In 1968, the United States Supreme Court ruled in favor of public school teacher Marvin Pickering who was terminated for writing a letter to the editor, subsequently published by the local newspaper, admonishing the school board's use of funds between educational and athletic programs. The school board declared his letter was "detrimental to the efficient operation and administration of schools" (*Pickering v. Board of Education*, 1968). Pickering filed a lawsuit claiming that his First Amendment rights had been violated by his dismissal. The decision, in favor of Pickering, held that public school employees do not forfeit their First Amendment rights and can express their opinions on issues of public importance without being dismissed from their position. Further,

> That ruling also established what is now known as the *Pickering* balancing test, in which the court weighs the employee's interest in commenting upon matters of public concern and the employer's interest in "promoting the efficiency of the public services it performs." (Will, 2020, para. 16)

In sum, the two-pronged test first asks if the employee's speech is a matter of public concern, and if so, the second prong of the test asks if the employee's speech disrupts the work environment or if the speech interferes with the performance of the employee's duties. In simpler terms, the two-part test first asks whether the employee's speech addresses an issue, topic, or event that is important to the public and affects the community. If it does, the second part looks at whether the speech creates problems at work or impacts the employee's ability to do their job. Again, this is why social studies teachers must be mindful of how they teach their subject matter, particularly controversial topics, as they may face heightened scrutiny due to the current sociopolitical climate.

Garcetti v. Ceballos (2006)

Richard Ceballos, a deputy district attorney, wrote a memorandum to his supervisors wherein he recommended a dismissal of a case, alleging law enforcement misconduct. Following the memorandum, he was transferred and denied promotion, and he alleged that these actions were retaliatory for addressing corruption on a matter of public concern.

While the *Pickering v. Board of Education* (1968) decision establishes that public employees do not relinquish their rights on matters of public concern, the *Garcetti v. Ceballos* (2006) Supreme Court decision, which did not favor Ceballos, held that "when public employees make statements pursuant to their official duties, they are not speaking as citizens for First Amendment purposes, and the Constitution does not insulate their communications from employer discipline" (*Garcetti v. Ceballos*, 2006). In sum, public employees are not entitled to First Amendment protection for speech when it is performed as an integral part of their professional roles and responsibilities. Further, the case clarified the distinction between speech as a private citizen and speech as a public employee.

Teacher Tip: It is important to reinforce that public employees are not entitled to First Amendment protection for speech when it is performed as an integral part of their professional roles and responsibilities.

Social Media and Digital Communication Trends

Social studies teachers are aware that advancements in technology have influenced the way people communicate in the shapeshifting sociocultural digital landscape of the 21st century. In 2021, Pew Research Center data noted that roughly "seven-in-ten Americans" use social media (Auxier &

Anderson, 2021, para. 1). Newer research from the Pew Research Center notes that about 83% of American adults use YouTube; 68% of Americans use Facebook; 47% use Instagram; "27% to 35% of U.S. adults use Pinterest, TikTok, LinkedIn, WhatsApp and Snapchat" and "about one-in-five say they use Twitter (recently renamed 'X') and Reddit" (Gottfried, 2024, para. 6). Further, while "YouTube and Facebook are the only two platforms that majorities of all age groups use," the early adopters to new and emerging social media platforms, as well as the use of multiple platforms, trend toward the youngest adult consumers (Gottfried, 2024, para. 14).

While the Pew Research Center data (Gottfried, 2024) does not delineate personal from professional usage of social media and digital communication platforms, a recent study conducted by RegisteredNursing.org (Burger, 2025), which is an advocacy organization for the nursing profession,

> examined the popularity of TikTok videos created by various professionals between 2016 and 2023. Those linked to the hashtag #teacher garnered 61.3 billion views—second only to those labeled with #doctor, which edged out those from educators with 61.5 billion views. (Heubeck, 2023, para. 2)

Further, the study

> showed that the short teacher-created videos (between 15 seconds and three minutes long) span a wide range of themes—from teaching-related tips, tricks, and hacks to venting on the challenges of the profession. Those that have gone viral include snippets of teachers showing grace to students, sharing strategies for teaching kids with ADHD, and offering tips for staying calm in a crisis. (Heubeck, 2023, para. 3)

It is an interesting sociocultural phenomenon to see professionals use these platforms, transcending the professional title of educator to influencer. Those who use these platforms to educate and highlight the profession, as well as bridge any and all communication gaps that might exist in this digital age (perhaps as a reaction to the collective existential crisis of isolation propelled by the COVID-19 years), do so to appeal not only to students and colleagues but also to those who may be interested in entering a profession that is experiencing a notable shortage. The increase in usage of TikTok has grown 12% since 2021, according to the Pew Research Center (Gottfried, 2024), and many "teacher influencers have been able to build invaluable connections with users on TikTok, often supporting them in their journey of becoming a teacher" (Hagerman, 2024, para. 1).

It is clear that technology is reshaping how we communicate, particularly in the education field, but how can this increased usage of social media and digital communication platforms potentially affect the employment of social studies teachers as well as other public sector employees?

Intersection of Free Speech and Social Media and Digital Communication Platform Usage for Public Employees

According to the most recent data, "In the 2020–21 school year, there were 3.8 million full- and part-time public school teachers, including 1.9 million elementary teachers and 1.9 million secondary teachers" (National Center for Education Statistics, 2023, para. 2). For these public school teachers, the school district is the government entity. As a public employee, if a public school educator plans to be a user of social media and digital communication platforms, then the educator must do so with the full awareness that teachers are held to a higher standard based on their standing in the community as role models. Administrators, parents/guardians, and the broader community all rely on educators to lead by example. With that, the use of social media and digital communication platforms to express thoughts, feelings, and opinions is now commonplace. *Packingham v. North Carolina* (2017) is a pivotal Supreme Court case that affirms that the First Amendment extends to social media platforms. When delivering the majority opinion on the case, Justice Kennedy acknowledged that "social media allows users to gain access to information and communicate with one another about it on any subject that might come to mind," and that social media and digital communication platforms are now "the modern public square," and added that to prohibit someone from social media altogether "is to prevent the user from engaging in the legitimate exercise of First Amendment rights" (*Packingham v. North Carolina*, 2017). In summary, while it is now commonplace to express one's thoughts, feelings, ideas, and opinions on social media and digital communication platforms, teachers still must be mindful of their role as community role models when using said platforms.

> *Teacher Tip: The two-part* Pickering *Balancing Test first asks whether the employee's speech addresses an issue, topic, or event that is important to the public and affects the community. If it does, the second part looks at whether the speech creates problems at work or impacts the employee's ability to do their job.*
>
> *In this political climate, can you think of a highly publicized statement made by a public official on social media and digital communication platforms where one could apply the* Pickering *Balancing Test? What was the outcome?*

Looking at the Pew Research Center data (Gottfried, 2024) and the popularity of TikTok as an emerging professional platform for educators, believing anyone could abstain from using social media and digital communication platforms is unrealistic. I believe the endeavors of teachers using social media and digital communication platforms to inspire others to enter the profession are altruistic, particularly in light of the many studies that address educator burnout and the studies that note some are leaving the profession altogether for various reasons. However, it is important to understand that anything expressed on social media and digital communication platforms pursuant to one's official job duties can potentially be problematic to one's employment if any of the content is deemed questionable or controversial. Additionally, due to the special characteristics of the school environment, a teacher's First Amendment right is tempered by other tangible constructs beyond Supreme Court decisions, including a school board's social media and technology use policies, employee handbooks, and, perhaps, a collective bargaining agreement (a contract that outlines the negotiated terms and conditions of employment between an employer and a union that represents a group of employees) if a teacher works in a unionized workplace.

This means that public school educators must always be mindful about what they say, inside and outside the four walls of the classroom. Specifically, when it comes to public educators' use of social media and digital communication platforms, they must be cognizant that the speech they post online,

A Classroom With Purpose: A Guide to Teaching Social Studies Today

in a personal or professional capacity, always has the potential to impact their employment. While the *Pickering* decision maintains that public employees as private citizens can exercise their right to free speech on matters of public concern, a school district has the aforementioned *Pickering* Balancing Test to rely on should they believe an employee's speech would have an impact on the district. A school district will always be wholly concerned with running an efficient, professional, disruptive-free working environment; it also has a greater obligation to its stakeholders, including taxpayers, parents/guardians, students, and the greater community. A school district will exercise its right to safeguard itself from negative publicity and damage to its reputation, and bound by law, it will certainly act on any disclosure of private or confidential information (e.g., student data). This means that if an educator posts something questionable on social media and digital communication platforms, there is a nexus between what that educator, as a private citizen, posts on said platforms—especially if it is controversial—and the impact it can potentially have on a district. The school district will look at the questionable and controversial speech through the lens of whether the speech is pursuant to the official duties of the educator or if the speech is related to a matter of public concern, in other words, whether the speech is part of the educator's job duties or related to a public issue. Speech related to job duties is usually not protected, while speech about public concerns may be protected by the First Amendment. While there may not be definitive case law regarding what information from online sources can be obtained without a person's permission, as a safeguard, educators should assume that anything they post on social media and digital communication platforms could be used as evidence against them should a school district want to pursue any disciplinary action, including termination of employment.

Even if one is adept at safeguarding social media and digital communication platforms through security measures (e.g., private accounts, two-factor authentication, etc.), the reality is that there are no bona fide safeguards, as nothing posted on the internet is truly private. This is why educators must be mindful of what they share on social media and digital communication platforms because there often is a greater audience beyond the intended audience. In my nearly twenty years in public education, I have seen this play out all too many times, and often not in favor of the public employee. For example, a colleague posted about his gripes with the school administration on a popular social media platform, only for one of his social media friends, who happened to also be a colleague, to take a screenshot and share said post with the administration. This educator never thought that his colleague would turn him in to the administration, as he truly believed that most of his colleagues felt the same way as he did (and clearly, at least one did not).

Increased usage of social media and digital communication platforms has given rise to the scrutiny of educators as professionals and private citizens. These days it is not uncommon to see an educator's digital presence unfurl on the larger stage of mainstream news, and it is usually centered around questionable and often controversial postings. For instance, in 2019, a high school teacher in Texas was terminated for "sending a series of tweets directed to President Donald Trump's Twitter account, asking him to 'remove the illegals from Fort Worth' and saying that her school district was 'loaded' with and her high school had been 'taken over by' undocumented students from Mexico" (Will, 2020, para. 7). One could opine that this teacher's opinions were a matter of public concern, but the 250th District Court of Travis County upheld the school's decision to terminate the teacher (Allen, 2022).

In the fall of 2023, after the Hamas massacre, a Jewish teacher in New York City found herself centerstage to student riots when she "changed her social media profile photo to a photo of her holding an 'I Stand with Israel' sign" (Lenthang, 2023, para. 6), which students screenshotted and circulated amongst the student population, wherein it was reported that about 30% are of Muslim faith. It was a student endeavor, which some attest started as a peaceful protest, where "hundreds of students stormed the hallway and tried to get into her classroom, cursing and threatening, and calling for her to be fired" (Marder & Weingarten, 2024, para. 6). This is a compelling example of the power of social media and the impact it can have on a school's operational functioning. Nevertheless, the New York City Schools Chancellor, school administration, and even the mayor of New York City supported the teacher; the Chancellor even "stressed that students and staff should be free to express themselves and their views, while not spewing hate" (Lenthang, 2023, para. 23).

Social Media and Digital Communication Best Practices

Should an educator choose not to abstain from personal use of social media and digital communication platforms, it is advised to approach with an abundance of caution and, most importantly, common sense. An educator who uses social media and digital communication platforms for personal use should take the time to research, review, and re-review, when necessary, all the privacy and security metrics for each platform. The National Education Association (NEA, 2023b) notes that "Some educators choose to use an alternate name on social media sites, so that it is more difficult for students and families to view their profile" (para. 8). As an aside, when I married my spouse, I purposely chose to take her last name, not just because I love her, but if anyone does a Google search of "Erica Kane," the algorithm will populate endless entries and images of the fictional character from the ABC daytime soap opera *All My Children* played by the famous actress Susan Lucci. The NEA (2023b) also encourages reviewing public posts and deleting "old posts that may be controversial" (para. 9). Additionally, educators need to be mindful of their social media audience when posting, sharing and resharing, as well as commenting or reacting to other people's content.

Teacher Tip: Think before you post! Your thoughts and opinions change with time, and you cannot outrun your digital footprint!

Further, if educators choose to interface with students, parents/guardians, or colleagues, in a professional capacity, it is advised that they do not do so through social media platforms but rather through digital communication platforms such as work email or applications compliant with federal, state, and education law, which will vary by state and school district, that are intended for such communications.

It should be obvious, but it is worth stating clearly: At this juncture, there is no way to completely erase one's digital footprint, and this is something to keep in mind before posting on social media and digital communication platforms. As an educator, I have reminded my students ad nauseam that what they share now can come back to haunt them later, especially when it comes to employment. The opinions and views they hold today may not age well, and this lesson also applies to everyone in the public sector, particularly educators.

Employee Protections

While outcomes related to educators caught in the ethical crosshairs of questionable and sometimes controversial social media and digital communication platform usage can fall asunder to the *Pickering* Balancing Test, outcomes can also vary by state, especially those that have tenure and due process protections.

Tenure and Due Process Protections

I recently engaged in a conversation with a young educator in her first year of teaching who was unaware of tenure and what it entailed. While I thought this was surprising, what should be commonplace knowledge truly is not. If you had asked me in my first years of teaching what tenure was, I am fairly certain that I would not have been able to define it either.

Earning tenure as an educator is heralded as a benchmark wherein an educator has earned employment protections under the law. According to the NEA (2023a),

> At the K–12 level, tenure laws prevent a school district from dismissing a tenured teacher without good reason.... These protections are not available to all educators—tenure is generally limited to teachers, and only teachers who have worked in the school district for a certain number of years are eligible. In addition, tenured teachers generally cannot transfer these protections to a new district if they change schools. (paras. 2–3)

In states with tenure and due process protections, if an educator has not yet earned tenure, there are certainly free speech protections (with limitations) but limited employment protection under the law, because in these states employers will have the "broad authority to dismiss K–12 teachers during their first years of employment in a particular school district" (NEA, 2023a, para. 6). If an educator has earned tenure in states governed by tenure protections, by no means does tenure ensure guaranteed employment, especially if a teacher's moral or ethical character, conduct, or competence is called into question, including questionable and controversial speech on social media and digital communication platforms. According to the NEA (2023a),

> Once a teacher has tenure, they can be dismissed only for specific causes outlined in state law.
> Common causes for dismissal are:
> - incompetency,
> - insubordination,
> - neglect of duty,
> - immorality,
> - violation of school board rules,
> - unprofessional conduct, and
> - reductions in the work force due to economic or enrollment conditions.
> Some states also include conviction of a felony or other specific crimes within their list of causes justifying dismissal of a tenured teacher. And most states have a catch-all provision allowing dismissal for "any good or just cause" (paras. 17–19)

A teacher's questionable or controversial speech on social media and digital communication platforms that disrupts school operations or interferes with an educator's job duties could be considered grounds for incompetency or immorality, depending on the nature of the speech. It may also be classified as insubordination (if the educator has received a specific directive from

A Classroom With Purpose: A Guide to Teaching Social Studies Today

administration), a violation of school board policies, or unprofessional conduct.

It is important to note that not all states have tenure and due process protections. According to the NEA (2023a),

> As of 2023, three states have effectively eliminated tenure for most teachers (Florida, North Carolina, and Wisconsin), and four other jurisdictions offer no tenure protections at all (Arkansas, District of Columbia, Kansas, and North Dakota).
>
> A few other states have significantly reduced tenure protections by providing for performance-based reversion to probationary status for permanent or tenured teachers (for example, Indiana and Tennessee), by allowing school districts to place teachers on indefinite unpaid leave without cause or a hearing in a number of circumstances (Colorado), or by permitting school districts to waive compliance with tenure laws when the district converts to a charter system (Georgia). (paras. 12–13)

Educators who work in a state with diminished or no tenure protections under the law will also have free speech protections (with limitations) but very limited employment protection under the law.

It is worth noting that if an educator works for a unionized workplace where there exists a collective bargaining agreement between the employer and a union that represents a group of employees, the collective bargaining agreement could further outline negotiated benefits in the form of job protections for the public employee. For example, if an employee's actions or conduct are not egregious enough to warrant immediate termination, a collective bargaining agreement may outline progressive discipline, which generally starts with a verbal warning then advances to subsequent written warning(s) oftentimes peppered with administrative support or training.

Cyberbullying: A Growing Trend in Education Impacting Employment

While the heart of this chapter is centered around a teacher's ethical obligation to the profession, both inside and outside the four walls of the classroom, I would be remiss if I did not touch upon the growing trend in education that could have an impact on one's employment status: teacher-targeted harassment and bullying. While this chapter appeals to expanding one's knowledge base when it comes to free speech as a public employee (tempered by all the aforementioned realities of the sociocultural digital landscape we live and teach in) the growing trend of teacher-targeted harassment and bullying in the form of cyberbullying is unsettling. An American Psychological Association (2024) study reports that the "percentage of teachers expressing intentions to resign or transfer rose from 49% during the pandemic to 57% afterward, the researchers found" (para. 2) due to an increase of threats and violence, including cyberbullying against educators post-COVID.

As consumers of media, we have seen an elderly bus monitor being bullied by middle school students, who posted their 10-minute video to YouTube, making national news (Botelho, 2012). We are aware of the countless YouTube and TikTok videos of students purposely acting out in hopes of digitally capturing their teachers acting unprofessionally, a tactic referred to as cyberbaiting (Duffy, 2011). We have learned of middle school students in Pennsylvania creating accounts on TikTok impersonating their teachers with posts "rife with pedophilia innuendo, racist memes, homophobia and made-up sexual hookups among teachers" (Singer, 2024, para. 4). We have learned about a student in Texas who created pornographic deepfakes of his teacher (Seedorff, 2023). It begs the question: What protections do teachers have when they are victims of targeted bullying and harassment?

If the acts against the teacher are criminal or teeter on the precipice of criminality, law enforcement should be involved. Further, reporting the acts against the teacher to the employer is also critical, as the

> Employer has an affirmative obligation under federal law to investigate and address certain kinds of harassment, even from third parties—but only if the employer knows about the harassment. Immediately reporting any issues ensures that the school or institution is responsible for taking steps to prevent further harassment. (NEA, 2023b, para. 18)

The NEA (2023b) also recommends that

> If you are ... experiencing threats or harassment, take steps to protect yourself by documenting the harassment.
> Take screenshots of all threatening messages or posts, including a timestamp and URL, and log other threatening communications...Keeping these records will preserve evidence of the harassment for use in any civil or criminal proceedings or school disciplinary action. (paras. 12–13)

While I have belabored that teachers are held to higher ethical standards inside and outside the four walls of the classroom, it should not be lost on the reader that you, too, as an educator have rights as well. Educators have the right to work in an environment free from harassment, which is often spelled out in most school board policies and typically reference all applicable federal and state laws. Much like school districts want to preserve their integrity against speech that is disharmonious to their daily operations, educators must also work to preserve their integrity in the face of harassment and bullying.

Checklist for Understanding Ethical and Legal Guidelines for Teachers

☐ If you use social media and digital communication platforms, what have you done to ensure that your privacy settings have been updated?

☐ If you use social media and digital communication platforms, personally or professionally, do you have posts that could be perceived as questionable or controversial?

☐ If you use social media and digital communication platforms, personally or professionally, have you observed posts from other teachers or colleagues that could be perceived as questionable or controversial?

☐ If you are employed by a school district, does it have a social media policy, and if so, what does it say?

☐ What are the tenure and due process protections in the state where you work or plan to work?

☐ If your workplace has a collective bargaining agreement between the employer and a union that represents a group of employees, specifically teachers, does the collective bargaining agreement outline any additional employment protections?

☐ For planning purposes, if you are a victim of teacher-targeted harassment and bullying, what workplace protections does your school district have in place, e.g. policies and safety plans?

Extension Activities

☐ Research and report on three cases involving educator speech issues that have arisen from social media and digital platform usage that have occurred in the last three years.

☐ Research and report on three cases involving teacher-targeted harassment and bullying that have occurred in the last three years.

A Classroom With Purpose: A Guide to Teaching Social Studies Today

References

Allen, S. (2022, May 9). Three years after Georgia Clark was fired, Fort Worth Schools face another racist incident. *Fort Worth Star-Telegram*. **www.star-telegram.com/news/local/crossroads-lab/article261166417. html**

American Civil Liberties Union. (2019, February 22). *Tinker v. Des Moines—Landmark Supreme Court ruling on behalf of student expression*. **www.aclu.org/documents/tinker-v-des-moines-landmark-supreme-court-ruling-behalf-student-expression**

American Psychological Association. (2024, May 30). *Violence, aggression against educators grew post-pandemic*. **www.apa.org/news/press/releases/2024/05/violence-against-educators-post-pandemic**

Auxier, B., & Anderson, M. (2021, April 7). *Social media use in 2021*. Pew Research Center. **www.pewresearch. org/internet/2021/04/07/social-media-use-in-2021/**

Botelho, G. (2012, June 23). *Emotional, widespread reaction to harassment of 68-year-old bus monitor*. CNN. **www. cnn.com/2012/06/22/us/new-york-bus-monitor-reaction/index.html**

Burger, C. (2025, February 8). *The most popular professions on TikTok*. RegisteredNursing.org. **www. registerednursing.org/articles/most-popular-professions-tiktok**

Duffy, F. (2011, November 28). *More students 'cyberbaiting' their teachers*. Education Week. **www.edweek.org/ teaching-learning/more-students-cyberbaiting-their-teachers/2011/11**

Garcetti v. Ceballos, 547 U.S. 410 (2006). **www.law.cornell.edu/supct/html/04-473.ZS.html**

Gottfried, J. (2024, January 31). *Americans' social media use*. Pew Research Center. **www.pewresearch.org/ internet/2024/01/31/americans-social-media-use/**

Hagerman, G. (2024, July 18). *Exploring the world of teachers on TikTok*. NEA Today. **www.nea.org/nea-today/all-news-articles/exploring-world-teachers-tiktok**

Heubeck, E. (2023, July 19). *Could TikTok be teachers' new best friend?* Education Week. **www.edweek.org/ technology/could-tiktok-be-teachers-new-best-friend/2023/07**

Killion, V. L. (2024, March 28). *The first amendment: Categories of speech* (CRS Report No. IF11072).

Lenthang, M. (2023, November 28). *400 students launch protest at NYC high school against teacher who posted pro-Israel stance online*. NBC News. **www.nbcnews.com/news/us-news/crowd-400-students-launch-protest-nyc-high-school-teacher-posted-onlin-rcna126954**

Marder, K., & Weingarten, R. (2024, April 15). *My students rioted after I said, 'I stand with Israel.' Here's how we came together after*. USA Today. **www.usatoday.com/story/opinion/2024/04/15/israel-sign-protest-new-york-high-school-free-speech/73274354007/**

National Center for Education Statistics. (2023, May). *Characteristics of public school teachers*. **https://nces. ed.gov/programs/coe/indicator/clr**

National Education Association. (2023a, April 4). *Teacher tenure & due process protections for educators*. **www. nea.org/resource-library/teacher-tenure-due-process-protections-educators**

National Education Association. (2023b, April 5). *How should educators handle harassment?* **www.nea.org/resource-library/how-should-educators-handle-harassment**

Packingham v. North Carolina 582 US 98 (2017) **www.law.cornell.edu/supremecourt/text/15-1194**

Pickering v. Board of Education 391 U.S. 563 (1968). **www.oyez.org/cases/1967/510**

Seedorff, M. (2023, April 13). *Houston-area student accused of creating "deep fake" explicit photos of teacher, sharing them online.* FOX 26 Houston. **www.fox26houston.com/news/houston-area-student-accused-of-creating-deep-fake-explicit-photos-of-teacher-sharing-them-online**

Singer, N. (2024, July 6). Students target teachers in group TikTok attack, shaking their school. *The New York Times.* **www.nytimes.com/2024/07/06/technology/tiktok-fake-teachers-pennsylvania.html**

Tinker v. Des Moines Independent Community School District 393 U.S. 503 (1969). **www.oyez.org/cases/1968/21**

United States Courts. (n.d.). *What does free speech mean?* **www.uscourts.gov/about-federal-courts/educational-resources/about-educational-outreach/activity-resources/what-does**

Will, M. (2020, March 17). *Teachers, politics, and social media: A volatile mix.* Education Week. **www.edweek.org/technology/teachers-politics-and-social-media-a-volatile-mix/2020/03**

Hope for Teachers: A Conclusion

Kristi Fragnoli and Timothy D. Potts

As we come to the final words and thoughts of *A Classroom With Purpose: A Guide to Teaching Social Studies Today*, we invite you to see this not as an ending but as a starting point for a wonderful career of meaningful, reflective, and impactful teaching of the social studies. Our hope is that you will forever develop and refine your practice, evolving into a thoughtful social studies educator. Our hope is that you return to this book throughout your career, using its key themes as a guide for reflection, inspiration, and hope.

In *The One Thing You Need to Know*, Marcus Buckingham (2005) summarizes the importance of keeping things simple, including your personal and professional goals. The lesson is that we get more done when we focus less and zero in on what matters. It is no mystery that teaching in a 21st-century world is extremely hard work. The key is to not spread yourself too thin; otherwise, you will not do anything well and will potentially be miserable. This book, *A Classroom With Purpose: A Guide to Teaching Social Studies Today*, provides a plethora of information on how to be a better teacher, but you do not have to implement it all or be an expert at everything. We strongly recommend choosing a few concepts or suggestions from each chapter to introduce over time. Then develop a plan to tweak specific areas with the goal of becoming a better social studies teacher. It is okay to scrap draft plans, but you must keep moving forward. One of the overall purposes of this book is to offer you ideas, inspiration, and the hope of creating a sustainable teaching career that will impact multiple generations. We truly hope this is your forever career.

Each author has contributed valuable insights, offering practical strategies and theoretical frameworks to support teachers in their work. The chapters are designed to have you engage thoroughly with their respective content, including teaching tips, checklists, graphic organizers, and images. Completing this process will help you explore the potential of a long-lasting career in social studies education. This book serves as a foundation for deeper pedagogical research, positioning you to become a dedicated teacher who builds meaningful relationships with students, going far beyond just teaching historical content.

If you are starting your career in social studies education, follow the recipe in Chapter 1, "The Art of Career Search: Finding and Landing the Perfect Job" by Jason Chevrier, Ed Finney, and Alyssa Sabbatino to land the perfect job. As you implement the authors' suggestions, it becomes evident to start with articulating your professional educational philosophy. It is critical to move through this process with a clear educational philosophy and mission. It is paramount to know what it is that you want to achieve by teaching young minds. If you are struggling to craft your own educational philosophy statement, it is recommended that you read Chapter 3 first. This chapter, "Teaching for Tomorrow: Social Studies as a Path to an Engaged Citizenry" by Kristi Fragnoli, Timothy D. Potts, and Paul Gold, guides a teacher through the purpose and definition of social studies, helping the reader craft their own philosophy that promotes students as active thinkers and engaged citizens. This mission must meet the needs and aspirations of the district, and when that happens, you have landed the perfect job.

The authors of the remaining chapters provide a solid framework for becoming a highly effective social studies educator, one that will significantly impact students and the overall school community. According to *A Classroom With Purpose: A Guide to Teaching Social Studies Today*, knowing and understanding the curriculum standards of your school district and state truly determine what you are teaching and, as a result, what the students learn. Many studies show that it is an empirical fact that how we teach determines how much the students learn. Within Chapter 4, "Building Bridges: Crafting Engaging Social Studies Units of Study," and Chapter 5, "Tapping Your Creativity: How to Create Engaging Social Studies Lessons," Karen Poland and Kristi Fragnoli break down the importance of thinking through your unit and lesson design. The importance of a well-thought-out teaching unit is the blueprint for a functional daily lesson plan that engages students in true thinking. It is the key to preparing our next generation of informed active citizens.

We can turn to Chapter 6, "Investigating History" by Bruce Lesh, to understand the importance of questioning and inquiry through primary sources. Sam Wineburg's seminal work *Historical Thinking and Other Unnatural Acts* published in 2001 significantly impacted the field of social studies by introducing the concept of historical thinking practices. Wineburg's work shifted the focus toward engaging students in the deeper, critical thinking processes involved in understanding history. Bruce Lesh, a pioneer in historical thinking skills, emphasizes the use of historical questioning and inquiry to design lessons that deeply connect students with historical documents. The ultimate goal of a social studies educator involves leading students to question and form their own interpretations of history.

In Chapter 2, "Navigating the Early Years" by Emily Wells and James O'Brien, the classroom environment sets the stage for all learning to occur. Safety, respect, and trust lay the groundwork for students to flourish. The importance of creating an inclusive, safe learning environment is topmost in social studies education due to the number of controversial topics that can show up in the curricula. Several chapters focus on creating inclusive learning environments, which is evidence of the importance and the need for educators to reflect and implement strategies that are aligned to students' needs. In Chapter 8, "Being the Best Social Studies Teacher for Students with IEPs," Darren W. Minarik provides guidance on supporting students with diverse learning needs, while in Chapter 9, "Just Remember the Peanut Butter and Jelly Sandwich: Supporting Multilingual Learners," Aja E. LaDuke highlights strategies for engaging students from multilingual backgrounds. In Chapter 7, "Dreaming of Resilience, Resistance, and Joy in a Culturally Relevant Social Studies Classroom," John Palella calls for educators to embrace culturally relevant pedagogy, ensuring that all students see themselves in the curriculum and develop a sense of belonging. It is crucial to recognize early in your career that you have both a moral and legal obligation to follow the learning strategies outlined in an Individualized Education Program or a 504 plan. Teachers are legally required to comply with local, state, and federal laws to ensure students' educational rights are upheld as outlined in these chapters.

The world has become much more dynamic and confusing with the emergence of technology, from AI to social media to legal or illegal applications. Two chapters, Chapter 10, "Transforming Social Studies Through Technology" by Ed Finney, and Chapter 11, "Teaching in the Digital Age: Understanding Ethical and Legal Guidelines" by Erica Kane, provide a foundation for integrating digital tools into the classroom beyond novelty or exposure level, protecting your legal and professional reputation, and protecting your students' privacy rights. As educators, we must navigate the ethical and legal dimensions of technology use while embracing innovative approaches to enhance student engagement, the actual use of technology, and techniques that integrate technology to broaden and deepen historical thinking content and practices.

Throughout *A Classroom With Purpose: A Guide to Teaching Social Studies Today*, common themes weave together to form the foundation of effective teaching. The various authors have all mentioned similar strands of "good social studies teaching." We start to understand the importance of being a reflective practitioner, having a growth mindset, and maintaining professional engagement. These components are not just stand-alone concepts of education, they are anchored in a teacher's philosophy of education and the individual personality of the teacher. All the wonderful information throughout the book is crucial to being an effective social studies teacher, but all the research, theory, and knowledge is screened by your own philosophies, personality, and life's filters.

Reflective Classroom Practitioner

What sets great teachers apart and allows them to sustain and grow over time is their commitment to reflective practices. Reflective practices—whether done individually or with colleagues—creates opportunities for continuous growth, improvement, and learning. Looking back on past lessons with a critical eye, identifying strengths and weaknesses, and making adjustments benefit both teachers and students.

The key to being a reflective classroom practitioner is always putting your ever-changing students and their needs first. You teach, assess, and reflect. You review in your mind how each student reacted during the lesson. Did they interact, question, answer, and discuss content, or were they silent and unresponsive?

The reflective classroom practitioner replays all key components of the lesson, from introduction to the dissemination of content to activities and assessment. You should be evaluating your role throughout this entire process. As a teacher, you rarely receive constructive feedback, maybe during an observation, but that only occurs a few times a year. Growth comes from feedback and change, so reflective classroom practitioners use their student assessment data and their ability to critique themselves and the lesson. Students provide a tremendous amount of information during and after a lesson. They might be excited to participate, or they may be resistant to participate. Additionally, all of the different and multiple formative and summative assessments utilized in a lesson provide great data for reflection. Reflective classroom practitioners use their students' engagement and responses as valuable data, considering both verbal and nonverbal cues. Through the process of personal reflection, you will continually develop as an effective educator. Reflective teachers understand that all teachers—novice and veteran alike—have room to grow.

Growth Mindset

The most successful teachers adopt a growth mindset and maintain a vision of both helping children grow and learn and allowing the same gift for themselves (Dweck, 2007). A growth mindset is strongly connected to the amount of passion that you exude with your students. It is absolutely essential to be passionate in all that you do for the students that you teach. Unfortunately, students can have a myriad of issues going on in their lives. Students know well which teachers are serious about their subject matter and care about them. They will often communicate their positive or negative viewpoints to their peers, parents, support staff, other teachers, and administrators. As a teacher, your continuous journey of reflection and growth will allow for your passion and inspiration to shine forth in the classroom. Your students are extremely savvy and will feel your passion the minute they walk into the classroom.

John Quincy Adams is often credited for this great inspirational quote: "If your actions inspire others to dream more, learn more, do more, and become more, you are a leader." Sorry to say, we would have to amend this quotation by changing "leader" to "teacher." You, the teacher, inspire others to dream more, learn more, do more, and become more because that is what teachers do. This is only possible when the educator has a growth mindset for self and others.

We wear many different hats during a day of teaching—teacher, nurse, friend, counselor—there are so many roles we assume. And we cannot be successful all the time, in all roles, but we must remember the growth mindset: "This growth mindset is based on the belief that your basic qualities are things you can cultivate through your efforts, your strategies, and help from others … everyone can grow through application and experience" (Dweck, 2006, p.7). As a person and a teacher, we are growing through all the varied experiences we live through. We take something positive from every failure or adversity. We change ever so slightly as we progress through our lives. Like a glacier moving over the land, scraping away bits of rock and leaving beautiful valleys and mountains in its wake, we are ever-changing.

Maybe education is not intended to fill a child with facts but to help a child develop into a unique person. So the true educator not only exhibits and shares a growth model but also curates a growth mindset in their students. We must celebrate and teach how to develop these unique attributes. Henry David Thoreau wrote, "Birds do not sing in caves." You, the teacher, and your students are birds, let's hear you all sing!

Professional Engagement

It is absolutely fundamental that in teaching today you cannot be an island unto yourself. Truly, in a 21st-century world, it is not a solitary profession but one of multiple interactions, and you may interact with hundreds of people daily. On your first day of teaching, you will meet many new faces. To be fully transparent and honest, some staff are there to help you, and some will be a hindrance. We strongly encourage you to develop your personal local professional support network, which may include your mentor, department colleagues, teacher leaders/coaches, administrators, school support staff, and personal friends. It is the first step in creating a strong support network or a personal "board of directors."

Relying on this network in the early years can be the first defense in preventing a loss of confidence when times get tough. Undoubtedly, there will be difficult days, and there could be many where you will question whether you have what it takes to persevere and carry on in a social studies teaching position. It is during those moments that your local network will inspire you to nurture strong supportive collegial relations, to develop coping skills, and to have the motivation to continue to the next day, month, and year. This network is absolutely essential to weather the various storms of teaching and to be a much-needed inspiration for sustainability. Although extremely important, your local support network is only one facet of true teaching longevity. Branching out beyond your physical locale, school district, and sometimes your region can lead to other strong supportive connections.

We highly recommend that you immerse yourself in local, state, and national professional organizations. In general, they are the key to staving off burnout, enhancing learning content, being immersed in fabulous discipline-related professional development, and developing lifelong professional connections outside your local network. Take advantage of the many free professional development workshops for social studies teachers that allow you to visit important historic sites around the country and world. Students are always fascinated when they learn and know that you have actually visited historic sites included in the curriculum. What a perfect way to demonstrate a growth mindset and a lifelong learning when you share photographs, videos, souvenirs, replica artifacts, and stories about being there.

Early in our careers, we became involved in our state social studies organization and then later the National Council for the Social Studies and its associated groups. Our involvement in these organizations is integral to fulfilling the mission of a growth mindset. We attended annual conventions to participate in workshops for advancing our content acquisition, to learn new pedagogy directly from teacher presenters, to visit off-site historical locations, and to network. As time went on, we submitted workshop proposals to present annually, and they were accepted. It allowed for us to share innovative ways for teaching social studies and to share resources with our attendees. Presenting helped us connect our classroom to our colleagues' classrooms around our state and share in the collegiality that is truly part of a growth mindset. Your students will pick up very quickly that you are involved and will ask questions about why you present workshops and travel to various locales. This is a great opportunity to share what you do as an educator and to model true lifelong learning.

Later, we joined professional and governance committees taking on more leadership roles. Getting involved at this level continues the process of solidifying your professional persona and demonstrates that you are a true leader, a leader who shows the qualities of giving versus taking. Involvement in a professional organization is one way to give back to your discipline and is a natural extension of your teaching.

Social studies organizations are a great way to shine in your chosen field. You can become a better teacher at multiple levels by joining and participating in these organizations. Unfortunately, professional organizations are suffering in membership recruitment, retention, and filling leadership positions due to a host of reasons. However, these professional organizations benefit from young and creative ideas and experiences. Your insights and enthusiasm will usher in new perspectives and will inspire veteran teachers. It is through this synergy that professional organizations stay current and effective.

Conclusion

A Classroom With Purpose: A Guide to Teaching Social Studies Today should accompany you throughout your educational journey. It is our hope that you refer to this handbook as a form of encouragement and inspiration that will lead to a forever career in teaching social studies. Mark it up, annotate the pages, and reflect on meaningful excerpts.

Consider our final thoughts as you enter the social studies classroom: You must be centered and focused on exuding the love of learning and sharing it every day. Your students must see you in action, practicing what you preach, motivating them to be their best selves. Read and explore all forms of social studies content, pedagogical theory, and research, but more importantly, be a role model and develop a love of learning in your students.

Through this pathway of continuous learning and reflecting, your students will evolve into astute citizens participating in civic engagement within their community. As you can see, it always comes back to the mission and purpose of social studies in creating students that are clever, shrewd, and full of intellectual discernment.

A social studies teacher is in a very powerful position: From implementing the purpose of social studies to modeling the discourse that is needed for an informed citizenry and a growth mindset, the teacher is a strong role model. We must realize our actions, words, and decisions impact all the students that sit in front of us. Teacher and child psychologist Haim Ginott (1972) captures this powerful position teachers are in:

> I've come to a frightening conclusion that I am the decisive element in the classroom. It's my personal approach that creates the climate. It's my daily mood that makes the weather. As a teacher, I possess a tremendous power to make a child's life miserable or joyous. I can be a tool of torture or an instrument of inspiration. I can humiliate or heal. In all situations, it is my response that decides whether a crisis will be escalated or de-escalated and a child humanized or dehumanized. (pp. 15–16)

So how we react, what we decide to teach, and how we decide to instruct all play a role in developing our next generation of citizens.

Great social studies teaching requires flexibility. There is an endless stream of issues, conflicts, and interruptions, and any event or student can throw a wrench into the best-made plans. The ability to adapt in the moment is essential. This resilience is what separates a struggling educator from a thriving one. Grit and tenacity are necessary traits for success. Angela Duckworth (2013) shares, "Grit is passion and perseverance for very long-term goals. Grit is having stamina. Grit is sticking with your future, day-in, day-out" (2:56). You will experience many setbacks, but a strong teacher learns from them and becomes better with each challenge.

Equally important is finding balance in work and personal life. Currently, there is much research and literature about the mental health benefits of balancing your daily employment needs and the various events of your personal life. In the early years, teaching can feel all-consuming, and exhaustion is inevitable. Over time, you will find coping skills and strategies to manage the workload while still maintaining a personal life. This process will take time and perseverance. Trust the process, as some days will be more difficult than others. The key to survival is finding a support system—colleagues, mentors, friends—who can make all the difference on difficult days. Lean on your support group and remember that balance is a journey, not a destination.

As we come to the end of the book, may your journey be filled with discovery, inquiry, and personal growth. The development of you, as a person and educator, is the ultimate goal. Follow your instincts and trust yourself throughout this evolving process. The true goal of teaching is about guiding students as they develop their own identities, perspectives, and abilities. You are the true practitioner who models the process of change and growth for your students. Embrace it!

References

Buckingham, M. (2005). *The one thing you need to know.* Free Press.

Duckworth, A. L. (2013, April). *Grit: The power of passion and perseverance* [Video]. TED Conferences. **www.ted. com/talks/angela_lee_duckworth_grit_the_power_of_passion_and_perseverance**

Dweck, C. S. (2007). *Mindset: The new psychology of success.* Random House.

Ginott, H. G. (1972). *Teacher and child: a book for parents and teachers.* Macmillan.

Glossary

A glossary is a vital resource for any educator seeking to create an intentional and impactful classroom environment. This glossary provides clear explanations of key terms, concepts, and strategies critical to effective social studies instruction. Whether navigating pedagogical approaches or established methodologies, this reference aims to empower teachers with the knowledge and language needed to foster engaged, thoughtful, and informed learners in today's classrooms.

academic intervention services (AIS). A system of academic support provided to students who are struggling to meet grade-level standards in specific subjects.

anticipatory set. A brief activity or strategy used at the very beginning of a lesson to engage students, activate their prior knowledge, and prepare them for what they are about to learn.

artificial intelligence. The integration and application of technologies that enable computers or machines to simulate human learning, comprehension, problem-solving, decision-making, creativity, and autonomy within learning environments.

backward design. A framework of planning that starts by outlining goals before selecting specific instructional methods.

Behavior Intervention Plan (BIP). A structured plan developed to support a student whose behavior interferes with learning. BIPs are often part of an IEP or 504 Plan and guide educators to support student success.

behaviorist approach. Also called *direct instruction model*. An instructional approach that emphasizes direct instruction, repetition, and reinforcement to shape learning behavior.

Children's Online Privacy Protection Act (COPPA). A federal law imposing certain requirements on operators of websites or online services directed to children under 13.

classroom management. Strategies and techniques used to maintain a productive, respectful, and safe learning environment.

code-switching. The practice of alternating between two or more languages, dialects, or syntactical systems during a conversation whether purposeful or unintentional, often based on a social setting or context.

compelling questions. Questions that are aligned to the standards, are intellectually rigorous, are relevant to students, seek to foster connections, provoke curiosity, and have academic value.

constructivist approach. An instructional approach that involves abstract concepts that require critical thinking or problem-solving for students to construct their own understanding.

content funnel. Explains the purpose, focus, and value of the unit to the rest of the school year, beginning with an enduring understanding. Used to develop a *content outline*.

content outline. A framework of the specific content students will learn throughout the unit including all relevant names, dates, definitions, explanations, facts, concepts, events, and places.

Culturally Relevant Pedagogy (CRP). An approach to teaching developed by Gloria Ladson-Billings that empowers students by connecting successful classroom learning to students' cultural backgrounds, lived experiences, and personal interests.

culturally responsive education (CRE). An approach to teaching that recognizes and values students' cultural backgrounds and incorporates them into the curriculum.

data-driven instruction. The use of student performance data to guide teaching practices and personalize learning.

differentiated instruction. Also called *differentiation*. Instruction tailored to meet individual learning needs through various methods, content, and assessments.

digital literacy. The ability to confidently and critically use digital technologies to find, evaluate, create, and communicate information in various formats, requiring both technical and cognitive skills for learning and collaboration in academic environments.

diversity, equity, and inclusion (DEI). The intentional efforts to create an environment that acknowledges, respects, and celebrates people's differences, while ensuring that all people, regardless of background or identity, have access to equal opportunities and support.

diversity. The inclusion of individuals from various backgrounds, perspectives, and abilities, contributing to a rich and varied learning environment.

due process. The legal rights and procedural protections that public school teachers, particularly those with tenure, must be afforded before they can be disciplined or dismissed from their position.

enduring understandings. The core insights and ideas learned in a specific context that students retain beyond that context.

English as a New Language (ENL). A structured program that provides specialized instruction to help students acquire language skills.

English Language Learner (ELL). A student who is in the process of acquiring proficiency in English while continuing to learn academic content in other subjects.

equity. Ensuring fair treatment, opportunities, and outcomes for all students by addressing individual needs and removing barriers.

essential questions. Open-ended, non-content-specific questions that promote critical and higher-order thinking and transferability of ideas and often lead to additional questions.

Family Educational Rights and Privacy Act (FERPA). A federal law that protects the privacy of student education records.

formative assessment. Ongoing assessments used to monitor student learning and adjust instruction as needed.

generative artificial intelligence. Artificial intelligence that uses user inputs and machine learning to create new content.

growth mindset. The belief that intelligence and abilities can be developed through dedication, hard work, effective strategies, and learning from mistakes, rather than being fixed or innate.

High-Leverage Practices (HLPs). Core practices for effectively teaching students with disabilities. Developed by the Council for Exceptional Children (CEC).

historical thinking. the process historians utilize when analyzing and interpreting the past by using sourcing, contextualization, and evaluating the reliability of information to construct well-reasoned conclusions.

inclusion. The practice of ensuring that students of all backgrounds, abilities, and needs are supported within a general education setting.

Individualized Education Program (IEP). A legally binding document that protects the right of students with disabilities to have a free and appropriate public education. See also *least restrictive environment*.

Inquiry Design Model (IDM). A framework for creating curriculum and instructional materials that centers student inquiry. IDM revolves around compelling questions, tasks, and evidence-based argumentation.

learning management system (LMS). A digital platform used to organize, deliver, and monitor teaching and learning. Examples include Google Classroom, Canvas, and Schoology.

learning objective. The purpose for creating and teaching the lesson.

learning outcome. The achieved result or consequence of instruction.

least restrictive environment (LRE). The practice of educating students with disabilities alongside their peers to the greatest extent appropriate.

Maslow's Hierarchy of Needs. A psychological theory developed by Abraham Maslow that organizes human needs in a pyramid, starting with basic physiological needs and progressing to self-actualization.

measurable learning outcome (MLO). The combination of a learning objective and learning outcome in one statement. It is a clear, specific statement of what students will be able to demonstrate in terms of knowledge, skills, or values.

multitiered system of supports (MTSS). A comprehensive, schoolwide framework that provides varying levels of support to students based on their academic, behavioral, and social-emotional needs. See also *social-emotional learning*.

pacing guide. A tool used by teachers and schools to outline the sequence of content and skills and provide the timing and duration of instruction on each topic. These guides design the length of lessons and units to serve as a curricular roadmap throughout the year.

personal learning network (PLN). A group of like-minded educators who share and collaborate on topics of mutual interest.

***Pickering* Balancing Test.** A test used by the courts for determining whether a public employee is entitled to First Amendment protections.

proactive restorative practices. Strategies that focus on building relationships, creating a positive community, and preventing conflicts before they occur.

project-based learning (PBL). A teaching method in which students learn by solving real-world issues.

reactive restorative practices. Approaches that address conflicts or harm after they occur, focusing on repairing relationships.

reflective classroom practitioner. A teacher who actively engages in a thoughtful and systematic process of examining their own teaching practices, beliefs, and decisions with the goal of improving student learning and professional growth.

response to intervention (RTI). A proactive, multitiered approach to identifying and supporting students with learning and behavior needs.

restorative practices. A set of practices focused on building positive relationships and resolving conflicts by repairing harm rather than focusing solely on punishment. See also *proactive restorative practices*; *reactive restorative practices*.

scope and sequence. A tool used by teachers and schools that outlines the content and skills that will be taught and the order in which it will be delivered.

sentence frames. An instructional tool with partially completed sentences that model how to express and organize ideas in writing or in speech.

social-emotional learning (SEL). Programs and practices that help students develop self-awareness, social skills, and emotional regulation.

summative assessment. A type of assessment that evaluates student learning, knowledge, and skills at the end of an instructional period.

supporting questions. Questions that are scaffolded to guide students' thinking and inquiry toward the content they need to investigate and master in order to craft an argumentative answer to essential and compelling questions.

teaching (or educational) philosophy. A set of beliefs and values about teaching and learning that guides a teacher's approach in the classroom.

tenure. The status granted to an educator after successfully completing a probationary period.

translanguaging. (1) A practice by multilingual individuals fluidly using all the languages they know, rather than using each language separately. (2) A pedagogical, asset-based approach that uses more than one language in the classroom.

trauma-informed education. An educational approach that recognizes and responds to the effects of trauma on students, incorporating practices that support emotional safety and resilience.

unit. The organization of curricular topics and content into a focused period of learning.

Universal Design for Learning (UDL). A proactive educational framework designed to remove any barriers before students enter the classroom.

Index

Figures and tables are indicated by "f" and "t" following the page numbers.

A Classroom With Purpose: A Guide to Teaching Social Studies Today

A Classroom With Purpose: A Guide to Teaching Social Studies Today

www.ingramcontent.com/pod-product-compliance
Lightning Source LLC
Chambersburg PA
CBHW080421270326
41929CB00018B/3110